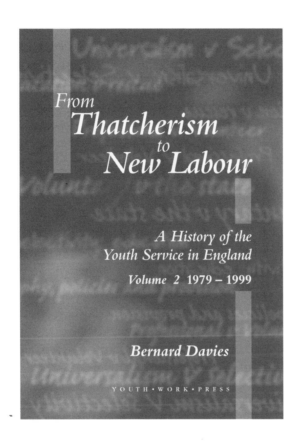

From
Thatcherism
to
New Labour

A History of the
Youth Service in England

Volume 2 1979 – 1999

Bernard Davies

YOUTH·WORK·PRESS

NATIONAL YOUTH AGENCY

9·H   Q   28129

A History of the Youth Service in England comprises two volumes:

Volume 1: 1939 – 1979
From Voluntaryism to Welfare State
ISBN 0 86155 207 5   £14.99

Volume 2: 1979 – 1999
From Thatcherism to New Labour
ISBN 0 86155 208 3   £14.99

Published by

17–23 Albion Street, Leicester LE1 6GD.
Tel: 0116.285.3700. Fax: 0116.285.3777.
E-Mail: nya@nya.org.uk
Internet: http://www.nya.org.uk

© September 1999

Editor: Denise Duncan
Cover design: Sanjay Kukadia

Y O U T H • W O R K • P R E S S
is a publishing imprint of the National Youth Agency

Contents

Glossary of Acronyms

AJY	Association for Jewish Youth
BYC	British Youth Council
BYCWA	Black Youth and Community Workers Association
CBI	Confederation of British Industry
CDF	Community Development Foundation
CHE	Campaign for Homosexual Equality
CETYCW	Council for Education and Training in Youth and Community Work
CHAR	Campaign for the Homeless and Rootless
CIPFA	Chartered Institute for Public Finance and Accounting
CYSA	Community and Youth Service Association
CYWU	Community and Youth Workers' Union
CRC	Community Relations Council
CRY	Campaign for Rural Youth
CSV	Community Service Volunteers
DES	Department of Education and Science
DfE	Department for Education
DfEE	Department for Education and Employment
EPA	Educational Priority Area
ESG	Educational Support Grants Scheme
GEST	Grants for Education Support and Training
GLC	Greater London Council
GMS	Grant Maintained Status
GREA	Grant Related Expenditure Assessment
HMI	Her Majesty's Inspectorate
ILEA	Inner London Education Authority
INTEP	Initial Training and Education Panel
INSTEP	In-Service Training and Education Panel
IPPR	Institute for Public Policy Research
IT	Intermediate Treatment
JNC	Joint Negotiating Committee
JOC	Juvenile Organisation Committee
LEA	Local Education Authority
LEATGS	Local Education Authority Training Grants Scheme
LMS	Local Management of Schools
LUYC	London Union of Youth Clubs
MAYC	Methodist Association of Youth Clubs
MSC	Manpower Services Commission
NACYS	National Advisory Council for the Youth Service
NABC	National Association of Boys' Clubs

NAGC	National Association of Girls' Clubs
NAYCEO	National Association of Youth and Community Education Officers
NALGO	National Association of Local Government Officers
NAYPCAS	National Association of Young People's Counselling and Advisory Services
NAYSO	National Association of Youth Service Officers
NAYC	National Association of Youth Clubs
NAYLO	National Association of Youth Leaders and Organisers
NCTYL	National College for the Training of Youth Leaders
NCVYS	National Council for Voluntary Youth Services
NCSS	National Council for Social Service
NOW	National Organisation for Work with Girls and Young Women
NUT	National Union of Teachers
NVQ	National Vocational Qualification
NYA	National Youth Agency
NYB	National Youth Bureau
OFSTED	Office for Standards in Education
OPCS	Office of Populations Censuses and Surveys
PAVET	Part-time Workers and Volunteers Education and Training Panel
RAMP	Regional Acceditiation and Moderation Panel
SCPYCO	Standing Conference of Principal Youth and Community Officers
SCNVYO	Standing Conference of National Voluntary Youth Organisations
SRB	Single Regeneration Budget
SSAs	Standard Spending Assessments
TAG	Training Agencies Group
TEC	Training and Enterprise Council
TUC	Trades Union Congress
YCWTA	Youth and Community Work Training Association
YMCA	Young Men's Christian Association
YODU	Youth Opportunities Development Unit
YOP	Youth Opportunities Programme
YSA	Youth Service Association
YSDC	Youth Service Development Council
YSIC	Youth Service Information Centre
YSWU	Youth Social Work Unit
YTS	Youth Training Scheme
YVFF	Young Volunteer Force Foundation
YVRU	Young Volunteer Resources Unit
YWCA	Young Women's Christian Association
YWU	Youth Work Unit

About the Author

Bernard Davies first got involved in youth work in 1948 aged 13, as a member of a youth club and a Jewish Lads' Brigade unit. He went on to professional training via senior member and part-time leader and, after graduating with a history degree, took the one-year course for 'youth leaders and organisers' at University College Swansea during the year of Albemarle, 1958–59.

During the early 1960s he was a tutor at the National College for the Training of Youth Leaders and, after 18 months in the USA, for seven years ran a teacher-youth worker course at a mature student teacher training college in Lancashire. He served on advisory and review groups for NYB and CETYCW during the 1970s and 1980s and also served on a local authority education subcommittee and on local youth service review panels. His extensive experience of the voluntary sector includes chairing and being a member of local management committees and involvement as a local community activist. In 1983–84 he was president of the Community and Youth Workers' Union.

Throughout his career Bernard Davies has written extensively on youth work, the youth service and youth affairs. He contributed regularly to *New Society* in the 1960s and 1970s, co-authored *The Social Education of the Adolescent* with Alan Gibson, published in 1967, and has written pamphlets and a book, *Threatening Youth* (1986), on youth policies. Since taking early retirement as youth officer (training) from Sheffield Youth Service in 1992 he has acted as consultant for a number of voluntary organisations and local authorities including, with Mary Marken, carrying out a review of Sunderland Council's youth services.

About the Publisher

The National Youth Agency aims to advance youth work to promote young people's personal and social development, and their voice, influence and place in society. It works to: improve and extend youth services and youth work; enhance and demonstrate youth participation in society; and to promote effective youth policy and provision.

The NYA provides resources to improve work with young people and its management; creates and demonstrates innovation in service and methods; supports the leadership of organisations to deliver 'best value' and manage change; influences public perception and policy, and secures standards of education and training for youth work.

Acknowledgments

Though I of course take full responsibility for what follows, I want to record my thanks to the many people who, often in passing and perhaps even without realising it, have contributed information and above all ideas to the writing of this history. They include all those who took part in the Durham History of Youth and Community Work conference in November 1998 but in particular Colin Heslop, Doug Nicholls, Sangeeta Soni and Jean Spence. I am grateful, too, to Lady Albemarle and Sandra Leventon for some specific information and responses and to the students on the Durham Youth and Community Work course who allowed me to try out some early ideas on key 'threads' emerging from the youth service's history.

Over nearly three years, the staff of the National Youth Agency's library and information centre have been infinitely patient with my cries for help, particularly Judy Perrett and Carolyn Oldfield. Mary Durkin, then at the NYA, provided early inspiration. Mary Marken's reactions to drafts have invariably gone straight to the weak points in my arguments, been incisive but constructive and so have added greatly to the analysis. Sally Davies has also flogged her way through long drafts, in the process contributing valuable comment on the content and language as well as identifying errors which have saved me from much later embarrassment.

Above all, however, I want to put on record my thanks to Tom Wylie and Denise Duncan. Through their consistent support, encouragement – and critiques! – I have come to understand and appreciate just how crucial editors are for writing for publication.

Bernard Davies
September 1999

Dedication

This book is dedicated to **Stanley Rowe** (1924–92) – youth worker, youth work trainer, trade unionist and youth service policy-maker – who had a permanent influence on my own work and thinking and whose contribution to the youth service over five decades helped to ensure its survival and development.

Preface

Bernard Davies has written the definitive history of England's youth service during the last 60 years of the 20th century. It highlights the contributions and achievements made by diverse individuals and organisations to the development of a distinctive form of practice – youth work – and of a distinctive, if nebulous, pattern of social education provision for young people – the youth service.

There are many ways of presenting history: as a nostalgic reverie of better times; as a set of accidents or contingencies with unintended consequences; as an elemental struggle by heroes and heroines. Bernard Davies's book transcends all of these. It is a tale of continuities, of enduring – and sometimes resolved – struggles towards a better life for our young people, more often by those who worked directly with them than by those who made national policy about them. It is the text for generations of youth workers, and also a spur to greater effort based on a deeper understanding of our roots.

Tom Wylie
Chief Executive
National Youth Agency

Foreword

Beyond objectivity

In setting out to write the history of England's youth service, pure objectivity has for me never been a realistic option. This admission is not meant to suggest that I have allowed free rein to my personal prejudices and biases. It is merely to own up to the subjectivity which is part of the analysis of any human enterprise as this is filtered through the values, feelings and preconceptions of the analyst.

This, however, is a history which has stood even less chance than usual of being neutral and stand-offish. For most of the period it describes, I have had some sort of personal involvement in youth work. In the late1940s, just after my 13th birthday, I joined a (voluntary) youth club and boys' brigade unit. From the mid-1950s my awareness of the wider organisational context of these personal experiences was being sharpened by my deepening contact with Stanley Rowe, a full-time leader who had been actively and influentially involved on the national youth service stage for at least 10 years. After studying history at university – a not insignificant influence in itself on what follows – I found myself doing full-time training for youth work during 'the year of Albemarle' (1958–59).

Though for long periods straying into the worlds of both teaching and social work, I have never since got youth work or the youth service out of my system. For good or ill, therefore, I have a considerable personal investment in the history which I here try to record and interpret – hardly an ideal platform for objective appraisal or distanced judgment.

My objectivity has been further restricted by my unashamed intention to write a history which addresses institutional and professional concerns which have stayed *current* through most of the youth service's development. Precisely because so much of my own personal and career development over the past 40 years has been intertwined with that of the service, I have become highly sensitive to (even impatient with) how easily even its immediate past slips away, unnoticed and undervalued. This is a service, I am tempted to conclude, without a history – and therefore, if it is not very careful, without an identity.

Losses like these have real everyday consequences. For one thing, they have prevented (and still prevent) those who come later from 'standing on the shoulders of those who went before' – an essential (and humbling) viewpoint for anyone caught up in the daily pressures and aggravations of today's struggles. This deprivation of insights into why things are as they are, these gaps in historical awareness, also cut off practitioners and policy-makers from crucial analytical tools for current planning and action. In offering a historical framework, however partial (in both senses of the word), I hope therefore to give some distant support to these ongoing activities and engagements and maybe even to contribute a little to them.

Limitations

On the assumption that another history of the youth service in England may not be written for some time, I have tried to make this one as authoritative as possible – that is, to put together a comprehensive and accurate document of record. Even so, some crucial limitations are built into what follows.

- In striving to give due weight and space to the range of cultural experiences and traditions which have gone to create the youth service in England, my class origins and my experiences as a Jew have hopefully added something relevant to my interpretations. Nonetheless, I have remained conscious throughout that this is history written by a white able-bodied heterosexual man.
- This is a history of the *youth service* and not of youth work. Moreover, it starts from the assumption that, far from being amenable to some non-controversial definition, this will always involve a degree of

arbitrariness. What follows sets this definition quite narrowly. It, for example, assumes that the service was created as an institution when the state achieved a recognisable and substantial presence in the sponsorship of youth work – and it dates this from November 1939 when the Ministry of Education published Circular 1486, *The Service of Youth*. It also assumes that, by definition, it constitutes a complex set of relationships and negotiations between the state and voluntary organisations – though conceptions of the latter, their boundaries and their much-hyped 'partnership' with the state are also treated as problematic and in crucial respects unresolved.

- This is quite explicitly a history of the youth service in *England*. It does make passing references to Scotland, the north of Ireland and particularly Wales, most often where significant overlaps into English events and learning occur. However – above all because the youth services in these other parts of the United Kingdom have developed in such often radically different ways – it makes no claims at all to writing their histories.
- This also is very largely a history *from above* – about national policies and policy-makers, statutory and voluntary, and how these have interacted with and helped to shape local developments. Though some use is made of local experience to illustrate and illuminate these top-down influences, no claim is made to in any way trace how local and national policies have worked their way out as provision and practice on the ground.

Sources

Though this account of the growth of the youth service in England is based on considerable 'research', only a small proportion of this has been archival in the sense that it has used original documents or records. Key published papers – government, voluntary sector and independent reports, policy statements and discussion papers, departmental circulars, HMI reports once they became public documents – have clearly been important sources. So, too have some 'semi-published' papers such as presidential addresses to union AGMs, other conference papers and reports, press releases and a range of similarly transient materials going back to the 1940s.

Most of the detailed 'evidence', however, has been drawn from the (often high-quality) journalism of what can at best be described the service's 'popular' press and periodicals. I have thus relied heavily on the monthly and quarterly publications of the Ministry and later Department of Education, the Youth Service Information Centre, the National Youth Bureau and the National Youth Agency. Most important here have been:

- The YSIC *Digest* of the late 1960s and early 1970s;
- *Youth Service* in its various forms;
- *Youth in Society*;
- *Youth Scene* and *Scene*;
- *Young People Now*;
- (*Youth*) *Policy Update*; and
- The *Newsletter* of the Council for Education and Training in Youth and Community Work.

I have also made use of NAYC/Youth Club UK's *Youth Clubs* and of cuttings from *Education*, the *Times Educational Supplement*, the *Times Higher Educational Supplement*, *The Guardian* and *The Observer*.

Other key sources have been trade union journals. Particularly important here have been *The Youth Leader*, the National Association of Youth Leaders and Organisers' quarterly published during the 1940s and 1950s; *Youth Review*, the National Union of Teachers' periodical published monthly in association with the National Association of Youth Service Officers and the Youth Service Association through most of the 1960s; and since the early 1970s the Community and Youth Service Association/Community and Youth Workers' Union journal and then newspaper *Rapport*.

Throughout, I have striven to remain critical of these sources – and indeed self-critical where I have drawn on my own previous writing and publicly expressed views. Though most would hardly be classified as respectable academic sources, they have nonetheless proved a mine of information on what happened, when, and with and through whom. They have also conveyed a strong sense of what was important to the service at different times and so have caught something of the mood, even the passion, driving events.

Where I have ridden on the back of others' original research and findings, references are listed at the end of each chapter. However, in order to avoid over-burdening further two already lengthy volumes, most of the detailed sources have not been listed. They are for the most part recorded and can be made available to anyone interested – either from me through the National Youth Agency or via the NYA website http://www.nya.org.uk

Hopefully, too, such exchanges will help to achieve one of the main objectives of writing this history in the first place: to set in motion further debates on issues and concerns which have deep roots in the service's past and which continue to engage and preoccupy it at yet another critical moment in its development.

Bernard Davies
September 1999

Introduction

Chronology – with attitude

The overall framework of this history depends on that rather simplistic trick of dividing the past into significant periods and key events. By coincidence – and it surely *was* coincidence – influential reports on the youth service have been published at or very near the turn of each of the four decades which provide this book's main focus: Albemarle in 1960, Milson-Fairbairn in 1969, Thompson in 1982 and Coopers and Lybrand in 1991. In shaping the overall plan, each of these is used as a major signpost and transition point.

Other critical transition events and developments will also be dated and placed as accurately and as objectively as possible. These include state papers such as the 1967 Hunt Report *Immigrants and the Youth Service* and government discussion papers and circulars; the periodic attempts to get 'youth bills' through parliament; and the ministerial conferences of the late 1980s and early 1990s. What follows therefore is in many respects a very conventional chronological exposition intended to tell 'the story' as logically as possible.

The reason for wanting to fulfil this basic task, however, is not just to satisfy those who see history as 'getting the facts straight'. In this account, these have the more important purpose of providing a skeleton on which to flesh out more analytical themes. Far from being conceived and constructed as a description of who did what when, this book seeks as far as is possible to understand some of the 'whys' of those 'facts'. Above all, it attempts to locate them in the (changing) ideas and social, economic and political conditions of their time and in their broader educational and social policy contexts. Youth work, youth organisations and the youth service itself are thus treated, not as special or exceptional but, first and foremost, as examples of the way educational and welfare activity has been organised *and institutionalised* in our society.

One of the ways this book seeks to do this is to filter the past through present preoccupations in order to construct a *contemporary* history. Such filtering is to some extent an inevitable part of the subjectivity of historical description and analysis. What follows therefore, far from trying to deny or mask this effect, seeks deliberately to embrace it in order to try and produce a usable set of insights and comments on our own times. Date-stamping is thus interwoven with engagement in debates on key policy issues which have swirled around the service across the decades and continued to do so even as this book was being written.

Though overlapping, inherently ill-defined and far from exhaustive, these – in simple terms deliberately intended to convey something of their inherent and unresolvable tensions – include the following:

- **Universalism vs selectivity** – that is: How far should the youth service be an open-door provision, working with those young people who choose to participate. Or – especially assuming limited resources – should it concentrate its efforts on identified sections of the youth population specifically targeted because they are in special need; or because they are discriminated against and oppressed?

- **Education vs rescue** – that is: How far should the youth service's 'mission' be concerned with young people's self-realisation and personal (and indeed collective) development; or with their rescue from personal, family and/or societal risks and difficulties?

- **Professionalism vs volunteerism** – that is: How far should the youth service move from a reliance on lay volunteers (that is, with limited training and specialist qualifications) to employing paid, trained and 'qualified' staff?

- **Voluntaryism vs the state** – that is: How far should the youth service move from sponsorship and control by 'independent' charitable bodies or self-help groups to state sponsorship and control underpinned by legislation, shaped by government policies and priorities and funded out of local and national taxation?

In negotiating these debates, other key elements of the service's philosophy, policies and provision are also passed through an analytical mesh. These include:

- **The changing perceptions of the youth service's clientele** including how, and how far, these have taken account of the ways in which young people differ because of their identity and self-identity – for example, as Black, female, disabled, gay, lesbian or bisexual, living in rural areas.

- **Changes in how the work has actually been delivered** – that is, in the methods and approaches adopted and the facilities provided; and in how these have been seen, described and justified by policy-makers and practitioners.

- **The service's changing structures and administrative arrangements**, including, for example, in some periods, the distinctive role and contribution of HMI; whether and how ministers have been provided with advice through national committees and councils; and the provision of 'intelligence' on what is going on (particularly information and research).

- **The changing nature and conditions of the workforce (paid and unpaid, full- and part-time).**

- **The evolution of training and qualifications for those workers.**

- **The rise and fall – and ultimately fall – of funding and other resources.**

In search of a critical history

Underlying this approach to historical writing, however, are some deeper assumptions – about the nature of society and the questions which need to be asked about its past development. These, too, need to be made explicit.

Inevitability

In reassessing any historical event, especially one which retrospectively is judged to have been significant, the wisdom of hindsight has huge power. Often its leads to the implicit (even unconscious) assumption that:

- the event was of course bound to happen; and
- it was bound to happen when it did.

A much more penetrating and textured history, however, demands a constant search for naivety. This helps to encourage a focus on what at the time individuals and groups thought and why they did what they did. Historical changes are then less likely to be treated as the result of some mysterious (and mystifying) process of inevitability than of human agency – of the conscious choices which people in the past have made. Though influenced by the dominant values and ideas of their time and constraints imposed by political or economic realities, events are then seen to unfold because women and men acted – and took responsibility for their actions.

Most often and influentially, these 'actors' have come from – or are seen to have come from – the more privileged sections of society. However, from the 19th century onwards, others who were less privileged and had had a less 'natural' grasp on power also gained some leverage on decision-making processes. This happened particularly as, 'from below', groups organised themselves, acted collectively and thereby much more consistently wrote themselves into history.

Absences

However, at (sometimes crucial) moments women and men also failed to act – perhaps because they did not think to do so, or because certain actions were considered and rejected or because others, individually and collectively, prevented them from acting. Absences then acquire great potential significance – sometimes as telling as 'presences' – and so need if possible to be spotted, analysed and their significance judged.

Contradiction

In the context of education and welfare, denying that events occur inevitably also opens up the question: is everything that happens really for the best – simply part of that great march of human progress driven by altruistic aspirations and rational decision-making? This book does not operate on this premise. Rather it assumes that what eventually emerges as social policy is almost always the result of contradictory, even contested, motives, many of which may have more to do with self-interest on the part of those promoting the policies than with an unsullied desire 'to do good'.

Conflicting interests

Such a perspective points to another, of equal influence: that underlying such motives are processes of policy-making which are often (some would say always) rooted in some fundamental conflicts of interests between competing groups within the society. These social divisions are often most starkly outcrops of the divergent experiences which citizens have particularly because of their class, their gender, their race, their sexual orientation and/or because they are disabled. On occasion, these differences can run so deep that they challenge the very concept of society when this simply takes for granted (and so helps to reinforce) commonsense notions of a largely unblemished consensual culture and social structure.

Negotiation

Because of these inherent societal differences and even conflicts, the social policies which do eventually get agreed and implemented are thus seen as the product of a complex if at times barely discernible 'negotiation'. This in effect occurs among a society's varied interest groups, and especially among those within it with usable degrees of power. Necessarily therefore such political processes embody and produce significant practice and even principled compromises for those involved in the negotiation.

The state

In carrying through this negotiation – especially during the period in which the youth service has been constructed and developed – the state has played an increasingly influential part, often taking on direct responsibility for designing and implementing social, including youth, policies. Notionally 'neutral' in these

negotiations, in practice it usually reflects and indeed replicates prevailing balances of power among the competing interests while acting as the vehicle for operationalising the political, economic and/or social priorities which these have produced at any particular time.

Thus, though often implicit and (again) contradictory, throughout the youth service's 60-year history the state's 'mission' has to varying degrees endorsed some important and influential aspirations for individuals and their personal development. However, particularly because the focus is youth, the state has paid very special attention to nurturing a section of the population openly defined as society's 'seed corn' – or its emergent 'human capital'. Induction into those values, beliefs and practices particularly endorsed by dominant interests in the society and seen as essential to a stable social order have thus also been given considerable emphasis.

Though a highly complex concept, the state's key ways of expressing itself have for the purposes of this book been greatly simplified. In effect it is thus conceived as those organisations, institutions, services and facilities:

- which have been created or sometimes backed up by legislation;
- which are at least in part paid for out of public taxes;
- which operate under the auspices of central and/or local government or (sometimes) other 'statutory' bodies; and
- which are administered by elected and employed public officials.

Youth service as social policy

Implicit in all the above is the assumption, too, that within this society the youth service does *not* stand alone as a free-floating provision for a specified section of the population. Rather it has to be understood as one, albeit somewhat peculiar, outcome among many of the broader social policy negotiations in which the state has this century played an increasingly influential role.

In the past much historical writing has treated the service and the most influential voluntary organisations within it as entirely novel inventions for dispensing education and welfare to young people. The youth service may indeed have, and may have had, a range of unique and positive features and an important internal rationale. On their own, however, these cannot explain why it was conceived of in the first place, by the particular people who did the conceiving, at the particular moment in time that they did this; or why its development took the particular twists and turns it did. Such events and explanations need continually to be located in the wider shifts of thought, belief and action of the periods during which it has existed.

In these ways and for these reasons, material towards the history of the youth service in England does not – indeed, cannot – simply 'speak for itself'. What this version of that history attempts to offer, therefore, is a critical pathway through some contradictory and 'unfinished' negotiations. Though the origins of these can certainly be traced back at least to the mid and late 19th century, Book One took as the proper substantive starting point the much later moment when Britain went to war in 1939. Book Two now takes up the story at one of the most decisive political break points in 20th century British history – Margaret Thatcher's general election victory in May 1979.

1 A Review for the Thatcher Era

From the optimism of Albemarle to the pragmatism of Thompson

The 1980s were ushered in for the youth service by a third review in just over 20 years. The first of these, published in 1960, had produced what turned out to be the landmark state paper on the service, the Albemarle Report. This led to unprecedented – and, since, unmatched – increases in resources and some fresh, if far from radical, thinking about the service's aims and methods. Over the decade these advances had been marked by:

- a 10-year development programme;
- constant monitoring, review and policy development through the work of a Youth Service Development Council (YSDC);
- a major building programme which had produced purpose-built premises across the country specifically designed with the 1960s teenager in mind;
- the establishment of emergency training at a National College which in 10 years more than doubled the number of full-time youth workers;
- the establishment of a committee to negotiate salaries and conditions of service for full-time workers in both the statutory and voluntary sectors;

- an increase in the number of paid part-time workers and the introduction of more systematic arrangements for their training which drew together both statutory and voluntary organisations;
- increased government grants to national voluntary organisations both for headquarters costs and for 'experimental' work; and
- the establishment of a Youth Service Information Centre committed to collecting, collating and disseminating information and research on young people, youth work policy and practice and relevant training.

In the process of carrying forward this programme, some crucial balances of power (or at least influence) had been tipped – for example, towards the state and away from charitable provision and 'the voluntary principle'; and towards full-time 'professionals' and away from part-time paid and volunteer workers.

The Albemarle reforms did not simply bring unblemished progress. As the service continued to be preoccupied with individual development, it often ignored or simply missed just how tightly this was constrained for many young people because they were working class, young women, Black, disabled and/or gay or lesbian or because they lived in rural areas. Partly as a result, the service continued to fret about its failure to extend its reach, especially to the more threatening elements of 'the unattached'. It also at times allowed itself to be seduced by the attractions of apparent panaceas – most notably community service – which, though having validity in their own right, were greatly over-blown as solutions to its take-up problem.

The service's second review report within a decade, *Youth and Community Work in the '70s,* was published in 1969 – the awkward amalgam of the work of two YSDC subcommittees. For some two-and-a-half years these had laboured to gather and then reconcile often contradictory evidence and recommendations on the service's relations with schools and with the adult community. For the service, this long drawn out and opaque process was in itself debilitating. The actual report then opened up treacherous philosophical and policy debates – particularly on whether and how the service could become more community oriented – which further divided it and often distracted it from its core youth-focused tasks.

For much of the 1970s, these internal doubts and tensions allowed central government largely to wash its hands of the service. Secretary of State for Education, Margaret Thatcher testily launched the service into limbo in 1971 by rejecting the central parts of the YSDC report out of hand – and then peremptorily abolishing the YSDC itself. Meanwhile, across the country, local authorities proceeded over the decade to add to the service's national incoherence by batting it, ping-pong style, first into, then out of and

then sometimes back into community education – or, indeed, sometimes, into other services such as leisure or recreation.

Cumulatively, the results of these disappointments were doubt, disillusion and significant differences of orientation and priority among both policy-makers and practitioners. As wider – and major – political and ideological shifts redefined the service's core values and style as at best unfashionable and at worst subversive, this confusion became worse.

In addition, economic policies, sometimes though not always driven by economic downturn, squeezed public expenditure generally. For the youth service this initially meant standstill budgets at best and cuts in planned growth. In the later years of the decade, repeating waves of real and often very harsh cuts again in effect reduced the service to non-statutory status within local provision as local authorities chose to fund it (or not) at highly unpredictable and variable levels. Though, in a growing anti-state climate, voluntary organisations generally became the rhetorical flavour of the month – and though the traditional 'big guns' in the youth sector continued to 'adapt and survive' – they too were subjected both to cuts and to tighter controls over the grants they did receive.

In so far as the service retained any political credibility during the 1970s, this came increasingly from government expectations that it could and would target 'areas of high social need' and the most potentially troublesome young people within them. Such targeting was far from new. Youth work had always prioritised those elements of working-class youth who were most vulnerable – and most potentially dangerous to the social order. As the state sought a greater measurable return from its investment in the youth service, these pressures to target built up substantially. These put at risk youth work's commitment not to start from the stigmatising (and demoralising) labels so often attached to young people. Often, too, they came close to breaching the principle of their voluntary involvement with the service.

Running alongside and often into such official forms of selectivity were streng-thening commitments to targeting from below. These concentrated particularly on those sections of the youth population who were on the receiving end of the discrim-inatory and oppressive practices built into British society. With increasing vigour and often passion, activist groupings within the service injected key messages from wider liberation movements which emerged or reinvigorated themselves during the 1970s. These built up their own pressure within and on the service – in this case for special attention and indeed separate provision for young women and for Black and Asian, gay and lesbian and disabled young people. Though somewhat different in origin, some increased campaigning attention was given, too, to young people living in rural areas. Attempts were also made to call to account those seen as carrying some responsibility for institu-tional as well as personal forms of oppressions (workers and managers as well as young people).

Conflict often emerged between those committed to such issue-based work and staff operating more traditional policies and provision. Sometimes this occurred when the former demanded (implicitly or explicitly) that the mainstream change or at least make room for the new anti-oppressive priorities and the alternative styles and methods these required. Contradictorily, tensions could occur too because, albeit at the margins still, some forms of issue-based work became flavour of the month and so attracted additional funds (and kudos) for their special projects or community-based interventions. In neither case did the outcome do much for the coherence or sense of identity of a service which, at the very start of the decade, was struggling anyway to clarify its collective goals and direction.

Internal division and uncertainty were further exacerbated by the service's stumbling progress towards the professional status which for its workforce had become one of its greatest aspirations. Flaws in such claims were exposed most clearly by the service's increasing difficulties in recruiting trained and qualified full-time staff, resulting in a growing dependence on substantial numbers of 'unqualified' workers. As such posts often provided the only route for many Black and Asian workers into the full-time workforce, bitter overlaps could occur with the service's debates on how to tackle its own internal discriminatory policies and practices.

Deepening professional self-doubt often surfaced, too, in round-in-circle debates between employers and the tutors responsible for training and qualifying their full-time staff. These most commonly focused on the quality of the workers emerging from the courses and on the adequacy of the field's treatment of these new arrivals. Given employers' increasing reliance on unqualified recruits to fill vital vacancies, the fact that by the end of the decade a majority of those qualifying on the specialist courses were choosing not to go into youth service posts added an extra sharpness to these exchanges. Most of the post-Albemarle momentum in the training of part-timers also ebbed away, undermining not only the joint voluntary-statutory course structures created in the 1960s but the wider notion of a common element running through the youth work practised by both sectors.

In due course external pressures – not least the rapid surge in youth unemployment – did kick-start effective collective and political strategies aimed at influencing the service's national policy-making. These efforts sometimes sought to emphasise young people's participation in what was being attempted. One high profile example of this was a Youth Charter conference addressed by two former prime ministers. Another which was sustained for much longer was a Parliamentary Youth Affairs Lobby which gave groups of young people some direct access to interested MPs. In the main, however, the service's efforts nationally to fill the long post-YSDC political vacuum relied on the top-down collaborative activism of key national voluntary organisations and professional associations working separately though also, increasingly, together.

One key focus for this activity was the need to persuade a reluctant government to set up a new form of national consultative machinery. Though this was eventually agreed in 1976 by the Labour Government which was by then in power, the work of the resultant Youth Service Forum had little long-term or substantive impact. Its size and constitution – 35 members coming as representatives of a highly divergent range of organisations and interests – made it both unwieldy and prone to debilitating internal conflicts. Though addressing some important issues, not least the resourcing of the service, it was often poorly prepared and ill-focused in its approach. By the end of the decade a new Conservative government with little love for such quangos (quasi national governmental organisations) had little trouble finding excuses for closing it down.

More promising and in the end of greater longer-term impact were four attempts between 1974 and 1980 to push through the Commons a private member's bill which would *require* local authorities to provide a minimum level of service for young people. By youth service standards, the last of these campaigns to strengthen its statutory base – led by Trevor Skeet, a Conservative MP – caused sufficient Parliamentary and extra-Parliamentary agitation to force a new Conservative government into a significant concession: a new review of the service. Though the remit for this did allow for some consideration of whether stronger legislation was needed, it also bought time for the Government to head off the more ambitious expectations and demands encouraged by the Labour Government.

Though both the two earlier reviews of the service had had some negative unintended consequences, they were marked by strong convictions, some personal commitment to the service – and even flair. The review committees had also displayed an (albeit cautious) determination to respond creatively to the world of youth as it was then developing. Indeed, as if to indicate that they were not just off the official review conveyor belt, both, somewhat riskily, had been chaired by 'enthusiasts'. Lady Albemarle was a woman of impeccable aristocratic credentials who nonetheless came with a reputation for sharp political manoeuvring. Denis Howell, a junior member in a Labour government, revelled in the unofficial title of minister for youth. As YSDC chair, he played a hands-on role in its work for the best part of six years, including its struggle to produce *Youth and Community Work in the '70s*.

By contrast, in agreeing to the new review, the Conservative government's mood in 1980 could be read as at best truculent and at worst sour and manipulative. In an increasingly controlling political climate, it also seemed to flag up some of its unspoken motives by appointing as the new review group's chairperson a retired civil servant whose last job had been as a deputy secretary at – where else? – the Department of Education and Science.

The impact of Thatcherism

What then were the distinctive features of this new ethos – of what very quickly came to be called 'Thatcherism'?

For most of those involved in the youth service during the 1980s, the most likely answer would probably have been 'cuts'. And why not? For state workers of all kinds, and for welfare state workers in particular, the threat or reality of financial devastation seemed ever present. Throughout the decade, three Thatcher administrations (and indeed the Major government which followed them) kept up an incessant, not to say obsessive, though largely unsuccessful search for the holy grail of minimal public expenditure. This pressure was especially focused on local authorities whose actual expenditure was steadily reduced and whose powers to spend were more and more tightly capped.

However, for state social policy-makers – including in 1981–82 the Thompson Review Group – Thatcherism meant much more than reduced budgets, fewer staff and increasingly ramshackle buildings and equipment. The 'Thatcher project' also set out radically to alter *political* priorities and ways of operating – and the control of these activities. Equally important, it aimed to get deep into the minds and beliefs of the populace – into taken for granted ideologies – in order to change fundamentally the 30-year-old welfare state explanations of why social problems occurred and how these should be tackled. Thatcher's guru in formulating these radical 'new right' ideas was Sir Keith Joseph who, as the Secretary of State for Education receiving the Thompson Report, played a crucial (largely passive and negative) role in youth service events early in the decade.

The anxiety to 'save money' was therefore not driven solely by a desire (real though it was) to eliminate 'waste' or even to enforce the Prime Minister's basic 'housewife's rule' of keeping Britain's spending within its means. For the Thatcher governments, every pound raised by taxes and expended on public services – that is, taken from individuals and given over to the state – was a pound withheld from private enterprise which, alone, could make Britain prosperous. An unshakeable faith in the capacity of the market to produce answers to all Britain's problems – financial, industrial *and social* – thus shaped government policy-making throughout the decade and indeed well beyond. Cuts therefore were not by any means a mere pragmatic or even economic necessity. They expressed, too, a basic social principle – summed up in Thatcher's stated credo that there is no such thing as society, only individuals and families. This was caught precisely by one of the questions asked by a secret committee of senior Cabinet ministers in 1983:

> *What more can be done to encourage families – in the widest sense – to resume responsibilities taken on by the state, for example … for the disabled, the elderly, unemployed 16 year olds?*

One quite simplistic element of this logic led, as noted earlier, to a renewed interest in voluntary organisations and indeed in old style charity. As the state withdrew, these were seen as needing to regain their proper place in the provision of personal and family services. However, the assault on the post-war welfare state went much further and much deeper. On the 'trickle down' principle, a redirection of the nation's wealth from the public to the private sector was in effect assumed to contain its own inherent welfare state. By creating more jobs and thereby giving many more people real incomes rather than miserly state benefits, it would, according to Thatcherite thinking, ensure that prosperity was spread much more widely (though of course not equally) throughout the population.

This form of welfare would have a further beneficial – and in this case moral – pay-off: it would wean millions of people from the dependency culture into which, for a generation or more, state mollycoddling had sunk them. Victorian values, for long a term of abuse, even derision, were thus unashamedly, indeed joyfully, reclaimed. In an all-out effort to repair the terrible ravages said to have been inflicted by the permissive sixties, the individualistic qualities of self-reliance, hard work, labour discipline and personal enterprise were all forcefully reasserted. So, too, were respect for the law and those who enforced it and, especially, for the 'traditional' family.

In all this, how to deal with that most unreliable segment of the population, youth, was, as Albemarle had pointed out 20 years before, *the* litmus test. Through what came to look like an increasingly coherent national youth policy, determined efforts were made to 'remoralise' young people – to ensure that they above all took on the new right's core social and economic values.

- Via a series of major Acts, by the end of the decade schooling had been radically restructured. In part this was done to increase parent ('consumer') power and give all pupils a more consistent entitlement. Equally important, however, was ministers' determination to make schools more responsive to the needs of industry and – though often this was seen as identical – 'the national interest'. A detailed national curriculum was therefore all but imposed and, through more centralised control of their training, efforts were redoubled to ensure that teachers conformed to this new educational world.

- For those who were unemployed special measures were introduced whose central premises were openly enunciated by a former chair of the Manpower Services Commission (MSC) and Thatcher's favourite minister, Lord Young. 'Young people,' he declared, 'are not worth much when they leave school … they have no God-given right to a good wage.' What is more, whatever vocational training they were offered must, he asserted, be 'employer dominated and ultimately employer-led'.

- Within months of taking power in 1979, the new government announced that, for the purposes of 'coping with delinquent young people', it would 'regard child care services as an integral part of the national pattern of law and order services'.

- Other services aimed at or used by young people were bent to this new national will. The careers service, for example, was required to become the instrument of MSC policies and programmes while Income Support rules were increasingly and punitively 'reformed' in order to enforce the new labour discipline on young people.

Given how amorphous its role was and how uncertain its impact on young people, the youth service always remained peripheral to Thatcherite plans and

therefore largely safe from such deliberate and radical make-overs. Towards the end of the decade, the DES did seem suddenly to rediscover, not only that a youth service still existed, but that it might even have something to contribute to the Government's overall educational and social priorities. It thus mounted a series of ministerial conferences with the stated aim of producing a 'core' curriculum for the service.

Given the overall policy climate, however, for most of the decade the best the service could expect or hope for was benign neglect. Not that this left it untouched by Thatcherism. Some financial rundown clearly was inevitable – and was often very harsh in its effects. More subtle was the seeping influence of the new managerialism required by the Thatcherite drive to knock these slippery welfare state services into shape. Nor was this to be targeted only on expenditure. Concerted efforts were made, too, to refocus policy-making and to direct practice on the ground – in the classroom, the Youth Training Scheme, the intermediate treatment project, the careers advice session, the benefits office.

In the context of the youth service, pressures to become more accountable were if anything long overdue. With their often free-wheeling not to say maverick style, youth workers were still often failing to demonstrate that, on their own terms never mind on those defined by young people, they were delivering on their promises. Their reluctance to take ownership of such criticisms helped to ensure that, usually unchallenged, the terms on which the new managerial arrangements were developed – for accountability, cost-effectiveness, monitoring and evaluation and the rest – were largely not youth workers' nor even necessarily their immediate managers'. Overwhelmingly these emerged out of derisive Thatcherite criticisms of youth workers' 'woolly liberalism' which often also reverberated strongly with the disappointments of users, parents and their communities. What should have been integral to core professional self-expectations and the requirements of good practice thus got converted into, and came to be driven by, often hostile political imperatives.

With this came another shift which also had serious long-term implications. Like all state services, the youth service developed an often unnoticed habit of voluntarily tacking to the period's new ideological and political winds. *Experience and Participation*, the report of the Thompson Review Group, provided an early warning of how just such a process could start and in due course take root.

The Thompson Review: Process and proposals

Stumbling into action

At the time the last Youth and Community Bill fell, the minister with responsibility for the youth service, Neil Macfarlane, told the House of Commons that he intended 'to pursue a review of *provision for youth*

which would include an assessment of the need for legislation during the life of this Parliament' (emphasis added). This was in response to a private member's motion, proposed by Trevor Skeet within days of the defeat of his private member's bill. The motion 'call(ed) attention to the problems of young people in contemporary society' and to 'the need of the Government to pursue a positive and realistic policy towards youth'. The motion particularly demanded that the provisions of the 1944 Education Act be reviewed in order 'better to coordinate all departments' efforts in this field' and 'to provide suitable financial resources within (government) expenditure plans'.

That was in July 1980. By the time the membership and remit of the review group were announced a full six months later, though the reference to possible legislation had been retained, the focus was only on the youth service. Macfarlane also rejected suggestions that he encourage his counterparts in Wales and Scotland to undertake parallel reviews, though a separate report on Wales was in fact published in 1984 which dealt with many of the same issues and concerns as the Thompson Report. (Even more decisively, after a period of consultation, in 1987 a national curriculum for the youth service in Northern Ireland was introduced together with a set of national targets.)

As the English review got under way, Thompson himself sought to reassure the organisations which had campaigned for the youth and community bills that the review group would not be bound by a narrow definition of the youth service – not least because such a definition did not exist. Indeed, he likened the service to a medieval map: clear in some parts but with regions of 'fogs and dragons' around its boundaries.

Thompson was explicit about the need to examine three of these grey border areas – the treatment of young offenders, vocational training and full-time schooling. However, he made no commitment to the more expansive youth affairs perspectives which had underpinned much youth service lobbying over the previous decade. In fact, the committee's remit now also required it to clarify whether 'available resources can be deployed more effectively'. As had happened when the Albemarle Committee was first set to work, it was thus widely assumed that retrenchment rather than an opened-out vision would be the guiding principle.

Nor in this case did the actual composition of the group seem to offer much of a reassuring balance. Thompson's own 'insider' background hardly suggested that he would be much of a risk-taker or bring even mildly divergent thinking to his task. Added to this was what one of the youth representatives on the group, John Collins, the chair of the British Youth Council (BYC), saw as a somewhat patronising manner not always best suited to resolving the tensions which emerged during the committee's deliberations.

Collins was one of only two of the group's members who could be said to be a youth service specialist. The other was the director of the National Council for Voluntary Youth Services (NCVYS), Francis Cattermole. Including Thompson, four of

the eight involved initially were senior figures from the world of state education. One was a Conservative councillor while another came from private industry. None brought the kind of outsider's critical and analytical view which, for example, rising academic Richard Hoggart had injected into the Albemarle Committee's discussion or which Fred Milson (an experienced youth work trainer and writer) had provided for the YSDC. Indeed, the evidence at the time was that Thatcher had personally vetted the group's membership. She was said to have taken a particularly hard line on who should fill the voluntary sector place and, even when a strong youth work track record could be shown, had rejected proposed names specifically because of Labour Party or even 'wet Tory' connections.

The group had other features which spoke volumes of ministerial and official failures of imagination or even of a grasp of contemporary youth service starting points and debates. As we have seen, only one of its members could be classified as young. Only one was a woman. None was Black. A further six months were needed to coax out of the DES even a token gesture towards filling these gaps. The response when it eventually came was a single extra appointment – of Jan McKenley, a 26-year-old careers lecturer and former inner-city part-time youth worker from London whose family had originated in the West Indies. The lateness of the move was justified by a DES official on the grounds that 'the group needed an injection of new blood to get a new perspective on the evidence'. By then most of this – written and oral – had been collected and the

Group was already in the process of drafting its position papers on key issues.

The review group did make efforts to collect the views of 'unorganised' youth. At what at the time was criticised by some as unnecessary expense, it commissioned a market research company to gather evidence on how young people preferred to spend their leisure time, what value they placed on organised youth activities and how far existing provision for them was meeting their needs. It also met a group brought together by BYC which lobbied hard for more provision for the 16-plus group, for more political education and, apparently taking the group by surprise, for increased democracy within youth organisations. More broadly, four questionnaires were circulated to guide responses from local authorities, national and local voluntary bodies and youth councils, prompting returns from about 700 individuals and organisations.

When it first came together, the review group said it would take 18 months to complete its work. By delivering its report to the then Secretary of State Sir Keith Joseph in August 1982, it came close to hitting this deadline. It also published an interim statement in October 1981, pushed by what it saw as ministers' simplistic responses to that year's race riots and by a strongly flowing tide in favour of compulsory community service to which most review group members were opposed. This three-page paper outlined its understanding of the social and economic factors creating widespread youth alienation and issued a rallying cry to the government 'to take seriously the (youth service's) informal and voluntary terms of social education of the young'.

Nonetheless, the review group's final report did not appear until well over two years after the defeat of the Skeet Bill. By then, with the first Thatcher administration getting fully into its anti-welfare state stride, the chances of legislation to strengthen the service's statutory base – or even of some less specific forms of positive affirmation for its role – were virtually nil.

First encounters with Thatcherism

In the best social democratic traditions, the report's 'take' on contemporary social developments certainly sought to go beyond the victim-blaming philosophy of Thatcherism. It, for example, insisted that young people mattered as young people – that they had a range of unrealised personal talents and so were not simply to be treated as malleable workers and citizens or as potential delinquents. After nearly three decades in which, it had been assumed, consensus and affluence were the defining characteristics of British society, it also recognised the fissures which persisted within that society, shaped particularly by entrenched differences of class and wealth, ethnicity and gender. And it highlighted how these had in turn helped to nurture an endemic alienation among so many of the young.

When it came to look for positive ways forward, the report reaffirmed the characteristic which, it believed, made the service 'potentially one of the most significant vehicles of social education' – its 'experiential curriculum'. It also endorsed the service's efforts to give young people opportunities 'to take and follow through collective decisions', the freedom young people had over whether to participate or not, and 'the non-directive relationship between workers and young people'.

In spelling out these positions, the report clearly stayed firmly within the service's historic individualistic values and practice parameters. Unambiguously and without even a nod in the direction of the growing Thatcherite insistence on national and especially vocational goals, it, for example, reasserted that the youth service's *sole objective is the personal development of the individual*' (emphasis in the original).

Somewhat contradictorily, however, it also gave strong endorsement to young people's participation (including the role of local youth councils in facilitating this), to political education and to the new 'political' issues of unemployment, racism and sexism and work with Black and Asian young people. In its apparent exclusive emphasis on individual personal development, however, could perhaps be found explanations of two of its more significant misses. One was its lukewarm attitude (at best) to specialist and separate work with young women; the other, its failure even to mention work with gay and lesbian young people. In both these (slowly) emerging areas of innovative youth service practice, developing collective identities and outcomes was seen as being as important as releasing personal potential.

When it came to converting its sole objective into curriculum 'offerings', its framework appeared far from original and even read as dated. Its '5 As', for example (association, activities, advice including information and counselling, action in the community and access to life and vocational skills), contained some strong echoes of Albemarle's 'association, training and challenge' while its enthusiasm for both school-based and community facilities recalled some of Fairbairn-Milson's more simplistic (and internally contradictory) aspirations.

Its broader social analysis, especially its descriptions and explanations of young people's increasingly dire condition, also lacked any of the more imaginative thrusts which had characterised the Albemarle or even the Fairbairn-Milson reports. It drew heavily on over-used generalisation about the mobility and materialism of modern society, the breakdown of family life and of community bonds, and the deterioration of young people's physical environment. As a result, its key messages contained little to stir the blood of youth service activists or provoke them into enthusiastic, still less passionate, defence of its perspectives and recommendations.

Even when it did address some more fundamental issues, its tactic was frequently to fend off the more searching and politically difficult questions. With the 1981 riots in Bristol, Brixton, Liverpool and other parts of the country occurring while the review group was actually at work, it did recognise that the experience of racism caused 'frustration, anger and despair leading possibly to deep-seated alienation' among Black young people. Even so, it managed to imply that it was only since the arrival of more Black people in the 1950s onwards that racism had become a significant feature of British life.

On unemployment – perhaps the youth policy obsession of the time – it decided that 'this is not the place to argue alternative models of future economic growth' even though it acknowledged that 'all commentators seem to be agreed that the present trends … will continue for some time'. The key causes of youth homelessness which it identified – the shortage and high cost of suitable accommodation for young people – were presented as rather unfortunate facts of life. By in these ways playing down just how deep these social divisions were, it was able therefore to conclude that, in spite of the alienation to which elsewhere it gave such emphasis, 'a comprehensive and realistic sense of identity with society' was well within each young person's grasp. It also fed the service's reluctance to address the continuing class nature of many young people's condition which had some significant consequences for its practice during the decade (see Chapter 6).

In due course the report turned to examining how the youth service should be responding to the disadvantaged segments of the youth population, including 'the handicapped' and (briefly) those in rural areas. As well as reinforcing the virtual invisibility within the service of gay or lesbian young people, however, on the barely implicit assumption that sexism was soon to be eradicated it discussed provision for girls and young women as an unfortunate temporary expedient. Indeed here as elsewhere it displayed a weak grasp of history, implying, for example, that it was only uniformed organisations such as the Guides which had a tradition of catering separately for girls and overlooking the deep colonial roots of the racist attitudes and practices which it condemned.

The report also listed a substantial number of weaknesses in current provision. These included failures 'to work out a coherent … theory of social education' and to exploit properly all the methods available to it; 'a patchy and incomplete response to newly emerging social needs'; and 'inadequate provision to meet the needs of the over 16s'. Few at the time would have quarrelled with this appraisal. Less convincing, however, was its conclusion that nearly all of these failings stemmed from 'aspects of management or training' – an explanation which seemed even less tenable when set alongside its admission that it had 'found no method of establishing whether current resources are sufficient to meet needs'.

Because, it concluded, the 1980s had 'brought the beginning of retrenchment', the report did recommend that 'the service should be funded at a high level'. Though justifying this on the grounds that the service had the 'potential for meeting crucial social needs', it was clear, too, that 'funding of the statutory sector should be channelled through the usual policy-making network of the local authority department responsible for the youth service'. This it saw as particularly necessary if the inequalities between different areas of the country resulting from governments' increasing resort to special area strategies were to be reduced.

However, after asserting this positive overall funding position, through some of its other proposals and ruminations the review group offered up some extremely vulnerable hostages to fortune. Not only did it fail to cost some of its recommendations – for example, proposing an age range extended from 14 to 20 (normally) to 11 to 20 which would still somehow allow the 16-plusses to get priority. As if to demonstrate that on financial matters in could be as macho as the new Thatcherite Government, it also offered an elaborate guesstimate of the total resources available to the youth service. What is more, it plunged enthusiastically into constructing this in great detail notwithstanding its earlier admission that it could not decide whether existing resources matched need nor its complaint that 'basic data are lacking, and the information which does exist … often appears contradictory'.

Part of its calculation of resources offered by the report relied on NCVYS 'estimates' of the maintenance costs of its 100,000 to 140,000 affiliated voluntary units. From this, the review group concluded, 'the voluntary sector must be able to draw on funds of at least £200 million a year'. Even though it acknowledged that 'the extent of this resource is almost impossible to quantify', the work of the volunteers involved was costed at another £500 million a year. These approximated figures were then lumped in with other published statistics such as the notoriously unreliable LEA expenditure returns.

The result: reassurance to a government actively looking for shifts of responsibility (including funding) from the public to the private and voluntary sectors that, as the *Times Educational Supplement* put it, the youth service was 'swallowing up more than £1,000 million of resources a year'.

For carrying out such a costing exercise, it is possible to imagine the calculator fingers of a well trained civil servant working overtime. Underlying it, however, was something deeper: a failure to give due weight to the economic knock-on effects of the shifting political and ideological climate in which the review group was operating. It particularly took too little account of how, even before Thatcher came to power, attitudes to public expenditure on the welfare state broadly defined had become increasingly sceptical and constraining. Though still not by any means in full flow, it was clear even in the early 1980s that the new Government was determined to think the unthinkable about such spending – and to try and act on it. Jan McKenley in effect acknowledged the review group's short-sightedness here when, shortly after *Experience and Participation* appeared, she commented on how 'naive' the group had been in its expectations of the political action which its report would stimulate.

On the other hand, even though the review group had been handpicked for their new right Conservative sympathies, ministers were still most displeased with some elements of the report. Its unambiguous faith in social and political education, for example, was bound to jar with a Secretary of State for Education like Joseph who made no secret of the fact that he found it difficult to distinguish between sociology and socialism. Such doubts would certainly have been deepened further by the boldness with which the report resorted to terms like racism and sexism or dared to suggest that anything other than personal or family defectiveness were causing young people's unemployment, homelessness and law-breaking.

Even less welcome to the Government was the report's flirtation with stronger state machinery for coordinating youth affairs locally and especially centrally and its support for a more explicit legislative base for the youth service itself. It certainly approved of proposals for improved agency liaison at local level – within and between local authorities as well as with other key youth providers such as the MSC and intermediate treatment schemes for young offenders. It was also likely to welcome the report's encouragement of a stronger voluntary sector role in the planning and delivery of the service locally, including its funding.

However, though stopping short of advocating a Cabinet office post for youth affairs or even a Ministry of Youth as had been fashionable during the 1970s, the report went on to recommend that a DES minister be nominated to oversee central state departments' collaboration and effectiveness on youth issues. And, though seeking to head off ministerial resistance by defining its role as 'to study, consult, and advise, not to act', it also proposed a national body for 'advising ministers on the exercise of their functions, in so far as these touch on youth affairs'.

When recommending on the need for legislation, the report adopted a similar pre-emptive strike tactic against likely ministerial criticism. Though recognising that 'the lack of a clear statutory framework is a source of confusion and uncertainty of purpose', it nonetheless concluded that the 'very specificity' of the Skeet Bill had been its downfall. It particularly pointed to its 'prescriptive character' which had, it believed, 'robbed it of support which might have been forthcoming for a statute which allowed for more flexibility and local variation'.

It also decided that the crucial question for determining whether a youth service was 'sufficient in itself' could not be answered:

> In view of the variations in context, the difficulty of evaluating community needs and the importance of variety in local provision, it does not seem sensible to define the standards of such provision.

It therefore concluded that any legislation which was passed should confine itself to defining the broad purposes of the youth service.

Despite this major reservation, the report came down firmly in favour of some such legislation. Indeed it went so far as to set out a 'proposed clause for inclusion in a Bill' which, it suggested, should lay a duty on local education authorities 'in respect of a defined age range'. The local state in the shape of the local authorities was not assumed to be the only potentially appropriate direct sponsor. Its duty therefore was not actually to provide 'an adequate service … in their areas' but to ensure only that this was available, especially through regular consultation with and the full participation of both the voluntary sector and young people.

Yet, despite these caveats, the implication of the report's recommendations was clear. In the provision of a youth service, the role and responsibilities of the state were to be confirmed and indeed in certain crucial ways extended and strengthened. Thatcher – she who over a decade earlier had personally cut the service down to size by dismissing *Youth and Community Work in the '70s* as irrelevant and by abolishing the YSDC – was now likely to be even less impressed by such ideas. After all, with the zealous encouragement of her anti-statist guru Sir Keith Joseph, reducing the role and power of 'officials' of all sorts was for her an article of ultimate faith.

The impact of Thompson

Is anyone listening?

By taking almost two years to make his formal response, Sir Keith Joseph gave perhaps the clearest indication of his ministerial detachment from the Thompson Report and many of its central tenets. (In this, he got immediate implicit backing from most of the media which either ignored the report completely or went for superficial human interest angles.) When Joseph's response did finally come, in July 1984 it was greeted as 'very little, very late' by BYC – a view echoed by most of the other youth service organisations which had been pressing for action on it.

After an initial and somewhat disingenuous hope that the report's

proposal for a new youth and community Bill would get a mention in the Queen's speech in November 1982, a year-long campaign started to get some form of legislation through Parliament. It was fronted by the Youth Service Partners Group, a loose alliance of national umbrella organisations and professional associations formed in 1980 after, for the second time, a Conservative Government had peremptorily abolished the service's national advisory body.

When none of the 20 MPs who won a place in the 1982 private member's bill ballot were prepared to take on the report's recommendation, the group considered trying to initiate legislation through the House of Lords. A year later, however, Sir Patrick Wall – like all previous sponsors, a Conservative MP – agreed to promote a Partnership in the Youth Service Bill, though his 12th place in the ballot gave it little chance of success.

Its failure to get a second reading in the Commons in November 1983 marked the last serious attempt by the service to strengthen its statutory basis via the route of the private member's bill. However, with the need for a firmer legislative basis for the service remaining firmly on its agenda, alternative tactics were adopted. In 1988, for example, NAYCEO expressed 'considerable regret' that no reference was made to the youth service in the Education Reform Bill then going through Parliament – dubbed the most radical reform of the education system since 1944. Working with the Scout Association and its Parliamentary lobby, NCVYS went one significant and opportunistic step further:

it persuaded Liberal MP and former youth leader Paddy Ashdown to try to insinuate the desired clauses into the Bill. In the event, neither this tactic nor a move spearheaded by the Scouts to tap what was said to be 'massive support' for the voluntary sector in the Lords proved any more successful than previous similar efforts.

In the two years after the Thompson Report was published, attempts were made to prod a largely indifferent Government into action on some of its other proposals. In December 1982, meetings of the Parliamentary Youth Affairs Lobby, which brought together MPs with an interest in youth issues, were used to jog ministers' memories. The following October, a NCVYS delegation met Joseph while in May 1984 Geoff Lawler, a Conservative MP and member of the Youth Affairs Lobby, got all-party support for an early day motion in the Commons urging the Government to legislate 'at the earliest possible moment'. In the build up to the 1983 general election, the Partners Group also started looking for ways of getting manifesto commitments on legislation from all of the main political parties.

Two of the report's recommendations did in fact get rapid and positive responses from the Government. As perhaps the report's most concrete long-term outcome, a Council for Education and Training in Youth and Community Work (CETYCW) was established in 1982 with powers to endorse and monitor initial and in-service courses (see Chapter 4). A review of the National Youth Bureau (NYB) was also set

in motion which was completed in 1983, well before Joseph had gone public on what he thought about the rest of the report (see Chapter 3).

However, despite the service's lobbying, for over two years the Government all but sidelined the report. By January 1983 Commons questions to William Shelton, the junior minister with youth service responsibility at the time, revealed considerable frustration over ministerial evasions among sympathetic MPs. With support from both Labour and the Liberals, Alan Haselhurst, who had been a sponsor of one of the 1970s private member's bills, asked why 'we have had talks about consultations about consultations for as long as anyone could remember'. As at that stage neither of the two bodies representing local authorities had yet responded to the report, Shelton was able to deflect the criticism simply by extending the period for consultation by a further three months, to the end of March 1983.

The following month, when Joseph himself faced a Commons Select Committee on Education, some of the deeper reasons for the delay became clear – particularly his personal distaste for many of the Thompson proposals. He was, for example, asked for his view on its recommendation that LEAs 'should be recognised as the prime focus for youth affairs by being given statutory responsibility for coordination'. His reply was sharp: 'Youth does most of its activities, mercifully, without taxpayers' money.' The Thompson proposal anyway, he suggested, implied a larger role for LEAs than either he or the Government regarded as necessary, especially for a service which was 'predominantly, overwhelmingly and properly voluntary'.

Joseph was equally dismissive of some other significant Thompson proposals. On the appointment of a Minister of Youth in his department, he confessed that his own reaction was 'not very warm'. When asked about the creation of some form of national consultative machinery for the service, he recalled: 'I have had experience in my previous incarnations of presiding over rather large advisory bodies and I must say my opinion is somewhat coloured by that experience.' As for the Thompson suggestion that political education should be a normal part of the service's curriculum, for him 'the processes of democracy are better articulated by the word "civic" than by the word "political"'.

Though refusing to make a firm commit-ment on when he would be making his formal response to the report, Joseph said he hoped this would come by the end of July (1983). With only two officials at the DES dealing with youth service matters, even this tentative deadline was missed by a full year – something which, as he publicly admitted in the summer of 1984, greatly embarrassed the latest incumbent as junior minister for the service, Peter Brooke.

Urging rather than acting

After getting Thatcher's personal approval, Joseph eventually made his statement to the Commons in July 1984 – that is, just before Parliament broke for its long summer recess. It contained evidence

that some of the service's pressure had paid off. An advisory council was after all to be set up. A 'publicly known unit' was to be created within the DES itself. A DES circular on the service was to be issued. Short-term grants were also to be given to voluntary organisations to run 'experimental projects in managerial innovation'.

Joseph's message, however, had at least as much bad as good news for the service. Explicitly denying 'any suggestion of a crisis among the youth of this country', he rejected the need for legislation on the grounds that 'existing legislation for post-school education remains broadly adequate'. Though later prompting a furious riposte from Thompson himself, not for the first time Joseph could not refrain from noting 'the youth service's considerable resources' (which anyway, he believed, were being underused). He then went on to assert that in this context the report's main recommendation had been that these resources needed to be better managed.

A number of MPs were highly critical of his line of argument. They included Trevor Skeet who urged him to reconsider the need for legislation and Paddy Ashdown who accused Joseph of 'a betrayal of the youth service'. Not surprisingly reactions from the main national bodies were also run through with disappointment and even foreboding.

The promised draft circular issued immediately after Joseph's statement, though making no concessions to these criticisms, seemed more inclined to preach than to propose. It thus made familiar token gestures to participation and to young people with special needs. Though separated out in the final version, the original draft once again collapsed into this single category 'those … who suffer from mental and physical handicap; those at risk; and those from ethnic minorities'. There were the well-worn references to the voluntary organisations' 'distinctive and varied contribution' and to the need to 'reinforce the partnership between the voluntary and statutory sectors'.

However, far from endorsing the Thompson notion of a youth affairs coordinating role for LEAs, local authorities were urged to keep 'a clear focus for youth service matters' while at the same time avoiding 'unnecessary duplication'. As their 'general expectation must be against increases in what they can afford', they were warned to 'appraise carefully their funding of the statutory youth service relative to other claims on their total expenditure' – that is, it seemed, to continue to treat the youth service as one of their lower priorities.

The final version of the circular eventually went to local authorities in March 1985, with a request that they tell the DES by the end of the year how they were responding to a report which had by then appeared over three years earlier. Perhaps as an indication of lost momentum if not of lack of enthusiasm for the report itself, fewer than 60 per cent of local authorities had replied by the deadline with, even four months later, answers still being awaited from 25 per cent of them.

This was not of course the full or final picture. A 1986 NYB survey suggested that, on the back of Thompson, between a third and a half of local authorities had reviewed and often restructured their youth services. In the process many were 'moving on to new ground and tackling new issues'. What was also clear by this time was that, given that it was largely the product of the first Thatcher Government's absence of mind early in its life, Thompson was the best state paper the youth service was going to get for some time. It had made public statements about the deprivations and the injustices facing increasing numbers of the young. It had endorsed some wholly out-of-favour humane and person-centred values and approaches to them. It had even argued for the continuation of arrangements in place at least since Albemarle which assumed that, without a central place for the state, an adequate service could not be provided.

Nonetheless, five and certainly ten years after it appeared, the positive gains flowing from the report were not easy to discern. Too many of its recommendations were framed in terms of 'more needs to be done …' or 'thought needs to be given …' and so appeared more as pious hope than as guide for policy-makers, managers and practitioner to concrete action.

Moreover, even when those with a harder edge were adopted, they were sometimes less the result of the review group's recommendation than at first sight appeared and did not always bring their promised long-term gains. Thus, though the review group's endorsement clearly helped, well before Thompson was appointed key interest groups including HMI, the professional associations and indeed NYB had been pressing for something like CETYCW. NYB was re-organised – but in ways which hobbled rather than released its greater potential. In spite of Joseph's strong personal reservations, a National Advisory Council for the Youth Service (NACYS) was set up – but was wound up immediately it reached the end of its experimental three-year period. Most significantly, perhaps, the review group's rather spurious costing exercise provided ministers who were at best uninterested in and at worst hostile to the service with just the evidence they needed for trying to return it to its 'voluntary' pre-Albemarle state – and status.

Certainly the Thompson Report was unfortunate in its timing, coming as it did at the beginning of the increasingly demoralising Thatcherite era. Nonetheless, even when judged in its own right, few in the youth service were to remember it as a stirring or challenging document, capable of providing them with a manifesto for hard-headed resistance to the coming onslaught.

Main references

Department of Education and Science, *Youth Service*, Circular 1/85, 1985

National Council for Voluntary Youth Services, *Facts: An introduction to Voluntary Youth Work in England*, NCVYS, 1985

Douglas Smith, *Reshaping the Youth Service: Developments in Youth Service Policy following the Thompson Report*, NYB, 1987

Thompson Review Group, 'Interim statement', 1981

Thompson Report, *Experience and Participation: Report of the Review Group on the Youth Service in England*, HMSO, 1982

2   Money, Politics and Organisations in the 1980s

'Strict controls on expenditure'

One of the findings of the NYB survey of the service post-Thompson was that a decade of 'strict controls on expenditure' had already produced 'cutbacks in provision, fewer workers ... and a deteriorating material infrastructure'. This proved to be the service's continuing experience throughout the 1980s and into the 1990s, in a context in which expenditure on the service nationally accounted for, at most, 1 per cent of the total education budget.

The cuts and their effects had been traced periodically during the 1970s by NYB's research officer Douglas Smith, particularly through surveys of projected LEA youth service expenditure – not always the best source of information on what was actually happening to budgets. The first of these, published in October 1979, showed that in the financial year 1979–80 three-quarters of local authorities in England and Wales were planning to reduce spending on their services by an average of 4.6 per cent. Continuing a trend which had started in 1976 and which had already led to a 17 per cent reduction in staffing, these planned cuts ranged from 2.5 to 15 per cent. Nine months later a

second report by Smith revealed that, for 1980–81, 75 per cent of local authorities were envisaging some level of cut, with 31 per cent proposing that this be above a 'severe' 10 per cent.

When Smith returned to re-examine the decade's actual against planned expenditure in 1985, he was able to paint a rather more up-beat picture. What, it seemed, had been reduced was hoped-for expansion rather than existing services:

> The pattern revealed is one of a real but declining rate of growth during the early 1970s and retrenchment or slight expansion during the mid-1970s ... There followed a period of recovery up to 1979 as public expenditure controls were eased. Over the course of the decade, in common with many other public services, expenditure on the youth service increased. By 1979 the youth service was receiving some 50 per cent more in real terms than it had in 1970.

What Smith's retrospective research showed, in fact, was that it was only after the first Thatcher Government came to power in 1979 that 'the political and financial climate changed' resulting in the youth service experiencing its first 'real cut' for 10 years.

Throughout the 1980s the cutting, it seemed, went on incessantly until it reached seriously damaging levels during

27

the later Thatcher and the Major administrations. At one end of the decade, as the budget cycle for 1981–82 got under way, Somerset, Leicestershire, Cumbria, Kirklees, Manchester and East Sussex emerged as posing serious threats to youth service resources. At the other end, in 1988 Kent and Brent were being headlined – the latter for 'a deliberate attempt to destroy the youth service' – with many other authorities planning major cuts to educational provision overall which inevitably filtered down to the youth service. Into the 1990s attention turned to Sheffield, Dudley, the London Borough of Camden, Northampton, Berkshire and Warwickshire. Indeed, the latter turned out to be something of a cause célèbre when it was taken to court for failing to fulfil its statutory duty by the Community and Youth Workers' Union (CYWU – recently converted from the Community and Youth Service Association).

What lay behind most of these headlines was the Thatcher administration's determination throughout the 1980s to get overall local authority expenditure under control – that is, to cut it back substantially. This showed itself most vividly in large reductions in the block grant which local authorities received from central government: between 1979 and 1985 this fell as a proportion of their overall expenditure from 61 to 49 per cent. From 1985 rate-capping, though widely opposed (including by groups within the youth service), tightened the vice further as did the vagaries of the poll tax when it replaced the rates. The result was that local authorities' scope for dealing with this shortfall by putting up local taxes was also greatly reduced.

What sharpened the debate on resources within the youth service, however, and fed the local and national campaigns against cuts was the Government's introduction in the early 1980s of a complex, mysterious and mystifying formula for deciding the size of its Rate Support Grant to each local authority. Known as the Grant Related Expenditure Assessment (GREA), this involved a calculation for each authority of what notionally it needed to spend in order to ensure the level of provision which the Government thought was required. With these figures being broken down for each of its services including the youth service, it quickly emerged that few local authorities were spending on the youth service up to their assessed GREA levels. Across the country as a whole this suggested a huge albeit notional under-spend on the service.

For those fighting the cuts, this information – which at the end of 1984 was pulled together in a NCVYS pamphlet, *GREA Today: Gone Tomorrow?* – provided some powerful rhetorical ammunition. It revealed, for example, that for 1981–82 expenditure on the service in 77 out of 96 English authorities was £28 million less than the GREA allocation. For 1982–83, the gap for 78 authorities was £35 million – though by 1987–88, for 85 authorities for which full returns were available, it had apparently fallen to £23m. These discrepancies came to seem even more unjust when, for 1985–86, the Government announced it was allowing LEAs to increase their spending on the youth service by 8 per cent above the rate of inflation. Its expenditure plans for the period 1988–89 to 1990–91 projected an extra £50 million for the service, producing an overall three-year increase of 38 per cent.

In fact, the resource situation on the ground was never as clear-cut as the headlines and overall figures suggested. For one thing the problem identified by Thompson – a lack of reliable statistical information on youth service resources – had still not been tackled. Indeed, in 1988 the DES was still being pressed (by CYWU) to undertake a comprehensive national audit of the service.

Secondly, 'considerable variations (existed) in the financial fortunes of individual youth services'. This was one of the conclusions of a 1992 survey of youth service funding and expenditure for 1988–89 carried out by the National Youth Agency, the organisation created out of a merger between NYB and a number of other national bodies in 1991. This showed, for example, that though over half of the services surveyed had apparently had increased funding between 1988–89 and 1991–92, within the period 1990–91 to 1991–92 nearly two-thirds had experienced decline.

The picture was complicated still further by policies deliberately designed to shift control of the use of some resources from local to central government in order to ensure that the money was used to address ministerial priorities. Strictly earmarked, some of it was then channelled back to local authorities. In part this was done through long-established programmes such as Urban Aid and Section 11 (grants to support work with ethnic minorities released under one of the local govern- ment acts). Specifically under the DES,

however, targeted resources of this kind were also provided as educational support grants – for example, for work with the young unemployed and young drug users or 'to promote social responsibility'. Though such projects were always time- limited, these allocations could boost local authority out-turn figures in ways which masked falls in mainstream – that is permanent – funding.

Even these short-term resources were far from secure, however. At various times both Urban Aid and Section 11 grants came under threat, while within the DES's own programmes, in competition with the schools, the youth service was always the very poorest of relations. These special programmes did to some degree help to compensate for the losses which the service was experiencing, especially in the second half of the decade. However, local authority funding generally was squeezed harder and harder.

Throughout the decade ministers continued to claim that the service was being protected and that there was no evidence of discrimination against it by local auth- orities. Indeed, a survey of staffing needs in 1988 produced 'optimistic predictions of modest and sometimes substantial growth … by employers' including 'for an overall increase in (full-time) posts of 12 per cent by 1995'. By the early 1990s, however, the experience on the ground was much less positive. Central government's unrelenting pressure for lower local government spending had created huge pain for the service with evidence accumulating by the early 1990s of deteriorating premises and reduced staffing.

What local autonomy?

As well as falling levels of government block grant, rate-capping and the other measures for limiting their spending, a series of education acts also reduced local authorities' autonomy and range of responsibilities. As part of a much wider Thatcherite determination to neuter or eliminate powerful alternative sources of opposition to its strategy, local government generally was downgraded. Thus LEAs were forced to substantially devolve control over schools' budgets to governing bodies and lost their responsibility for polytechnic and further education colleges altogether.

This latter piece of legislation – the 1988 Education Reform Act – turned out to have another less direct but still potentially serious resource implication for the service. With councils needing to give maximum protection to school budgets as a way of convincing them not to use their new powers to opt out of local authority control, local funding for the youth service came increasingly to be treated as discretionary (see Chapter 8).

For the youth service, one of the most directly damaging applications of the Thatcherite strategy for taming local government was the abolition of, first, the large metropolitan councils and the Greater London Council (GLC) and, then, of the Inner London Education Authority (ILEA), all of which were under Labour control. Though having no direct responsibility for the service, the loss of the GLC was nonetheless seen as meaning that potentially there would 'no longer be real youth service provision in London'. The metropolitan councils, too, had helped to underpin often experimental forms of youth work. Despite some interim arrangements through, for example, a London Borough's Grant Unit, up to 200 voluntary groups, including voluntary youth groups, were said to have closed across the country shortly after abolition in 1984, many of them Black and unemployment projects.

However, the damage inflicted by the loss of these tiers of local government was minor in comparison with what happened when the Inner London Education Authority (ILEA) was abolished. Per capita of the youth population, its provision was far and away the best resourced in the country with a total budget by 1990 of £30 million. Nearly £20 million of this was spent on supporting youth clubs and centres and a further £7 million on grants to voluntary organisations. Though sometimes seen as exercising too light a touch on the accountability tiller, it was nonetheless widely regarded as the flagship for a wide range of progressive field projects, equal opportunities policies and practices and training developments. It also acted as a significant force for redistributing resources across the capital, from the richer boroughs to poorer areas. As the new right backlash gathered force, it was these very characteristics which were reinterpreted as 'evidence' of the need to abolish the authority.

First murmurings about abolition came in 1984 when Joseph claimed that the ILEA was 'overspending' its GREA assessments

– and that the youth service was partly to blame for this. Though subsequently denied by his junior minister, Peter Brook, the accusation came with suggestions that the London youth service might be dismantled – and even perhaps handed over to the MSC.

The abolition of the ILEA did not in the end come until 1990. Despite a strenuous campaign in its defence, its youth service facilities, along with the rest of its education responsibilities, were dispersed among 12 London boroughs, most of which were already under intense financial pressure. The Government did set aside £500,000 a year for three years to replace the ILEA's £700,000 a year grant aid to London-wide voluntary bodies such as the Federation of Boys' Clubs and the Union of Youth Clubs. However, the latter was forced to cut back its services as a result of a £60,000 drop in its funding – over a half of its total income.

Within weeks of the abolition its effects were being felt, too, by some of the more cutting edge – and politically unfashionable – field groups. The Westminster Girls' Project, for example, had its grants withdrawn immediately while over the following years many of the facilities and staff of the other services were run down by attrition (at the very least). Some of the boroughs' arrangements for fitting the youth service into their local structures – for example, in Lewisham where it was linked to more formal forms of adult education – also seemed to risk lowering the priority for youth work approaches in their areas.

In comparison with what happened to some other education-based youth services, however, Lewisham's solution was highly conventional. More radical shifts in the youth service's location within local authority structures had begun to happen after local government was reorganised in 1974. Though some were prompted in part by the fashion for 'going community', others stemmed from the decision of some councils to define youth work as leisure or recreation. In the 1980s, this trend continued, though on a much smaller scale than debates at the time often implied. In 1983 a NCVYS survey of LEA-voluntary sector relationships revealed that only five councils had gone down this route. Even though they were later joined by three large authorities – Birmingham and (briefly) Liverpool in 1985 and Wolver-hampton in 1988 – the national audit of the service carried out in 1998 revealed that 90 per cent of youth services were still by then within education departments.

Wolverhampton was anyway something of a special case since the move followed a comprehensive review and analysis both of how local services catered for young people and of their 'social condition' following the collapse of the youth labour market. Undertaken by Paul Willis, an academic sociologist with a long personal connection with the borough, the result was a report which generated considerable interest, including within the youth service, well beyond Wolverhampton itself.

Over the decade, youth services in other authorities retraced their steps back into education. In 1988, for example, Kingston returned its service to the education department because, it concluded, in the leisure and marketing department 'it was almost completely ignored – there was insufficient funding and no recognition of the work being done'. Later that year Manchester decided to the same. Indeed by 1990, though with little noticeable effect, the DES was urging authorities where the service was still located in leisure to follow suit.

Even youth services which had stayed within education were by no means guaranteed security or status. The 1983 NCVYS survey, for example, showed wide variation in where the service fitted into the education service. Only 23 out of 89 councils had followed the Thompson recommendation that it should have its own policy-making committee.

However, though it reached only a very few services, the drift to leisure and recreation had a wider if more subtle effect. This after all was a time when the perception and often the reality were that the service's local financial base was being steadily and significantly eroded – even that it had no statutory right to exist. It was also the time when other major state agencies, in particular the MSC but also local social services departments via a rash of intermediate treatment projects, seemed to be in the process of constructing their own 'alternative' youth services. The very last thing the youth service needed during the second half of the 1980s was a fundamental debate about its identity and core function even when this was provoked by apparently whimsical local decisions on where to locate the service within a particular local authority.

'Voluntaryism' in the Thatcherite era

Depending on the state

During the 1980s the impact of the resource pressures on the service was often felt particularly acutely by a voluntary sector which had become heavily dependent on local as well as central state funding. Indeed a prominent right-wing academic, David Marsland, urged the voluntary youth organisations to return themselves to a 'real voluntaryism' by, for example, seeking more resources on 'the open market' (see Chapter 3). From a Thatcherite point of view, these organisations now provided a stark example of that 'welfare malaise' and the mind-set underpinning it which the new Government was determined to root out.

Indeed very quickly after the 1979 general election, the minister with youth service responsibility, Neil MacFarlane, set about trying to convince the voluntary youth organisations that it was up to them to fill the gaps left behind as public sector money was withdrawn. Clearly echoing Marsland's thinking, he encouraged them to do this by finding private and business benefactors. In 1980 he spoke at a seminar for industrialists and youth projects' representatives organised jointly by the Industrial Society and NCVYS – in itself a sign of the changing times. At this he forthrightly suggested that voluntary agencies should be looking for commercial sponsorship, given in kind (for example, through staff secondments) as well as in cash. Setting his ideas within the wider government educational agenda, he also stressed that voluntary organisations should be helping to bridge the gap between industry and young people. His message was driven home even more bluntly by a leading industrialist. His main attack was on 'the non-existent attributes of the jean-clad commune' and on academics and professionals operating on the 'basic political belief that people want to be transported from the womb to the tomb inside a cotton wool bed of roses'.

Against this shifting ideological and funding background, the DES announced in 1981 that it would no longer make direct contributions to voluntary capital projects. Instead its 50 per cent share would (notionally at least) be channelled through the local authorities' rate support grant system. Faced with what NYB's monthly broadsheet *Scene* called a 'disastrous' plan, NCVYS proposed – unsuccessfully – that a Voluntary Youth Service Trust Fund be set up to administer the DES's allocation and thereby make sure its was kept within the voluntary youth sector.

Throughout most of the 1980s, DES headquarter's grants to 63 English national voluntary organisations did survive. So too did the (time-limited) funding it provided through development grants for innovatory work and through an experimental grants scheme to support local projects doing work of national significance, administered by NCVYS. Nonetheless, though the Royal Jubilee trusts continued to support voluntary projects including,

for example, national developments for the YMCA and PHAB, the business world seemed much less ready to make substantial or ongoing commitments and the voluntary organisations' financial situation deteriorated over the decade.

In 1980–81, for example, the Boys Brigade's reported deficit was £55,000, in 1981–82 £80,000. Though headquarter's grants from the DES in 1984–85 rose overall by 13 per cent over the previous year to £1.6 million, over half the organisations applying reported deficits, 12 in excess of £20,000. A Policy Studies Institute report in 1986 again highlighted the difficulties faced by many voluntary youth organisations in raising non-statutory funds.

None of this, however, deterred the DES from pushing on with its policies of reductions in funding and tighter financial controls. The 1987 report on the headquarter's grants scheme questioned how well the voluntary sector was responding to young people in inner-city areas – often a code for work with Black young people. A consultation exercise followed which led to a DES decision in 1989 to seek radical reform of the whole system of providing grants to the voluntary organisations at national level.

One of the objectives of this exercise was to ensure that organisations' work was focused much more on 'ministerial objectives for the youth service'. Another was to make them accountable 'in a clearer and more precise way for the support given'. Though for the first year 80 per cent of their grant was protected, the (now 67) eligible organisations were in future to be required to bid to the DES for specific pieces of work under new programme-based funding arrangements. These were to have two main focuses: organisation and management and curriculum, with the latter covering 13 areas. In addition to sport, arts, adventure training and spiritual development, these included work with both young women and young men and work with ethnic minorities, with the unemployed and with young people in rural areas.

For the voluntary organisations, these proposals meant some serious heart-searching. Not surprisingly, they saw the Government's move as a very direct threat to their independence and especially to their right to decide what they should be doing to fulfil their, often century old, 'mission'. Some of the larger ones with the greatest financial autonomy even considered opting out of the grant scheme altogether. They also led the resistance to the DES proposals. Nonetheless, these were substantially implemented, leading to a strengthening of the state's diktat over the service by a government whose ideological (and very public) commitment was to reducing the state's role and powers.

At local level, though financial support for the voluntary sector also continued, the NCVYS survey in 1983 confirmed the Thompson Report's verdict: LEAs often lacked reliable information on what they were offering. The survey did, however, throw up sufficient information to show that per head of the local youth population variations were 'so wide as to

be beyond rational analysis: from inner London's £66.29 to Rotherham and Solihull's nil'. Again, with significant differences from place to place, support for the voluntary sector was also liable to be a prime target whenever cuts were called for with, for example, panics and protests occurring early in the decade in East Sussex, Liverpool and Birmingham and at the end in Ealing.

Within local authorities, committee structures not only repeated this confusion. They also reflected the low priority given to partnership where it seemed to matter most, in decision-making and especially over decisions about resources. In 51 of the 89 authorities responding to the NCVYS survey, the voluntary sector had no representation on the appropriate policy-making committee and in 42 no representation on any kind of advisory committee.

Though recognition of a consortium representing the voluntary youth sector overall was more widespread, some at least of the bodies which LEAs saw as playing this role were not actually claiming it for themselves. In authorities where such a consortium did genuinely exist, however, the revenue grant aid to voluntary youth organisations per head of the youth population was on average £5.65 as against only 55 pence where it was missing. At a time when another attempt was being made to push a private member's bill through the Commons, this evidence was used as a further argument in favour of legislation which tightened up local authorities' commitments to youth service.

The MSC: Saviour or coloniser?

By 1987 virtually all local authorities were claiming in their responses to the DES circular on their implementation of the Thompson Report that they had in place some means of consulting with the voluntary sector. By then, however, more and more organisations within the sector, national as well as local, seemed to be concluding that they had found a new saviour. Far from being, as MacFarlane had urged, the business and industrial world, this turned out to be another even more powerful and controlling public body: the Manpower Services Commission (MSC).

Set up in the early 1970s with a broad brief for manpower planning and development, by the early 1980s the MSC had converted itself into the Government's spearhead agency for dealing with mass youth unemployment. By 1987 its budget was £2,000 million and forecast to climb to £3,000 million – more than double the amount central government was committing to the country's universities. In addition to a target of half-a-million school leavers for the Youth Training Scheme (YTS), through its Community Programme (CP) it was by that stage recruiting half-a-million long-term unemployed adults onto one-year work-based training programmes. Many of these were being offered in the voluntary sector.

Though clearly driven partly by an anxiety to alleviate the effects of unemployment, even before the end of the 1970s voluntary youth organisations were drawn increasingly tightly into the MSC web by the need to cover the funding gaps left by repeated cuts to mainstream grants. By the middle of the 1980s, the practice had spread much more widely. The YMCA, for example, was running a range of MSC-funded programmes. These included 200 Youth at Work YTS projects for some 3,000 trainees and a Training for Life scheme which, with 50 per cent more staff than the 300 involved in its mainstream work, threatened to grow into the dog to the rest of the organisation's relatively insignificant tail.

Even more striking was the enthusiasm with which voluntary (and also often statutory) providers took to the Community Programme (CP), even though the one-year limit on appointments imposed severe constraints on what CP youth workers could achieve. Despite a determined campaign by CYWU against the threat to salary levels and established posts posed by the programme, it was widely used by voluntary youth organisations as a source of subsidised labour for running projects clearly requiring youth work skills. In 1983 in Manchester, for example, MSC was investing £4.8 million in CP schemes in the voluntary sector overall – a larger amount than local authority support to the voluntary sector through grant aid and the urban programme. A significant amount of this money was by then being used to underpin organisations like the Greater Manchester Youth Association.

For the youth service, the MSC posed problems both of style and values. In addition to the very short-term nature of its financial support, it was highly prescriptive. Its determination to monitor what was happening on the ground as precisely as possible could make the tactic of 'taking the money and running' very risky. Often, too, especially for small organisations, its operation was unnervingly erratic, with rules and procedures constantly being changed and apparently well established programmes being abandoned at short notice. Over time therefore some organisations found themselves weakened and even de-stabilised as MSC money was withdrawn and strategies for winning more secure funding remained seriously under-developed. In 1988, with the third Thatcher administration finally deciding that an arrangement which left the trade unions with a say in a key area of government policy had to go, the MSC was abolished and its doubtful beneficence removed.

However, the MSC's impact on the service was much more than financial. During its lifetime it also uncom-promisingly set agendas for work which after 1979 was increasingly shaped by tough Thatcherite stands on economic and social issues. As these ideas penetrated its thinking and planning, another vigorous stir was given to the youth service's internal confusions and divisions. In particular, in interaction with the MSC's much more authoritarian values and its highly targeted programmes geared specifically to meeting employers' needs, in a drip-drip way the service increasingly found itself compromising its participatory liberal education principles and non-stigmatising approaches.

Adapting and surviving – again

Both the new ideological and the tightening financial constraints, though not always easy to separate, showed themselves quite explicitly on occasions. Most dramatic was the NAYC's sudden – indeed overnight – closure of its Girls' Work Unit, with the sacking of all the staff involved and the decision to stop publishing the unit's influential newsletter. The action was justified on budgetary grounds and was accompanied by assurances that girls' work would continue to get attention within the organisation. Nonetheless, at a time when a wider anti-feminist backlash was already well under way, considerable political significance was read into the fact that, under a new (female) management, the unit was the only part of the NAYC to suffer this extreme fate (see Chapter 6).

From time to time, other voluntary youth organisations were also brushed by the new ideological and political winds. In 1983, for example, a suggestion by the (Labour) leader of the GLC that the Woodcraft Folk was a more 'relevant' organisation than the Scouts produced an immediate reaction in the right-wing press. Because of its stances on peace and nuclear disarmament and its contacts with Eastern Europe – and notwithstanding the fact that, in doubling its membership, it was rapidly and substantially tipped from working to middle-class – the organisation found itself being compared with the Pioneer movement of the Soviet Union.

In fact, as in previous decades, the Woodcraft Folk was by no means the only 'traditional' voluntary youth organisation striving to establish its up-to-date credentials. The Guides, for example, were permitting members to wear saris and other forms of traditional dress. They were also justifying their continuing single-sex policy on the grounds that:

> ... a Guide unit is a rare opportunity for girls to assert themselves ... They can learn about themselves ... without struggling to be heard.

In 1981 the Boys' Brigade sought to push itself forward by announcing a strategy for programme development aimed both at combating 'obvious threats to our work' and at making the organisation 'more outgoing'. The Scout Association – which through Scoutreach, for example, had for some time been working hard to bring Scouting into the inner city and to ethnic communities – did something similar in 1984. Its plan gave particular emphasis to work with disabled young people and – like the Boys' Brigade and indeed other organisations such as NABC and NAYC – gave specific priority to the young unemployed. By 1990 young women – who had been allowed to join the Venture (senior) Scouts since 1977 – were being accepted into troops aimed at a younger age group.

The non-uniformed organisations, too, sought to keep their affiliated groups and their leaders in tune with new thinking and new approaches. Guests speakers at the National Federation of Young Farmers' Clubs annual conference in 1984 included the leader of the GLC and the chair of the Campaign for Nuclear Disarmament. In spite of the negative publicity generated

by the amputation of its Girls' Work Unit, NAYC continued to offer clubs over 100 'inspirational' programme ideas through its Youth Work that Works programme and promoted a Youth Work in the '80s project to counter youth clubs' poor image. In 1987 it went even further and, for at least the fourth time in its history, gave itself yet another 'modernised' name – Youth Clubs UK.

NABC also went down the modernising route. One of the clearest signals of its intentions was the appointment in 1982 of a general secretary with considerable business experience in the tobacco industry and as a general commissioner of taxes. The next year independent consultants recommended major changes to its management structure and urged that – 'once and for all' – over the following two years some serious confusions of purpose and image should be resolved. These included disagreements over the association's single-sex policy. For some within the organisation, the report suggested, this meant a sharper focus on the 'true boys' club'; for others it created difficulties justifying boys-only provision. Three years later the junior minister responsible for the youth service, Bob Dunn, though seeing NABC as an essential element of youth work provision, also reminded its AGM of a possible need to modify itself to meet modern circumstances.

For The Duke of Edinburgh's Award scheme changes in its direction became particularly pressing in the aftermath of major teachers' disputes over pay and conditions which resulted in fewer volunteers to run extra-curricular activities. The scheme thus turned increasingly to the youth service as a source of recruitment and by the end of the decade had achieved impressive growths in take-up. It was also, according to an HMI report published in 1990, offering a 'remarkably successful' personal development programme. The report also concluded, however, that the scheme was still widely perceived as elitist and in practice was attracting mainly young people who were 'self-motivated, white, above average ability and with parental support'. Another of its newer objectives thus remained elusive: reaching more inner-city young people.

In addition to these longer established bodies, more recent arrivals on the voluntary sector scene added their ideas to the more conventional fare. The National Organisation of Work with Girls and Young Women, for example, founded in 1983 gained a renewed significance after the closure of NAYC's Girls' Work Unit. The National Association of Muslim Youth was by the second half of the 1980s giving some specific attention to providing for Muslim girls. Interaction, founded in the 1960s as a community-based organisation was into the 1990s presenting itself as an exponent of entrepreneurial social enterprise for young people.

As residential care for children and young people fell increasingly out of fashion, older organisations – the Children's Society, Barnardos, Save the Children Fund (SCF) – also began to take on more community-based youth work roles. SCF particularly sought to develop approaches

and support systems which allowed young people to find their voice and have it heard by decision-makers. Though rarely identifying themselves with the youth service as such – at no stage, for example, did they affiliate to NCVYS – their traditional focus on more vulnerable, at risk (and threatening) young people added to youth work's drift towards targeting special needs.

Despite these shifts and sometimes advances, some of the long-standing limitations of the voluntary sector continued to constrain its role and impact. Many of the modernising policies of the uniformed organisations were openly aimed at stemming the loss of older young people. The Boys' Brigade, for example, lost over 3,500 11 to 18-year-olds during 1982 in addition to nearly 6,000 in the 8 to 12-year-old age group. The Scout Association, after using its response to Thompson to call specifically for a fairer share of resources for work with under-14s, also gave specific emphasis within its new strategy in 1984 to holding onto older young people.

More fundamental were debates about values and purpose, with emerging equal opportunities demands from time to time forcing the strains out into the open. These were liable to show themselves particularly in relation to gender and sexual identity though, as a NCVYS report revealed in 1984, voluntary youth organisations were often also complacent in their approaches to work with ethnic minorities. Indeed, the report concluded, despite their claims to being pioneers, many of these organisations were trailing behind the statutory sector in promoting racial harmony.

As in previous periods, for some organisations these pressures meant a continuing balancing act – between on the one hand staying true to basic principles and rationales while at the same time responding to new social conditions and aspirations, especially as these were taken on by young people themselves. Often this debate – for example, within the NABC over whether and why to accept girls into its clubs – was not so much explicit as implicit in its policy changes. Just occasionally, however, it would burst into public discourse, as when the Chief Scout, a retired major-general, used a phrase which was later to have much wider and overtly political reverberations. Urging the organisation in 1982 to 'get back to basics', he went on:

> I wish I saw more alert, smiling Scouts … who called me Chief, or even Sir … It is not Scouting to carry out at camp … pastime hobbies like brass-rubbing, model-making or to play with electronic toys.

Clearly, converting the rhetoric of 'moving with the times' into a practical guide to policy and action was for some organisations and their staff continuing to prove extremely challenging.

Main references

Tony Addy and Duncan Scott, *Fatal Impacts? The MSC and Voluntary Action*, William Temple Foundation, Manchester Business School, undated

Maggie Jardine, *Analysis of Youth and Community Service Staffing: The supply and demand for full-time staffing*, CETYCW, 1989

National Council for Voluntary Youth Services, *Facts: An introduction to Voluntary Youth work in England*, NCVYS, 1985

National Youth Bureau, *Youth Service Funding and Expenditure 1988–92*, NYB, 1992

David Smith, *Partnership in the Youth Service: A survey of local authority policy and practice in England*, NCVYS, 1983

David Smith, *GREA Today: Gone Tomorrow: An analysis of the public spending on youth work, 1981–82 to 1984/85*, NCVYS, 1984

Douglas Smith, *Expenditure on the Youth Service 1978–1983*, NYB, 1985

Douglas Smith, *Taking Shape: Developments in Youth Service Policy and Provision*, NYB, 1989

Paul Willis, *The Social Condition of Young People in Wolverhampton in 1984*, Wolverhampton Borough Council, 1985

3   Resisting Thatcherism

Opposition to the ideological and financial pressures on the service during the 1980s was not (quite) total. Most notably, in 1981 David Marsland, who had maintained an active presence in youth service thinking and policy-making throughout the 1970s, was given space to pose some provocatively contrary questions in CYSA's house journal *Rapport*. Why, he and his co-author Digby Anderson wanted to know, were the voluntary organisations in particular not going for some 'real voluntarism … (by) seeking (their) own support and funding in the open market of ideas and value for money?' And, more broadly, when was the youth service going to do the 'important and difficult work … (of) thinking, researching, coherently deciding and planning about our purposes, our values, our methods, and our priorities?' Their bottom line was unambiguous:

> We should retrieve our steps before we find ourselves taking entirely for granted the absurd notion that "the youth service" means a bureaucratic centralised state apparatus funded and controlled for purposes which are quite possibly altogether incompatible with honest educational principles and contrary to the interests of young people.

Marsland and Anderson's assault was not just significant for the way, clearly and forcefully, it brought into the heart of youth service discourse new right arguments which Anderson had just spelt out in a book which challenged state welfare's conventional wisdoms even more broadly. Indirectly, they also gave a push to the kinds of managerial thinking which gained growing credence in the service as the decade progressed.

They did not go unanswered of course, least of all in the columns of *Rapport*. Indeed, over the decade as a whole, for most of the service's key interests the overriding priority remained defence of its already tiny share of the public purse and political leverage. Most obviously this was mounted by key national bodies, acting separately but also increasingly together in sometimes overtly political campaigns. More circumspectly, too, the core beliefs and ideas of the service as well as its resources were given the best defence possible from within 'the system', on occasions by some unlikely protagonists.

Advising the minister

The national advisory council: A three-year 'experiment'

Though noting the issue of declining resources, the NYB report on post-Thompson developments provided a much broader mid-decade assessment of the outstanding issues – and tensions – with which the service was struggling. Based on an analysis of documents from two-thirds of the local authorities in England and Wales and on a more detailed examination of 27 of those which responded, it found that:

- Resource constraints had put the statutory-voluntary sector partnership 'under considerable strain'.
- Coordination with other services and agencies had become something of a buzz word. When applied within education departments, though some authorities were resisting the trend on the grounds that it 'diverted youth workers away from their main task of working with young people', it was encouraging further shifts towards incorporating the service into a community education model.
- Greater lip service was being paid to 'creating new participation opportunities for young people', including giving them and their communities 'a greater hand in the operation and control of the service'. However, issues of devolution of responsibility and control, equality of participation among different groups and accountability had usually still to be resolved.
- Faced with pressure to extend the age range at least to cover 11 to 20-year-olds, 'the service is being stretched in two directions simultaneously, but with an elastic that is already as tight as it would go'.
- Though the service was also 'setting itself more detailed priorities in terms of issues, approaches or groups of young people', this was bringing with

it a move away from being 'purely responsive and demand-led' (see Chapter 5).
- Though evaluation was clearly beginning to take its place in the youth service's language, little progress had apparently yet been made in actually implementing this through service-wide processes and procedures.

For a National Advisory Council which had been foisted on an unwilling Secretary of State – see Chapter 1 – all this seemed to add up to a pretty formidable agenda.

As with his other youth service initiatives, Joseph did not hurry actually to set up the Council. Though in February 1985 his junior minister Peter Brooke promised action 'in the very near future', its full membership was not announced until the end of the year – 18 months after it had been trailed in Joseph's Commons statement on the Thompson Report. Even then, in its design, it was clearly meant *not* to repeat Joseph's previous unhappy experiences of 'presiding over large advisory bodies' (confessed to the Commons Select Committee in 1983). Its work would be reviewed at the end of its initial three year 'experimental' period while its members, though drawn from 'the broad range of interests in the youth service field', were to serve only 'in a personal capacity'.

In the event, with a membership of 23, the Council turned out to be a larger body than Joseph's initial cautions had indicated and, though dominated by professional educationists, including from the youth service itself, brought in people from industry and the equal opportunities field. Despite pressure from the service's emerging collective voice, the Partners Group (see below) as well as from others, only six of its members were women, only three were Black and only four could be classified as young people – though the last two groupings did each provide a joint vice-chair. The chair was Walter James, a former professor of educational studies at the Open University, who also had a long list of previous youth service commitments on his cv. Most recently, he had been chair both of CETYCW and of the Community Projects Foundation which, having started life as the Young Volunteer Force Foundation, was by the 1980s using community development approaches to work with young people and other community groups.

The Council took up its task against the background of the unhappy 1970s experience of the Youth Service Forum which, because it too often lived up to it, never managed to escape its reputation as a 'mere talking shop'. The new Council also needed to loosen itself from some of the constraints embedded in Joseph's proposed terms of reference and work programme. These reminded it of the need for 'the most effective deployment of available … youth service resources', 'for restraint in public expenditure generally' and – though relations with other relevant services could be considered – for an 'explicit focus on the youth service'. At its first meeting, the DES junior minister now overseeing the service's work, Bob Dunn, did recognise that 'the strength of the youth service lies in its broad provision for a wide variety of young people'. However,

he too stressed the importance of targeting, particularly the young unemployed, young drug users and young offenders.

As it got down to work in May 1986, the Council displayed some resistance to these pressures. Though accepting as one of its first two priority focuses 'young people, work and enterprise', it identified the other as 'increasing young people's effective participation in society'. Subcommittees were set up to report on the potential youth service contribution to each of these areas, one to report by January and one by May 1987. By the end of 1986, with a brief covering Wales as well as England, it had held a residential event in Cardiff during which it met those working in local projects and national organisations. At this meeting, it also drew up plans for a number of other subcommittees to work on other key youth service issues.

This strategy led to further consultation meetings outside London and to a series of publications. In addition to the ones produced by the Council's first two subcommittees, reports appeared at regular intervals on youth work in rural areas, work with girls and young women and with disabled young people. (Its work on the needs of Asian and African-Caribbean young people never saw the light of day.) It also produced a carefully researched and analysed report on resourcing the youth service. At national level this was simply left to gather dust, even though it could have helped to clarify those elusive but – in the context of securing a firmer legislative base – crucial terms in the youth service's vocabulary: adequacy and sufficiency.

One council's consultation paper – on 'a strategy to raise the effectiveness of the youth service' – led in due course to the release of a position paper, *Directions for the Youth Service*. This sought – albeit much more briefly – to revisit many of the areas of provision and the issues and choices facing the service which had been considered by Thompson. The paper again confronted the service's long-standing strategic dilemma over how far to move from its historic 'responsive and demand-led' approaches to more targeted forms of provision. At a tactical level, it largely repeated many of its traditional mantras – on, for example, statutory-voluntary sector partnership, young people's participation and collaborative work with the schools, intermediate treatment projects for young offenders and the MSC's Youth Training Scheme (YTS). However, it also pressed for greater autonomy for local youth clubs within their own communities, explored how the standards of youth work on the ground might be raised and asked whether local voluntary units needed to conform to all parts of their national organisation's programmes.

A month before this last report appeared, in January 1989, the last incarnation of a national consultative machinery for the youth service went the way of all its predecessors: it was abolished by a Conservative government. As on previous such occasions, the service was assured that it was to be replaced by 'periodic meetings between ministers and representatives of the voluntary and local authority sectors'. However, the DES statement also talked of 'consultations … about selected major issues of common concern (which) will take the form of national conferences'. The ground, it seemed, was being laid for the series of ministerial conferences, the first of which took place 12 months later (see chapter 7).

Like its predecessor, NACYS did not escape criticism. Shirley Williams, for example, speaking as president of the Social Democrats just before the 1987 general election, called it 'a somewhat toothless body' while a senior youth officer suggested that it had failed to offer workers in the field clear enough overall direction. And why, one prominent lobbyist asked, had it not offered the Secretary of State advice on 'one of the major youth service issues of the decade' – the need to strengthen its legislative basis?

NACYS survived only three years and was operating in uncomfortable, not to say hostile, political and economic conditions. These included working for much of its life to a Secretary of State for Education who was deeply sceptical about whether it was needed at all and to even more immediately influential civil servants equally unconvinced about its usefulness. Not surprisingly therefore it had much less to show for its work than did the YSDC during the 1960s. Indeed, as the last in a line of such bodies which goes back to the 1940s, it left behind the question: what is the long-term impact of such a structure, certainly on practice on the ground or even on policy-making at the top?

However, in comparison to its most immediate predecessor, the Youth Service Forum – of which memories for many were still only too fresh – it was energetic and grounded, in some significant ways affirming often less fashionable areas of practice. Though inevitably partial, Walter James' own obituary assessment did not seem too far short of the mark. In pursuit of 'consensual development on an extensive scale' he concluded that:

> NACYS might not always have succeeded ... (but) it attempted to produce reports in which the analysis was not superficial and the proposals were likely to be regarded by the field as authoritative and acceptable.

Encouraging and supporting by 'inspection'

Her Majesty's Inspectors had played a role in the service's development at least since its first national advisory council recommended in 1943 that an extended system of grants to the voluntary organisations required some measure of public 'scrutiny and inspection' of their work. Over the succeeding decades the role of HMI expanded significantly, not only through inspections of specific services and units but by more collective inputs into national policy formation. Indeed, as one former HMI subsequently put it:

> Youth and Community HMI, though often relatively few, were often at the sharp end of intelligence-gathering for the Inspectorate and the Department (the DES) about street-level, community-based activity designed to ameliorate youth issues.

Within the youth service itself, they had a strong influence on post-Albemarle developments including the shape of the capital building programme and qualifying training. By the 1970s this was felt too in the creation of NYB and of the machinery which validated first in-service training and then full-time qualifying courses. By the 1980s, the Inspectorate was also offering the DES advice and a professional judgment on its grants to over 70 national voluntary organisations.

At a time when ministers were becoming increasingly disenchanted with officials claiming independence and 'professional objectivity', HMIs during the 1980s found themselves having to tread very delicately. They were anyway as yet some distance from defining clear and publicly explicit criteria or methods for evaluating youth work. In 1986 one provocative analysis of their reports concluded that, though there was 'an inevitable tendency to see their comments as 'expert' or authoritative', there was little evidence that 'inspectors are any further advanced in ... assessing youth work than any other team of informed or experienced workers'.

Such 'ambiguities in their role' became more significant after the Conservative Government decreed in 1983 that, in order to introduce a form of market forces into all educational provision, HMI reports must be published. For the youth service, this attempt to provide consumers with more information on which to judge what was on offer led to a series of public statements on local facilities characterised by, as one reviewer put it, 'a diminishing reluctance ... to beat about the bush'.

Some of the harshest judgments concerned services' lack of clear policies, practice guidelines and evaluation procedures and practice which, by being too recreational in its orientation, was educationally undemanding.

Within these criticisms, however, were some deeper – though on occasions quite explicit – messages. These, for example, gave strong endorsement in principle to what the service had to offer even when flaws within its actual practice were being acknowledged. By highlighting that 'in most authorities there was insufficient funding to provide resources and sustain and develop work with young women', it gave official backing to the need for local authorities to support with more than just words what remained a marginalised and sometimes suspect form of provision. Though sometimes reinforcing the push to concentrate the service's mind on 'problem' young people, HMI also repeatedly made the point that it had gone well beyond its 'coke and ping pong' image and was making a distinctive contribution in some specialised areas.

By the mid-1980s the youth service team of inspectors numbered about 14 and were all (including the senior HMI heading the team) specialists with previous first-hand experience of the service. At that stage they concluded that there were more effective and helpful ways of playing their role than simply publishing one report after another on individual youth centres or projects. They thus chose instead to concentrate their still limited resources on running specialist courses within the DES's Teachers Short Course programme –

and on disseminating experience of good practice by examining and commenting on professional training and youth service responses to specific youth issues.

The result was a series of reports in the second half of the 1980s which demonstrated how – and often how effectively – the service was providing for the young unemployed and for young people in the inner cities and on urban housing estates; how it was offering forms of health education; and how it was contributing to youth arts and youth counselling.

Even more significantly, in two reports – *Effective Youth Work* published in 1988 and *Responsive Youth Work* released in 1990 – HMI used their accumulated experience and insights to identify some of the core features of the work in both the mainstream service and in projects catering for young people experiencing difficulties. The main messages of these flowed subtly but strongly against the current ideological tide. The first in particular went some way to defining the distinctiveness of a person-centred practice and indeed of youth work itself and so provided some much needed defence of the youth service generally. These were followed up in 1993 with a further report, *Effective Youth Work in Clubs and Projects*, which again took the opportunity to spell out the person-centred values which the service sought to embrace.

Behind the scenes, HMI also took up some, for DES minister and officials, sceptical positions. They were unhappy about what they saw as the department's cherry-picking of the Thompson Report.

They unsuccessfully opposed the abolition of NACYS. They were also, at the very least, uneasy about the way the department tried to force the service into agreeing its own core curriculum via the ministerial conferences set up after NACYS was abolished.

In the end these stands could only add to ministers' disenchantment with the relative autonomy of what they saw ultimately as a branch of the civil service needing to be held much more accountable to its political masters and mistresses. By 1992, youth service HMIs were thus to be overwhelmed anyway by the tide which swept the whole process of educational inspection into the new Office for Standards in Education (OFSTED) and, for the further education sector, into a Further Education Funding Council.

Inspiration and pressure from within

Important though they were in raising the profile of the youth service and in stimulating it to refresh its thinking and practice, both NACYS and the Inspectorate had some in-built limitations. For one thing both in the end were impositions from above. For another, both had to tread very gingerly within some hard-line official agendas.

Over a decade in which the struggle to advance or even sustain the service intensified, it therefore had to continue to rely heavily on its own internal resources

and resilience. Much of this work was done locally, often in ways which, when it was not actually invisible from a national perspective, could seem extremely modest. More visible – though still in part shaped by this grassroots activity – were the campaigns of key national umbrella bodies broadly defined, particularly NYB, NCVYS, BYC and the National Youth Assembly and the organisations representing youth workers and officers, CYWU and NAYCEO. Working within their own philosophies and styles and backed up by some of the bolder of their constituent groups and branches, throughout the decade these organisations went beyond just providing their established services to users or members. In an increasingly unsympathetic economic and ideological climate, they interpreted their different remits in more political ways, adopting a range of tactics to defend the service which they had first begun to test out in the 1970s.

Beyond the dissemination of information: The role of the National Youth Bureau

Having evolved in 1973 out of the Youth Service Information Centre and expanded its staff from less than 20 to 70, by 1983 NYB defined itself as:

> A national resource centre for information, publications, training, research and development, and as a forum for association, discussion and joint action, for those involved in youth affairs and the social education of young people.

After the establishment in 1978 of a unit with a specific remit for supporting mainstream youth work, it adopted an increasingly developmental interpretation of its information and training relationship with the youth service. This was perhaps most clearly illustrated by the Enfranchisement Project which from 1978 to 1982 encouraged youth workers to conceive of and implement the content of their work and their methods in ways which for young people would be liberating and empowering. More routinely, the bureau's brief was expressed too in a wide range of publications and in sustained work on, for example, the training needs of part-time and volunteer workers, work with girls and young women and anti-racist youth work.

However, the references in the bureau's remit to providing a forum for joint action on youth affairs were used by its first three directors, John Ewen, David Howie and Janet Paraskeva, as a mandate to address key youth issues *proactively* on the national stage. This approach meant that NYB repeatedly approached very close to, and indeed sometimes crossed, that boundary with political activity which in a period of relatively consensual politics had been left ill-defined. This was perhaps most starkly illustrated by the support given in the mid-1970s to a high profile campaign headed up by Ewen to get Edward Heath, the Prime Minister of the day, to coordinate youth policy more effectively through a Cabinet Office appointment.

Though largely funded by the DES and other central government departments, throughout the 1970s and into the early 1980s NYB maintained this implicitly politicised interpretation of its role. Its

periodicals, for example, in both their editorial and news columns, took up strongly committed positions on contentious youth issues. They attacked slow government responses to rising youth unemployment, police harassment of Black young people and 'harsh deals' meted out by the police and the courts to youth workers carrying out their professional duties. They expressed serious doubts about the way in which the law on cannabis was criminalising young people. They even pin-pricked one Prime Minister on the rapidity with which ministers were moved into and out of the youth service ministerial brief.

Though somewhat more circumspectly, NYB sustained this approach after the new Conservative Government came to power in 1979 – until, that is, a characteristically over-optimistic foray by the Thompson Review Group into the Thatcher maelstrom opened the bureau up to external review. The Review Group's motives were impeccable. Particularly as back-up to the national advisory council it was recommending, it wanted NYB to fill the information gap the group (like others before it) had identified. It therefore wanted the bureau to give more priority to gathering, selecting and making available basic data on the service and to disseminating this and the lessons of good practice in more effective ways. It more specifically proposed that, rather than being organised in 'inflexible' separate units focused on youth work, youth social work, youth unemployment and youth volunteering, 'its resources, particularly its staff, (should) be kept as manoeuverable as possible'.

However, the report also assumed – as it turned out, rather unrealistically – that its proposed national council would not only get rapid ministerial endorsement but that it would be permanent. It therefore argued that this should take over NYB's responsibility 'for the development of new policy-thinking' with the bureau continuing with 'some modification and clarification'. It thus opened the way for a fundamental review of NYB's work and structure by a government with a deep distaste for all such quangos and an increasingly dismissive and anti-pluralist attitude to their claims to independence.

The NYB review was initiated and completed during 1983 – that is well before Joseph had responded to the Thompson Report and certainly before he had agreed to set up any kind of national advisory body. It was carried out by Geoffrey Cockerill, like Thompson a retired senior DES civil servant who in this case had had oversight of the youth service earlier in his career. He was also just finishing a review for the DES of arrangements for inter-national youth exchanges.

Cockerill's recommendations on NYB's future role and organisation were agreed by Joseph in September 1984, though they were not fully implemented until January 1986. The most obvious result was a radical restructuring of the way the bureau decided policy, was managed and, with the abolition of its specialist units, delivered its services. In addition, the crucial agenda of trimming its policy – that is, political – wings, far from remaining hidden, got very explicit attention. Cockerill particularly homed in on the practice of including

editorial comment in NYB periodicals, especially on 'sensitive political questions'. This he saw as putting the bureau's credibility at risk. He also urged that, 'editorials aside, a continuing aim should be to achieve balance by a policy of broadening the argument to include opposite points of view'.

Given NYB's inherently ambiguous and often uneasy relationship with its field, reactions to Cockerill's proposed changes were understandably mixed. Most of them were, for example, supported by NCVYS whose director, Francis Cattermole, had been a member of the Thompson Review Group which had recommended them in the first place. CYWU on the other hand interpreted the Cockerill proposals as 'an attempt to contain and muzzle the bureau and youth work', arguing strongly that, since it 'must be seen to be opinionated', it should have a political role. NAYCEO too expressed concern that Cockerill's proposals might mean that NYB's campaigning role would have to stop.

The most obvious immediate effect of the review was that, from early 1984, NYB periodicals ceased to carry editorial comment. However, Cockerill's warning shot left deeper scars. These the Conservative governments of the 1980s and early 1990s constantly re-opened as they became less and less prepared to pay for what they saw as critiques of – even subversive opposition to – their policies. As a result NYB found itself needing carefully to adjust its work programmes to the demands of its main funder, to self-censor its public pronouncements and play its neo-political roles more covertly.

Though still defined broadly and in developmental ways, the bureau's core functions remained focused on providing information and training services. These were specifically committed to supporting social education within the youth service, initiatives on youth employment, education and training, young people's volunteering and work with young people at risk of offending.

However, its work at the national level on often contentious issues did not cease completely, even if the approach at times seemed more one of firing from the hip than of careful analysis and a strategic choice of priorities. It continued to focus, for example, on the needs of Black young people and young people's experience of the police. As it also persisted in declaring a role in examining youth service policies, strategies and structures, it went on making an ostensibly servicing contribution to the campaigning activities of the Youth Affairs Lobby and the Youth Service Partners Group.

Speaking for the voluntary sector: The role of NCVYS

Throughout the 1970s and into the 1980s, individual voluntary organisations also pursued such campaigning activities in their own right, sometimes in non-public but still effective ways. Indeed the initiatives of some of these bodies – such as the National Association of Youth Clubs' Community Industry scheme for responding to youth unemployment – could have considerable impact on national policies and programmes.

However, within and on behalf of the voluntary sector it was NCVYS which most consistently and overtly took up political positions during this period. It had emerged in 1972 from the Standing Conference of Voluntary Youth Organisations to act as the collective voice of the national voluntary youth organisations and of local councils of voluntary youth services – hardly an easy task given their often divergent philosophies and approaches. Despite occasional internal tremors – for example, at the end of the 1970s over responses to gay and lesbian young people – it succeeded under Francis Cattermole's direction in raising the profile of the voluntary youth sector within key national debates and took up forthright stances on some contentious issues. The fact that during the early 1980s its chair, Robert Aitken, was an ex-director of education with a national reputation also helped increase its leverage on a government keen to nurture most things voluntary.

As the financial situation had deteriorated, NCVYS had from early on challenged government funding policies for the voluntary youth sector. In 1980, for example, it criticised the DES's decision to stop giving direct financial support to capital projects. Three years later it published an influential (and again critical) report on the working of the government's mysterious funding formula for local authorities – grant related expenditure assessment or GREA. By 1984, too, it was looking to adapt its own role and analysis to these changing times and, following six months internal debate, ratified a five-year development plan. This started from a presumption of young people's powerlessness and set voluntary organisations the goal of 'remaining true to their established aims (while) developing their provision in the light of changing circumstances'. It also specifically committed NCVYS to working for a more secure legislative basis for the youth service.

With this agreed mandate, over the decade NCVYS did not hesitate to take on its own member organisations – for example, for their complacency in responding to young people from ethnic minorities. In 1986 it adopted as a model an equal opportunities policy which was both comprehensive and explicit and two years later produced a detailed briefing, *Disability – a Youth Work Agenda*, which clearly influenced the NACYS subcommittee's report on this area of work. With the equivalent organisations in Scotland, Wales and Northern Ireland it also pressed the Government in 1986 to pursue more sympathetic and coordinated youth policies, arguing that the youth service was well placed to act as 'honest broker' between other agencies. Within the Youth Service Partners Group and in its own right, it also continued to campaign hard for a Youth Service Bill, winning support – though not the argument – within Parliament in 1988 for amendments to the Education Reform Act then going through the Commons.

The voice of young people

With the National Youth Assembly (see below), the British Youth Council was one of two organisations which claimed to be 'run by young people for young people'

and to act as 'the voice of young people'. Dating back to 1948, it was created by the Foreign Office as a propaganda vehicle to carry the flag for British young people in Europe. It took on its new name in the 1960s and a new format in 1976. At that stage its most influential activist was its chair, Peter Mandelson, for whom, as for a number of others over the years, it provided a route into national politics. With a view particularly to tackling young people's political apathy, the 1976 reorganisation aimed to integrate BYC's political education work and its work with local youth councils and to strengthen, among other things, its lobbying potential. This seemed to have an almost instant effect when Mandelson's successor as chair, John Collins, was invited on to the Thompson Review Group as, in effect, the token youth representative. It also helped to place the organisation at the centre of a range of youth affairs activities for much of the 1970s.

By the end of the decade BYC had a membership of 6.5 million young people belonging to organisations ranging from party political student groups to the Guides and the Catholic Youth Service Council. Though in the 1970s its leading figures had straddled the party spectrum, in a Thatcherite climate increasingly intolerant of individuals and organisations which were 'not one of us', its campaigning stance on a wide range of, now, politically sensitive issues put its much prized consensus under increasing strain.

As early as 1980 one Conservative MP was accusing it of being run by Communists and was urging ministers to cut its funding. In 1982 there were the first of a series of skirmishes over its positions on sex education and work with gay and lesbian young people. At its 1983 AGM, Conservative students launched a carefully planned assault on its 'disproportionate publicity' for homosexuals and demanded that it support Government policies on the nuclear family, council house sales and reforming the trade unions. Their failure to make progress on these and other issues led to their withdrawal from the organisation for most of the rest of the 1980s. This was backed up by a campaign by the Conservative Bow Group that BYC's £100,000 government grant be withdrawn because of the Council's fraternisation with Eastern bloc youth organisations.

Though at that point the rest of consensus survived, the following year it was the turn of the Labour students' organisation to feel aggrieved. With the aim of safeguarding the Council's survival, careful and sustained lobbying among the more traditional voluntary organisations such as the Scouts led to control of BYC passing to non-party political organisations and local youth councils. Nonetheless, BYC continued to sharpen its radical edge. In 1986 it stepped up its efforts to increase Black representation and participation and in 1989 promoted a conference to highlight young people's losses in the areas of training, benefits and employment. By then, too, it had produced an information pack on gay and lesbian young people which appeared to a DES official 'to be predicated on one set of assumptions only about this matter'. It thus directly contradicted Government policy which by then had been embedded

in legislation forbidding the use of grant aid by local authorities to 'promote' homosexual behaviour.

Perhaps it was not surprising therefore that, by the end of the decade it found itself seriously at odds with the then Secretary of State for Education, John Macgregor. Its international work – for example, participation in a major tripartite conference of delegations from the two parts of Ireland and Britain as well as in East-West conferences and exchanges – was not at issue. Deep differences had emerged, however, over its domestic work, for which funding was actually stopped in 1989. At their root was a conflict between BYC's definition of its role as 'the forum which represents young people's interests' and the DES's, which saw BYC as a voluntary youth organisation like any other – 'little more than a vehicle through which "ministerial objectives for the youth service" could be delivered'. The result was suspension of BYC's political activities and delay for a year of a planned relaunch.

When this finally came BYC, having negotiated a new relationship with the DES and found itself new sources of income, was able to go on presenting itself as 'a national platform for the voice of young people'. Included among its six main programme areas was work on the environment, disability, anti-semitism, and education and training as well as preparation for the next general election. It also continued to contribute to the activities of the Youth Service Partners Group and to play a leading role in the Parliament Youth Affairs Lobby, often being the route by which young people were recruited to meet MPs.

Though less prominent – perhaps because it was less well resourced and based well away from the heart of national political activity in Lancaster – the National Youth Assembly also claimed to act as a channel for young people's ideas and opinions by promoting and supporting a national network of local youth councils. On occasions, the blurred lines of demarcation between it and BYC helped neither their working relations nor the clarity of the National Youth Assembly's own identity or role. (In 1982, for example, it was BYC which investigated and presented evidence to the Review Group on the changing role of youth councils.)

The specific attention given by the Thompson Report to youth councils and its broader emphasis on young people's participation and political education did help in the short-term to boost interest in the assembly's work. At that stage, too, the assembly was supporting affiliated councils to take on wider youth issues such as street violence and the impact of MSC policies and practices on young people. However, as Thompson pointed out, its local reach and vitality were often constrained by 'the ceremonial trappings and the formal machinery of holding committee meetings', approaches which in turned limited its credibility as a broadly representative vehicle for what young people were thinking and feeling. Thus, though keeping alive the youth council idea locally, it remained a junior partner in national debates and campaigns, including as a listed member of the Youth Service Partners Group.

Professional association – and trade union

Though their bottom lines could be sectional and inward looking, to varying degrees the organisations representing the service's paid staff (officers and workers) also defined themselves as key contributors to its wider development – and defence.

By definition, the National Association of Youth Service Officers' conversion into the National Association of Youth and Community Education Officers (NAYCEO) broadened – perhaps over-stretched – its remit while maintaining its philosophy and style as a professional association. At times it struggled as an organisation to take on some of the service's emerging concerns and priorities – for example, in relation to some of the wider implications of equal opportunities.

However, as well as being active in efforts to get new legislation through Parliament, it continued to contribute to the core professional debates within the service – for example, on training and on the range and quality provision on the ground. Writing directly to the Secretary of State, it was one of the first organisations to raise concerns about the effects of the 1988 Education Reform Act on the youth service. It pointed particularly to proposals to allow some schools to opt out of local authority control which could have the effect of depriving many youth organisations of the use of buildings and other school facilities on which they relied.

Faced with local authority cuts which were threatening members' jobs, the youth workers' body which started the decade as the Community and Youth Service Association became the Community and Youth Workers' Union (CYWU) in 1982. The adoption in 1983 of a new constitution completed its transformation into a trade union, with a clear commitment to a more overtly political campaigning philosophy and style.

Though attracting strong support, this move left a residue of dissatisfaction and even resistance among some long-standing and previously activist members, resulting from time to time during the 1980s in significant internal tensions. Indeed in 1986 they threatened the union's very existence when its secretary general, three of its most influential officers and a number of national committee members all suddenly resigned, insisting that the organisation was bankrupt and trading illegally and so should be wound up. At the end of the decade a proposal that the union seek amalgamation with another larger public sector union – eventually rejected – also produced strains within the membership.

From this relatively isolated position, some of CYWU's longer-term strategies – for example, for improving part-time workers' pay and conditions, for affiliating to the Trades Union Congress in 1989 and on pay – brought it into conflict with the local government workers' union, NALGO. Differences between the two unions flared most fiercely in 1992 when NALGO suggested that youth workers should be moved off their own JNC rates of pay and conditions of service and onto those for local government employees.

However, as the largest union in the field (with 2,500 members as against NALGO's 1,200), CYWU provided the chair of the staff panel on the joint negotiation committee for youth workers' salaries. Like NAYCEO, it was also represented on key national bodies such as CETYCW. It continued, too, to press for stronger youth service legislation and on other core youth service issues. (At a meeting with DES officials in 1988, for example, it sought and to some extent got reassurances on the threats to school-based youth service provision posed by the new Education Reform Act's delegation of school budgets to governing bodies.) With its internal women's, Black workers' and socialist caucuses taking up some highly critical positions, it also continued to campaign – both on its own account and in alliance with other organisations – on policy issues affecting young people.

Partnerships, alliances and lobbies

These six organisations had been forced into recognising the collective vacuum at the heart of the youth service when in 1971, Margaret Thatcher, then the Secretary of State for Education, had brusquely abolished the Youth Service Development Council. Though reaction was somewhat delayed, by the late 1970s wider social and economic developments – not least the effects on young people of the collapse of the youth labour market – forced greater coalescence on them. As well as continuing to act in their own right, they thus became active in developing two overlapping joint initiatives: the Youth Service Partners Group and the Parliamentary Youth Affairs Lobby.

For most of the 1980s, the Youth Affairs Lobby consistently strove to put key youth affairs matters, including what was (and was not) happening to the youth service, on the national political map. It was serviced administratively by BYC and supported by the National Youth Assembly, NYB, NCVYS, CYWU and NAYCEO, each of which appointed a liaison officer and on occasions arranged prior consultations and briefings. Without claiming that it was achieving major shifts in Parliamentary opinion or decisions, its tactic was to give on occasions up to 250 young people from all over Britain a direct contact with sympathetic MPs and peers. Through presentations and questioning, the young people were thus able to pass on their first-hand experience of the impact on them and their age group of Government policies and other developments.

Though overall attendance was inconsistent (indeed often extremely low!), a hard core of MPs from all three main parties gave the lobby a high priority. Over the decade most of the main policy areas and issues concerning young people got an often highly critical airing, sometimes more than once. These included Government proposals for young offenders and the young unemployed; the implications for young people of the 1984 Police and Criminal Evidence Bill and of the reform of social

security; problems of rural and of gay and lesbian young people; youth homelessness; and the environment. During Joseph's long silence, the lobby was also used to press for specific action on the Thompson Report; and for new youth service legislation. Lord Scarman was subjected to a grilling on his report on the 1981 urban disturbances and on race relations more generally. Special events were also organised to counter young people's growing disillusion with party politics by giving them a more direct experience of Parliament in action.

As all the same national organisations were involved, considerable overlap existed between the agendas of the lobby and the Youth Service Partners Group. However, the group gave particular priority to following up the Thompson Report, the need for legislation, the reorganisation of NYB and the long delayed promise of an advisory body. The group finally ran out of steam by the end of the decade, in part perhaps because of changing priorities within NYB after Janet Paraskeva took over as director.

However, at just this moment a new collective forum emerged in the form of a National Youth and Community Work Alliance. Two CYWU members had suggested such a grouping even while the Partners Group was still operating, to provide a more 'grassroots friendly' national voice for the service capable of having an impact on national policies and resources. Prompted initially by a national conference held at the end of 1989 on 'field-led influence on youth service policy', it brought together NAYCEO,

CYWU, BYC, NCVYS and the Training Agencies Group, itself an umbrella body for the youth and community work qualifying courses. Aiming to act as both an information-sharing network and a campaigning group, it became involved in 1992 in yet another unsuccessful attempt – this time through a Further and Higher Education Bill – to persuade the Government to strengthen the youth service's statutory basis.

Faced with the Thatcherite and post-Thatcherite tide of the 1980s and 1990s, all these networks and collaborative groupings could, even at the time, seem pathetically Canute-like. Repeatedly they failed to hold back the breakers which were swamping both young people, especially in the labour market, and some of the more liberal educational and welfare facilities inherited from the 1960s and early 1970s. They failed, too, to get major projects launched, particularly new youth service legislation, or even to keep afloat for very long others which did get started – such as the new National Advisory Council. Meanwhile on the ground, it looked as though the drip, drip, drip of cuts might eventually wash away the foundations of the youth service structure altogether.

Nonetheless, perhaps entirely against the odds, a recognisable youth service survived into the 1990s. Moreover, despite the best efforts of Sir Keith Joseph in particular, it had not been wholly returned to a 19th century model which assumed that the state would merely fill the gaps left by volunteers and voluntary organisations. Most local authorities,

albeit in some varied formats and with increasingly scarce resources, continued in most places to play the role of a (if not the) senior partner in local youth service policy-making and provision. And, albeit reluctantly and of course on its own terms, by the end of the decade even the central state was showing some renewed flickers of interest in the service as it began to plan for the DES-inspired core curriculum to be constructed by a series of three ministerial conferences (see Chapter 7).

Main references

Her Majesty's Inspectorate, *Education Observed 6: Effective Youth Work*, DES, 1987

Her Majesty's Inspectorate, *Education Observed, Responsive Youth Work – The Youth Service and urgent social needs*, DES, 1990

Walter James, *Life After NACYS: A personal view*, 1989

Peter Keunstler, *Youth Work in England*, University of London Press, 1954

Marion Leigh and Andy Smart, *Interpretation and Change: a history of the Enfranchisement Development Project*, NYB, 1985

David Marsland and Digby Anderson, 'Escape from Bureaucratic Serfdom? A Positive Perspective on Economic Stringency', *Rapport*, February 1981

National Advisory Council for the Youth Service, *Consultation paper on a strategy to raise the effectiveness of the Youth Service*, DES/Welsh Office, 1988

National Advisory Council for the Youth
Service, *Directions for the Youth Service:
A Position Paper*, DES/Welsh Office,
1989

National Council for Voluntary Youth
Services, *Disability – A Youth Work
Agenda*, Briefing No 8, NCVYS, 1988

National Youth Bureau, *Youth Service
Funding and Expenditure 1988–92*, NYB,
1992

Neil Ritchie, *An Inspector Calls: A critical
review of Her Majesty's Inspectorate*

reports on youth provision, NYB, 1986

David Smith, *GREA Today: Gone Tomorrow:
An analysis of the public spending on youth
work, 1981/82 to 1984/85*, NCVYS, 1984

Thompson Report, *Experience and
Participation: Report of the Review Group
on the Youth Service in England*, HMSO,
1982

Tom Wylie, '"Those that guard I do not
love": A memoir of HM Inspectorate
and youth work in the Thatcher era',
(pending)

4   Staffing and Training

The full-time workforce

The Thompson Report found the service's figures on staffing 'confusing and difficult to interpret'. Nonetheless it made a 'rough estimate' of the numbers involved, suggesting a total of 1,500 full-time officers (600 of whom were working for voluntary organisations) and 3,500 full-time workers (1,100 employed by voluntary bodies).

Though, the report concluded, the part-time workforce depended heavily on married women, the ratio of men to women among full-time workers was 3:1 and among officers 10:1. It also noted that 'the proportion of full-time workers drawn from the ethnic minorities is small'. According to the report, only a quarter of full-timers had come into the service through the youth and community work courses as compared with 50 per cent who had a teaching qualification – with or without some specialist focus on youth work. The report did point to the need for a revised grading structure for full-time workers to help reduce staff turnover. However, it had nothing to say – in relation to recruitment or training policies – on what during the 1970s had become a significant issue for a workforce which for decades had been claiming professional status: the 'substantial number' of *unqualified* full-timers.

By 1984, this issue was again emerging as something of a priority. Research by Barbara Kuper for the Council for Education and Training in Youth and Community Work (CETYCW) – the body which Thompson had recommended to oversee the validation of professional courses – revealed that 13 per cent of full-timers (by then estimated at 4,100) were unqualified. These workers were clearly helping to fill the recruitment gap between the 350 annual output of the specialist courses – not all of whom anyway went into 'youth service' jobs – and the 400 new entrants needed each year to deal with turnover.

Even more significant here, however, were those coming out of teacher training who were particularly strongly represented in an estimated 600 youth tutor and teacher-leader posts. By 1984 they still constituted 43 per cent of the workforce overall. The Kuper Report forecast a shortage of workers later in the decade mainly because after 1988 qualified teacher status would no longer automatically bring qualification as a youth and community worker. After that date, the report forecast, only 3 per cent of trained teachers (some 50 a year) would have taken a youth work option within their training. (By then these anyway were available in only five colleges and, following a review of teacher training, were about to disappear altogether.) With teacher training as a source of recruitment to the service thus likely to all but dry up, CETYCW committed itself to exploring 'alternative routes to qualification'.

By the time Maggie Jardine again reported for CETYCW on youth and community work staffing in 1988, the effects of this new policy were unmistakable. Indeed one of her main conclusions was that 'the trend is towards a declining shortfall until 1992–93, when the supply and demand of qualified workers will balance'. Over the decade that followed the proportion of trained teachers in the youth service's full-time workforce dropped. At the same time within it both Black and women workers came to constitute a higher percentage, though more men than women continued to become officers.

By 1998 when the service's national audit was carried out the statutory sector alone was employing nearly 3,200 full-time workers. Strikingly, given the budgetary pressures of the previous decade, this total was exactly a third higher than that reported by Thompson. By then, too, the proportion who were unqualified had fallen to 10 per cent.

Part-timers and volunteers

The Thompson Report concluded that 31,000 *full-time equivalent* paid part-timers were working in the service at the start of the decade, a surprisingly high figure

given evidence collected subsequently. An NYB questionnaire sent to local authorities in England and Wales in 1983, for example, produced a projection based on a 65 per cent response rate of nearly 28,300 paid part-time workers, including those within the voluntary sector who were grant aided. For the statutory sector in England, the 1998 youth service audit of all the youth services offered a not dissimilar figure: nearly 24,000 workers or 4,000 full-time equivalents.

Though not giving overall figures, the Jardine Report did produce some revealing evidence on how the pressures facing the service were impacting on part-timers. The casualness of their labour meant that, when cuts had to be made, the money for their posts was often used as a buffer against full-time redundancies. At the same time, service re-organisations which transferred full-time staff into area roles with management responsibilities or into issue-based or detached work programmes resulted in more part-timers being pressed into service as youth centre leaders-in-charge and into still more of the face-to-face practice.

With more women and Black workers in the part-time than in the full-time work-force, managers were also increasingly seeing them as potential recruits to specialist full-time posts – perhaps in the process adding to the numbers of full-time 'unqualified' workers. Substantial part-time workers – those employed for six or seven or even more sessions a week – were becoming more common while more authorities were beginning to pay part-timers on a pro-rata basis with full-time staff. This finding seemed to echo one of the conclusions of the 1983 NYB survey which had indicated that 65 per cent of the responding authorities were by then claiming to link their pay scales for part-timers to the Joint Negotiating Committee (JNC) scales for full-timers. However, not only was the strength of these links not clear from the returns: considerable variations in rates of pay among authorities showed up here too.

Findings such as these were of particular significance as pressure built up through-out the 1980s to redress an imbalance – indeed some of the injustices – in the relationship between part-timers and full-timers which dated back at least to the immediate post-Albemarle period. It was exerted particularly by CYWU which, as the Community and Youth Service Associa-tion, had first admitted part-time workers to a limited form of membership in 1977.

As early as 1982, as a starting point for negotiations with employers on part-timers' pay, conditions and training, the union surveyed its part-time members. Though the response rate was very low, the results confirmed more anecdotal evidence, not only on variations in their pay scales, but also on their lack of employment and other rights and their restricted training and qualification opportunities. The survey also revealed that, for over half of the 55 respondents, their youth work was their main source of income – a figure which rose to 81 per cent for the 27 women who replied. This finding was confirmed by a survey of part-time workers in the Sheffield Youth Service carried out at the end of the decade.

The insights gained from the 1982 CYWU survey and through the campaign which then followed took well over a decade to bring part-timers parity with full timers' pay and some key employment conditions. Indeed, it was not until 1988 that the Joint Negotiating Committee agreed to consider part-timers at all. It then set nationally agreed minimum rates of pay and conditions which CYWU's national organiser, Doug Nicholls, claimed at the time represented 'a major shift in the status of part-time staff'. Two years later, with CYWU and NAYCEO now working together, JNC set up a working party to examine the issue of full pro-rata pay for part-timers. This was finally agreed for some, mainly substantial, part-timers in 1992 and, together with wider parity arrangements, for all part-timers in 1996.

These, however, were the *paid* part-timers. What about the unpaid ones – the volunteers who, since youth work was invented in the second half of the 19th century, had done most of the direct service delivery? The Thompson Report estimated that there were over 500,000 of them, 80 per cent working in voluntary organisations. It was clear that those relying on voluntary effort needed to put resources into recruitment, support and training as well as into paying out-of-pocket expenses. At least implicitly, they treated their contribution as self-evidently good and indeed essential, regretting that, in conditions of rising unemployment and increased pressures on full-time staff, they were becoming more difficult to find and hold. Others, too, though also emphasising the support structures required, continued to discuss them in largely uncritically glowing terms, with the youth service minister, Bob Dunn, talking in 1986 of their often 'unsung' contribution.

Concerns remained, however, about their status and even their survival which dated back at least to the 1930s. At the end of the decade, for example, Francis Cattermole of NCVYS warned that a wedge could be driven between volunteers and paid part-timers as the latter were increasingly 'professionalised' by their incorporation into the JNC machinery. On the ground, however, the dividing lines seemed to be far less sharply drawn. Twenty-four per cent of the paid part-time workers responding to the Sheffield survey, for example, said they were working more than six 'voluntary' hours a week while overall this unpaid time was increasing part-timers' working week by about a third.

However, as the protection of children against abuse became an increasingly pressing issue for the youth service as for other services during the 1980s and into the 1990s, the rhetoric which had previously given volunteers unqualified approval came to be tempered by caution and even reservation. Volunteering, it turned out, had a more complicated and even darker side. The first suggestion that police checks might need to be carried out on those volunteering to work with children came in a draft government circular in 1986. By 1993 the Home Office was circulating a code of practice to all voluntary organisations dealing with children which it called *Safe from Harm?*

It was the Cullen enquiry into the Dunblane Primary School murders in 1995

by someone with a youth work involvement (albeit often discouraged) which confirmed the need for 'substantial checks on the suitability of leaders and workers who have substantial unsupervised access to (young people)'. As parents now needed to be assured that their children were being given 'an adequate degree of protection against abuse', such checks, already in place for paid staff, were now accepted as necessary for volunteers, too. Even so, the procedures for implementing this commitment were still not in place in 1999.

Opening up access to training

Monitoring and validating

One outcome of the Thompson Report with a clear developmental impact on the service was the creation in 1983 of CETYCW – the Council for Education and Training in Youth and Community Work. This began with a staff of eight and a budget provided by the DES of £120,000. With much groundwork having been done already by other groups and organisations, over its decade and a half of life the council was given or acquired a variety of responsibilities. Though sometimes criticised for being too liberal and flexible, under its first professional adviser and then director, Don Grisbrook, it used its relatively open and pluralistic structure to promote influential developments in three areas in particular.

- On behalf of the JNC, its newly created Initial Training and Education Panel

(INTEP) monitored and validated initial courses leading to the nationally recognised qualification in youth and community work.

- In 1986, through a Part-time and Volunteer Education and Training Steering Committee, it took on the task of developing part-time leader training in much more systematic ways.
- When it was set up, it took over the monitoring and validation of in-service training and staff development courses and programmes from an existing Panel – INSTEP.

From the start, CETYCW used a peer assessment process involving a representative range of service (including field) interests to carry out its on the ground appraisal and validation tasks. Many of these same interests also had some purchase on the council's policies and directions of movement through formal representation on the council itself or on one of its panels. In addition to national political bodies such as the local authority associations, they included NCVYS, NAYCEO and CYWU and the two organisations specifically concerned with training in the service.

One of these was the Training Agencies Group (TAG) which, as the body representing the providers of qualifying training, broadened its membership over the decade to draw in the growing number and range of courses and schemes which emerged under CETYCW's auspices (see below). The other, a forum for individuals with a specialist training interest or role, was the Youth and Community Work Training Association (YCWTA) though, as

its significance declined, this lost its place when CETYCW was reorganised in 1990.

This restructuring process, which occurred at a time when the council was seen as more necessary than ever, produced some ruffled feelings over 'heavy-handedness' and lack of consultation, particularly among the JNC's representative organisations. Barely a year later, however, uncertainties re-emerged over the priority to be given to the validation of youth service training, and especially its peer evaluation procedures, when CETYCW and NYB merged in April 1991 into the new National Youth Agency (NYA).

For many in the field, the CETYCW and subsequently NYA structures left them feeling distanced from its operations anyway and with only a tenuous influence on its work. It was therefore perhaps not surprising that the council often struggled to confront, and then relieve, some long-standing tensions between field and training interests which continued to play themselves out most sharply in the context of initial qualifying training.

New routes to professional qualification

As the Thompson Report pointed out, the roots of the youth service's training structure at the start of the 1980s could be traced back 20 years at least, to the one-year emergency course recommended by the Albemarle Report. After running for 10 years – twice its intended life – this was replaced by two-year full-time courses in six higher education institutions already involved in teacher or social worker training.

The number of these courses had expanded to 11 by the time Thompson reported with two (at Westhill in Birmingham and Goldsmith's College in London) also awarding a Certificate of Qualification in Social Work. By then, too, a three-year part-time course had been established (at Avery Hill College in London) and a distance learning course (at the YMCA National College, also in London) was just starting.

From then on CETYCW more than fulfilled its commitment to increasing the number of routes to youth and community work qualification. With these having risen to 10 by 1991, some 60 different courses and schemes producing over 1,000 newly qualified workers had been approved and the threat of a shortfall of staff removed entirely. Instead, the service was facing the possibility of an over-supply of professionally trained staff. Moreover, this was occurring even though the youth and community options within four teacher training (BEd) courses were withdrawn from 1991 because they no longer fitted teacher training regulations.

How had this potential glut of qualified staff come about? Much of it was the result simply of an increase in full-time two-year courses from 12 to 16 and of full-time one-year postgraduate courses from two to six. More striking, however, was the appearance or substantial extension of what an HMI report called 'several innovative and creative programmes'. In

part these were made possible by the introduction by the DES in 1976 of funding arrangements for in-service training which gave a specific priority to youth worker training which had been absent from the previous one.

One of these new routes was the three-year part-time course which allowed unqualified full-time workers to combine college-based study with continuing, usually full-time, employment. Between 1984 and 1991, with courses on this model being established all over the country, their number grew from one to nine. In addition one two-year and one one-year postgraduate course running on a part-time basis also gained CETYCW endorsement.

Even more striking by 1991, however, was the existence of 17 recognised apprentice-ship schemes. Though not with CETYCW validation, the first of these had originally emerged out of Sheffield's economic crisis in the early 1980s as an 'earn while you learn' approach to re-skilling unemployed manual workers for community work roles in their own areas. By the late 1980s CETYCW had endorsed three such schemes – a 'repeat' one in Sheffield and new ones run by Turning Point in London and Interface in Birmingham.

In 1989, however, with HMI inspiration, the DES began directly to fund 15 such schemes in England and three in Wales to the tune of £4 million. Given the overall title of Youth Leaders in the Inner City, these offered 'indigenous young people' three-years' employment in youth and community work together with day release for related training, leading to the JNC-recognised qualification. Though most of these schemes proved to be a one-off, in 1992 over 200 qualified workers emerged from all the apprenticeship schemes then running. Significantly, however, the average age of these new recruits was much lower than that of students on the two and three-year courses, and, in line with expectations which had underpinned the DES decision to fund the schemes in the first place, almost half of them were from either African-Caribbean or Asian backgrounds, over half of them were women and 9 per cent were disabled.

Though on a much smaller scale, there were other new arrivals on CETYCW's approved list. These included a two-year full-time trainee scheme, an in-service course for part-time workers and a validating learning from experience (VLFE) scheme. This last approach enabled experienced workers to provide evidence of the skills and understanding they had developed from past practice through a portfolio-building process and then have this assessed and accredited. CETYCW had been working proactively to encourage such a route at least since 1986 when it won special funding from the DES for a feasibility study. The report which resulted, *Taking the Experience Route* published in 1988, provided detailed analysis of what the model required. Though CETYCW's subsequent efforts to raise funds for a pilot scheme failed, a long established project in Greater Manchester with roots in community work broke through the validation barrier in 1989. It was followed by three other schemes in the early and middle 1990s

though by the end of the decade only one of these survived.

Simultaneously – if less obviously and perhaps even accidentally – a trend counter to that of widening access could be seen to be developing, however, which at least contained the potential for redirecting qualifying training down more 'academic' paths. This could have been 'read out of' the appearance of four degree course routes by 1991, one at MA level. More serious, however, was the conversion during the early 1990s of virtually all the established two-year full-time courses from certificate to diploma status.

The drive here seemed often to have had less to do with the requirements of training or of practice as such than with the need to solve a problem which had plagued these courses since the 1970s: their students' eligibility at best for only discretionary grants. For the students themselves, when this did not force them actually to give up their course place, it often meant working their way through college – or simply surviving in poverty. For the courses themselves, the grant situation often seemed likely to threaten their very viability. With Secretary of State Keith Joseph rejecting the Thompson Report recommendation that youth and community work students should get mandatory awards, they thus went into the highly competitive 1990s urgently needing a solution to the grant problem.

This emerged with the recognition in the 1980s of the diploma of higher education both as a qualification in its own right and as two-thirds of a first degree – and therefore as attracting a mandatory award. According to Terry Cane, a CETYCW adviser, by 1991 this was 'fast becoming the level for qualifying training in youth and community work'. Though it could well have implications for entry requirements, course content and assessment methods, this was happening even though 'there has been no policy announcement by the JNC, NYA or the DES. It is purely a market driven phenomenon.'

Albeit via a somewhat incoherent range of the formats or orientations, after at least a decade of pressure CETYCW's generally expansive and open access approach had gone a long way to relieving the service's chronic overall staffing shortage. Indeed, with great urgency, it had overcome the problem identified in 1984 by CETYCW's own research: that a gap could open up between demand for and supply of qualified full-timers once qualified teachers ceased to be recognised automatically as qualified youth and community workers.

Over the decade, however, other (often closely connected) motivations for extending qualifying opportunities existed. One was the need to give access to often very experienced and competent workers, many of whom had already been employed full-time in the service in order to fill vacancies for which there were no qualified applicants. In the process, some of the more fundamental and sensitive curriculum gaps in the workforce were also made good, as skilled members of ethnic minorities, disabled workers and those (especially women) with childcare responsibilities found ways of achieving 'qualified' status. Many in these groups, having earlier in their lives strayed or been forced off conventional educational paths, had looked on entry into a higher education institution as, for them, neither feasible nor, perhaps, desirable. The 'alternative' routes helped to remove or at least lower some of these barriers.

The diversification of qualifying training was driven, however, by at least one other set of agendas, often submerged, sometimes right out in the open: employers' dissatisfactions with the way the full-time training agencies operated and, especially, with the quality of the workers they were 'producing'. Their concerns were often heightened by evidence on the 'export' of youth service training to non-youth service agencies. This, according to the Jardine Report, by 1988 accounted for 41 per cent of the students coming off the two-year courses – a finding very similar to those produced by studies done in 1978 and 1984.

Though these tensions between employers and trainers had existed at least since the early 1960s, communication across the divide had if anything become even more uneasy during the 1970s following the adoption by both of ill-defined and often conflicting notions of community. By 1988, the Jardine Report was thus talking of employers 'feeling frustrated because they do not believe they are listened to by the training agencies' while in 1991 Cane was referring to 'employers' lost confidence in the training provided by the established training agencies'.

In a 1990 report on initial training, HMI did concede that the quality of experiences and opportunities offered by the field work placement – that is, the up to 50 per cent element of professional training which relied heavily on an employers' contribution – was for many students 'poor'. Nonetheless, the main thrust of their criticisms all but endorsed employers' judgments on the courses. Many of these, they said:

> ... concentrate on teaching about social issues, often from a sociological perspective. These issues provide the context of young people's development, but as much attention should be given to the development of such skills as counselling, group work and curriculum development.

In 1997, Tom Wylie, former HMI and chief executive of the NYA, was still reiterating many of the same reservations.

In these 'debates', CETYCW (and later NYA) were often caught in the crossfire, trying to sustain dialogue and extend mutual understanding through balanced representation on the validating groups visiting training institutions and by running the occasional consultative conference. Most significantly, in 1984, as one of its first initiatives, it circulated its guidelines to the endorsement of courses which, adapted as more and more routes came on stream and radically revised in 1997, offered a flexible pathway through the validation process for institutions and schemes.

By the end of the decade, however, the wider demand, encouraged by the Thatcherite revolution in vocational education and training, for much greater responsiveness to employers' needs was starting to intrude into the youth service's thinking about and arrangements for professional training. The service had already begun to spell out the competencies required for effective youth work practice. These had come both from the Bainbridge VLFE feasibility study and a highly influential report on part-time leader training (examined below) which had strongly recommended a portfolio-building approach.

By the mid-1990s, however, pressures for another radical re-plotting of the routes to qualified youth and community work status were impinging on the service. Disciplines as close to youth work as community work and play work had both accepted National Vocational Qualifications (NVQs) as a – perhaps *the* – appropriate model for enabling many more of their staff to progress to nationally recognised qualifications, and for ensuring employers got the kinds of workers they needed. Despite some deep reservations in certain sections of the field and a vigorous campaign of opposition by CYWU in particular, from the mid-1990s the NYA started to do the preparatory work likely to be needed for NVQs to be applied to youth and community work qualifications.

Starting from the strengths of the part-time worker

Even as the Thompson Review Group was at work, stirrings of dissatisfactions over the state of part-time worker and volunteer training began to appear. With sponsorship by the Royal Jubilee Trusts – long-time supporters of youth work training – NCVYS organised a consultation in 1981. In addition to its own training committee members and staff, this brought together representatives of 26 national voluntary youth organisations, nine local councils of voluntary youth services and the Inspectorate. The recommendations which emerged were hardly radical, concentrating largely on improved cooperation between organisations in the delivery of training (including training the trainers). They did, however, propose that new joint initiatives were needed to meet young people's changing needs in a changing society.

Nor, when it did appear, did the Thompson Report push much beyond these somewhat constrained boundaries of analysis or perceived need. It was certainly again anxious to stress how dependent the youth service was, as it had been throughout its history, on 'the huge numbers' of part-time paid and especially volunteer workers. Yet, like almost every other previous such document, it gave their training needs little more than token attention – and much less than it devoted to the training of full-timers.

The review group confirmed what a substantial research report published in 1978 had discovered: that few of the local committees, set up in the 1960s to produce joint training provision across the statutory and voluntary sectors, had 'had the degree of success hoped for'. Nor did the group see any point in trying to resurrect the concept of 'common element' training for which these committees had striven. In effect, this had sought to extract and then train workers for the essence of youth work embodied in the practice of uniformed and non-uniformed organisations, statutory and voluntary.

Instead the Thompson Report argued that it was better 'to start from the situation on the ground'. This it saw as characterised by:

- big national voluntary organisations who were getting on with their own training (even though in 1980, for example, the NAYC wound up its 30-year old King George VI course for volunteers);
- LEAs which had developed a substantial training capability of their own based on their local needs; and
- little external monitoring or moderation of these largely independent operations.

In seeking to fill this latter gap, the review group specifically rejected proposals for a national body to oversee developments. It did, however, note the developing work of the Consultative Group on Youth and Community Work Training on part-time workers' training which in the event turned out to be genuinely ground-breaking. Though not a formally representative body, the consultative group, which from its inception in 1972 had been serviced by NYB, included representatives from CYWU and NAYCEO, NCVYS and the full-time training agencies. Its Part-time Panel (PAVET) spent two years surveying the field and produced a report in 1983 which, at best, painted a 'patchy' and often an unflattering picture of training provision for part-timers.

Two of the survey's findings were to acquire special significance over the next decade. One was that training was by and large still treated by almost all services as meaning courses; the other that, in only two regions of the country was there a structure which guaranteed reciprocal recognition of qualifications among authorities. Building on this research, the following year the Part-time Panel produced a set of proposals which its chair, Duncan Scott, said were 'designed to promote fresh thinking on the training of part-time workers'. Written by Scott and Steve Bolger, one of NYB's youth work training advisers, its title captured precisely its core message: *Starting from Strengths*. It very specifically gave voice to part-timers' own concerns and motivations and in particular the priority they attached to the quality both of the relationships they developed with young people and to on-the-job support.

After reviewing existing training provision across both the statutory and voluntary sectors, the report suggested that the very form this took actually reinforced part-timers' and volunteers' low status within the service generally. Thus, course content was largely determined by the trainers; it was subject and topic-led rather than being shaped by a reading of participants' personal and practice requirements; and it was underpinned by a deficit model of part-timers as 'non-professional trainees'. Not surprisingly, therefore, *Starting from Strengths* advocated that training should be grounded in trainees' current experience so that they became active participants in a learning process. This could then, very deliberately, set out to identify, build on and accredit their existing strengths in the work.

The impact of the report, which was considerable when it was published, was

accentuated by the release at the time or shortly afterwards of six 'extension reports' dealing, for example, with the training for work with Black young people, young women and volunteers. The immediate follow-up by Bolger and the Part-time Panel was extremely vigorous and imaginative and was given additional status (and staff resources) in 1986 when the panel's work was taken over by CETYCW. Conferences for authorities which were implementing *Starting from Strengths'* ideas were arranged, further guidelines and handbooks were published and a video on portfolio-building released. A great deal of grassroots developmental work with agencies and workers was also carried out, backed up by new literature and training the trainer initiatives promoted by other agencies.

As a result by 1988 Bolger was clear that many organisations and authorities had undertaken wholesale reviews of their training provision, often after many years of trundling along without any change. He was specifically able to identify 28 local authorities and 15 voluntary organisations in which over the previous two years 'genuine experimentation and significant development (had) taken place in the training programmes'.

What particularly seemed to touch a highly responsive chord among training providers and part-time workers was *Starting from Strengths'* (initially quite exploratory) notion of how workers' existing practice strengths might best be identified, made explicit and then accredited. This, the report suggested, might be done by a worker constructing a portfolio which gathered together the evidence on her or his competences in the work – on 'what she or he claims to know, be able to do and the values that inform his or her work'. Over the decade after the report's publication, an apparently unstoppable swing to portfolio-based approaches took place, to the point where courses for training and qualifying part-timers became unmistakably unfashionable.

By blowing its fresh breeze through part-time worker training, *Starting from Strengths* undoubtedly rid it of some very old and dusty cobwebs. Its impact, however, was far from one-dimensional. At the time it had its critics, one of whom worried both about the eclecticism of its theoretical sources and its failure ('in the existing politico-economic climate') to address the service's 'central problems of purpose' – specifically over where and how to draw the line between its caring and its control functions. By glossing over these kinds of unresolved dilemmas, over time some unhelpful (if usually unintended) con-sequences did in fact flow from the report.

These were seen particularly in the way its notion of competences almost immediately bumped into and then became confusingly entwined with the concept of competences embodied in a development coming from a very different historical tradition and value base – the drive to establish a structure of National Vocational Qualifications (NVQs). By the early 1990s, long-established external examination bodies such as the City and Guilds Institute in London (to say nothing of some much newer commercial

consultancy agencies) were showing increasing interest in part-time youth worker qualifications. Partly as a result more mechanistic models of portfolio-building and accrediting prior learning began to achieve some credibility within the youth service.

The service did, however, fight back. The Thompson Report's aspiration that Regional Advisory Councils for Further Education (RACs) should in effect become a national network of accrediting bodies for part-time worker training had been realised only patchily. However, once established, the PAVET committee within CETYCW and then later NYA proceeded much more proactively, encouraging and then validating regional accreditation and moderation panels (RAMPs). In effect, in relation to part-time worker training, these were designed to act within their regions as mini-CETYCW's for consortia of local authorities and, sometimes, voluntary organisations. Some were stand-alone bodies, others operated within a host organisation such as an RAC (while they survived) or with one of the regional youth work development units which began to appear during the 1990s. Once the network of RAMPs covered the whole country, their transferable qualifications ensured that in practice a national route to part-time worker qualification had come into existence.

At a time when credit accumulation arrangements were increasingly treating past qualifications as steps towards new and higher ones, the creation of this (long-overdue) structure acquired an even wider significance. At the very least it could be read – indeed, was read by some – as representing a convergence between on the one hand this so-called 'non-professional' route to youth work qualification and on the other the existing 'professional' (especially full-time course) routes. This interpretation was given added credibility as, towards the end of the 1990s, an NVQ route to a professional youth work qualification seemed to come steadily closer. The ultimate rationale of NVQs was, after all, not to provide workers with training as such but to accredit what they knew and could do (including the training they had already completed). Approval of new NVQ standards for youth work, therefore, would inevitably invigorate a question which had been stirring among youth service personnel for some time: 'How much will my RAMP or City and Guilds qualification count towards my recognition as a "professionally qualified" worker?'

In-service training

The creation in 1976 of the In-Service Training and Education Panel (INSTEP) gave the youth service a process and criteria for coordinating and validating its in-service training courses and staff development programmes. The Thompson Report saw INSTEP as having 'laid a good foundation and … (as) beginning to show results'. It talked too, however, of resourcing being slow to appear and, seeing the INSTEP approach as being too reactive, looked to it to play a more 'initiatory role' once it was merged into CETYCW. Doubts were also expressed occasionally by those in the field: David

Anthony, for example, writing in CYWU's journal *Rapport* in 1983, questioned how well tuned INSTEP was into the 'real world' of local authority processes and workers' practice needs.

Certainly some boost to INSTEP's work – and fortunes – seemed necessary. In the six years up to 1984, it had, according to research carried out by Mike Dobson, endorsed only 50 local courses and five staff development programmes. This same research did, however, have one significant before-and-after finding. Whereas before INSTEP was set up 'few local authorities had given much thought to staff development', by 1984 90 per cent of the service (voluntary as well as statutory bodies) was aware of its role and 75 per cent had actually been in touch with it. Though course endorsement was not apparently regarded as a major advantage, its consultancy function and, especially after guidelines were published in 1980, its accreditation of staff development schemes, were particularly valued.

This of course was a period when, as one commentator on INSTEP's activities put it, local youth services resembled 'so many blasted heaths'. Though never flowing freely, more resources for youth service training programmes did, however, become available after the 1986 Education Act put in place new arrangements for funding in-service training generally within the education sector. Known as the LEA Training Grants Scheme (LEATGS), it was unashamedly designed to target this training on central government priorities, and then to monitor what was done much more strictly.

For the first time the LEATGS programme specifically earmarked funds for full and paid part-time youth worker training, though not for training youth officers nor volunteers. In addition to the £1 million set aside in the first year for local youth service training priorities, youth service bids for meeting some national priorities such as combating drugs misuse among young people were also 'strongly encouraged'. With the DES making a 70 per cent contribution towards costs, the result in some (especially low spending) areas was an immediate five-fold increase on what had previously been available for in-service training for youth workers.

By the early 1990s the money committed to the youth service through the scheme (now renamed Education Support Grants – ESG) was being targeted even more precisely and spread even more thinly. (A substantial proportion of it between 1989 and 1993, for example, was used to fund the 'Youth Leaders in the Inner Cities' apprenticeship schemes.) In 1990 the DES's contribution to the grants was cut anyway – from 70 to 60 per cent.

In 1991 the local flexibilities built into the scheme finally proved too offensive to a government still intent on exerting fierce controls on the volume and use of local authorities' spending. At the very moment that the youth service minister, Alan Howarth, was telling a ministerial conference on the youth service how highly he valued youth workers' training, the ESG programme was replaced by a new Grants for Education Support and Training scheme (GEST). This removed the freedom of authorities to spend in-service

training money on locally defined priorities, thereby cutting the levels of grant to some local youth services by as much as 85 per cent.

Despite these increasing constraints, DES funding policies during the second half of the 1980s did seem to have a noticeable impact on in-service training, broadly defined, within the service. By 1990, HMI were reporting, for example, that INSTEP had endorsed 108 different courses and had accredited 19 LEA and two voluntary organisation staff development policies. On INSTEP itself the overall conclusion of the HMI report was that it had 'played an important formative role … nationally' and had had 'substantial influence on the development of (in-service training) practice and staff development policies for youth and community workers in England, Wales and Northern Ireland'.

On LEA policies and practices as such, the HMI report seemed almost to be offering some indirect encouragement to the search for a core youth service curriculum then being pursued through the ministerial conferences. It painted a picture of a very wide and apparently disconnected array of youth service training priorities across the country – counselling and group work; outdoor activities and creative arts; management skills; equal opportunities and much else. The report also threw a little public light on the service's Cinderella status within many local authority structures. 'Too many LEAs,' HMI decided, 'subsume all their (in- service training) funding for the youth and community service under LEATGS budgets' while senior LEA officers 'do not always consult effectively about (the service's) needs'.

Nonetheless the report's overall conclusion was that, in the provision of in-service training, good procedures were being used to assess individuals' needs and that, usually using methods which drew on workers' practical experience, 'the quality of training (itself) ranged from good to excellent'.

Main references

Steve Bolger and Duncan Scott, *Starting from Strengths*, NYB, 1984

Terry Cane, *Professional Training in Youth and Community Work: In Confidence or Crisis?*, CETYCW , 1991

Coopers and Lybrand, *External Evaluation of Training Scheme for Youth Leaders in the Inner Cities in England (ESG XXX) and in the Valleys of Wales (ESG XXIII): Final Report*, DfE, 1993

HMI, *Initial Training for Professional Youth and Community Work*, DES, 1990

HMI, *Inservice Training for the Youth and Community Service in Local Authorities*, DES, 1990

Bernard Harper, *Better than Bessey?*, NYB, 1983

Bernard Harper, *Part-time Youth and Community Workers Survey: Interim Report*, NYB, 1984

Maggie Jardine, *Analysis of Youth and Community Service Staffing: The supply and demand for full-time staffing*, CETYCW, 1989

Barbara Kuper, *The Full-time Staffing Provision in the Youth and Community Service and the "Supply of Training"*, CETYCW, 1984

Mary Marken et al, *England's Youth Service – the 1998 Audit*, Youth Work Press, 1998

Duncan Scott, *Positive Perspectives: Developing the Contribution of Unqualified Workers in Community and Youth Work*, Longman, 1990

Thompson Report, *Experience and Partici-pation: Report of the Review Group on the Youth Service in England*, HMSO, 1982

Tom Wylie, *'Where Hope and History Rhyme': Training Youth Workers for the New Millennium*, NYA, 1997

5 Shifting Targets

The period of Thatcher dominance laid to rest the popular truisms of the 1960s and early 1970s: that Britain was an affluent society which had finally overcome its basic material problems and its deepest social divisions. The 'crisis of capitalism' of the mid-1970s set in motion a train of events which, even before Thatcher came to power, had re-created economic insecurity and re-introduced basic conflict into political life.

Though these changes had their most direct effects on (Labour as well as Conservative) governments' commitments to public expenditure, for the youth service their ripples spread much wider. They placed extra pressures on the service's person-centred philosophy and purposes as a much more demanding governmental ideology penetrated every element of public policy and created new and insistent priorities for all areas of the welfare state. Increasingly, too, the focus of its work was shifted to high-profile 'social problems' – or, looked at from the young person's point of view, the material facts of daily life.

Reaching the unattached

The background to the youth service's debate on take-up and unattachment during the 1980s was some major demographic shifts particularly involving those in their teens. Overall the 15 to 19-year-old population was expected to fall by some 16.5 per cent between 1989 and 1994, resulting in about 30 per cent fewer school-leavers by the end of the decade.

As earlier studies had done, the Thompson-commissioned survey, *Young People in the '80s*, confirmed that, as in other spheres of leisure activity, young people's use of the youth service varied according to age, gender and ethnicity as well as class. It also showed that, although some two-thirds of 14 to 19-year-olds had attended a youth club at some time, at best the proportion actually involved at the time of the survey had remained stuck at only 3 in 10. The Thompson Review Group was particularly disappointed that these included so few 16-plusses.

This not unfamiliar evidence put renewed pressure on the service to adopt detached and outreach approaches. Even by the time Thompson reported, most authorities were employing detached workers. From initially being regarded as a luxury to be cut, when times got hard during the 1980s and 1990s forms of detached and/or outreach work moved increasingly into the mainstream. A study of London's Youth Service in 1995 revealed, for example, that even after the abolition of the ILEA, levels of detached provision increased in 20 of the 33 new local authorities (and declined in only four). Across the country detached workers were being used by 1998 in all but one local authority area.

However, as in the past, such work homed in particularly on those most likely to be in or to be causing 'trouble'. In London by the mid-1990s most of the detached work was focused on drugs misuse, crime prevention, racial harassment and sexual health (often largely a euphemism for anti-AIDS programmes). The 1998 Youth Service Audit also concluded that, as well as being capable of reaching and engaging older young people, detached approaches were particularly amenable to targeting, especially those who by then were being defined as 'disaffected'.

Supportive initiatives for such work were also mounted. During the early 1980s NAYC's Project in Support of Alternative Work provided resource materials as well as a report offering guidance on policy and action. The annual detached workers' conference which had been running at Keele University since the early 1960s continued to attract high numbers and by 1996 had spawned a National Federation of Detached Youth Workers which continued to survive on a shoe-string budget.

Though often free-standing, this growing detached and outreach capacity was sometimes interwoven with another expanding youth service response to those many young people who would never have dreamed of going near a 'conventional' youth organisation:

information, advice and counselling services. These were not of course new – the Thompson Review Group received evidence from 14 local groups, reflecting the growth of such provision across the country since the 1960s.

An umbrella and servicing body for such work, the National Association of Young People's Counselling and Advice Services (NAYPCAS), had existed since 1975, acting as a pressure group, a clearing house for information and training and a lobby to increase funding for existing field agencies. An HMI report covering 1987 and 1988 talked of 85 specialist agencies and of 100 agencies affiliated to NAYPCAS. It also paid the organisation itself – which in 1993 gave itself the telling new title of Youth Access – an unusually unqualified tribute, noting its 'significant contribution to the development of youth counselling' and that it was 'well known, recognised and valued'.

The Thompson committee had taken the submissions made to it on information, advice and counselling seriously, recommending that 'an assured place should be given to such provision within planned local provision'. This encouragement contributed to the subsequent development, with Home Office money and under NYA general oversight, of a network of local youth information shops. The first of these was launched in 1991 in Bradford, with the next three planned to open in Wolverhampton, Nottingham and Accrington. By 1994, 11 were operating across the country.

Youth unemployment and the loss of the wage

A role for the youth service

Despite these continuing efforts to reach out to young people not using the service, neither Thompson nor most subsequent commentators displayed the same level of overt anxiety, even panic, about unattachment which had characterised previous such analyses of the service. This restraint may have had something to do with the emergence of a new and much more specific way of seeing and defining youth's 'outsider' status – 'the unemployed'. In fact, Thompson's own survey of youth activities showed that unemployed 16 to 19-year-olds were more likely to use youth clubs than those who were employed (29 per cent as against 19 per cent). Significantly, this was a finding which the researchers interpreted as indicating that these young people were behaving more like younger adolescents.

Nonetheless, on youth unemployment the Thompson Report simply took it for granted that the service must take some decisive initiatives:

> The youth service has to consider what its role should be, both in providing facilities and activities for unemployed young people, and in sustaining their social confidence, skills and motivation.
>
> It seems to us ... critically important that the youth service should participate fully in the planning, delivery and management of the new Youth Training Scheme.

Moreover, though Keith Joseph, the Secretary of State for Education, might dither over what to do about most of the Thompson recommendations, here at least he had no reservations. A DES circular on *The Youth Training Scheme: Implications for the Education Service*, published in September 1982, unusually devoted a whole sub-section to 'the contribution of the youth service'. This described the service as 'well equipped with expertise and premises to provide the social education necessary to complement vocational training'. It thus saw it as particularly important for:

> ... devising and using learning experiences (especially in group and residential settings) which can often motivate those who do not respond to more formal methods – especially in "outreach" provision.

The expectation that the youth service would make this expertise available 'to all those involved in providing MSC programmes' was reinforced two years later by the minister of state for employment, Peter Morrison. He described an NYB leaflet on the service's contribution to YTS as 'an important resource for the scheme's operation' and thanked youth workers for their role in its development.

Some youth service responses to youth unemployment did indeed follow, with youth workers even (implicitly) 'going political' in 1981 by organising a youth protest rally in London. On the ground, however, these were patchy and often knee-jerk. Across the country clubs and projects opened their doors to unemployed young people, in the main to provide a well intentioned but, in its aspirations and impact, 'lowest common denominator' daytime drop-in facility for filling empty and aimless hours. The title of the NYB support materials published in 1985 – *Beyond the Drop-in* – told its own story. An 1988 HMI report, though concluding that the service was making some distinctive responses to youth unemployment, criticised the lack of clear policies in most authorities and their failure to implement effective curricula for young people's personal development. In 1987 *The Better Possibilities*, produced by NAYC's Dayspace project, very specifically set out to fill this gap by offering a theoretical and practice framework which would give such work greater structure and direction.

As it had done since the very earliest days of this latest youth unemployment crisis, so too did NYB's Youth Opportunities Development Unit (YODU). This was established in 1978 to support youth work involvement not just in youth unemployment but also increasingly in youth training initiatives. Throughout much of the decade it produced a stream of publications all of which simply took for granted the need for a full-hearted and developmental youth service role. In 1982, the head of YODU, Graham Swain, compiled a position statement on employment, education and training on behalf of the Youth Service Partners Group while in 1987 the bureau itself sponsored a major conference on the place of youth work in vocational training and education.

In their own right, most of the national bodies continued to debate and plan how best to respond to what was repeatedly being treated as *the* youth issue of the decade. Though some were sucked more deeply into a funding relationship with the MSC (see Chapter 2), many adopted an increasingly critical stance towards it.

With male unemployment among 18 and 19-year-olds rising by 219 per cent between 1979 and 1984 and by 176 per cent among 18 and 19-year-old women, the nub of these criticisms was often simply: 'very little very late'. However, disillusion with the MSC did go deeper. In an NYB pamphlet, *The State We're In*, published in 1981, Bernard Davies argued that the 'colonising' approach of the MSC represented probably the crucial building block in the construction of an increasingly oppressive national youth policy in Britain. The 'grave concern' about MSC's special measures which had surfaced at the 1982 CYSA annual conference led the newly constituted trade union to call a special delegate conference later that year to consider policy and strategy for dealing with the Commission. By 1983, this unease was being given a more specific focus by MSC's new guidelines on the political content of YTS. These threatened to terminate contracts with off-the-job trainers who failed to deal in objective and neutral ways with 'the world outside employment'.

Community service – military, compulsory or voluntary?

In working out how to respond to the growing number of young people who were neither in school or college nor at work, contending with the MSC was not the youth service's only major diversion.

The collapse of the youth labour market also forced back onto the policy agenda a longer standing solution to the historic 'problem of youth' – the somewhat euphemistically labelled 'community service'. Though in the 1960s this had been an undisputed youth service issue, it in the 1970s and 1980s acquired a much wider political momentum.

This resulted in part from the Conservative governments' aim of placing volunteering of all kinds firmly within their wider social policy strategy. During the 1980s additional pressure came from the accumulating evidence that, even where organisations existed and young people were willing, their philanthropic urge was often blocked by lack of resources and poor cooperation among key organisations. Indeed in 1981 internal stresses almost forced the closure of Task Force, the London organisation which in the 1960s had helped to pioneer young volunteer work with older people.

The Government did attempt to underpin the more traditional forms of voluntary activity in 1982 by putting £4 million into an Opportunities for Volunteering scheme aimed specifically at the unemployed. However, the new moral panic over youth unemployment pushed policy-makers into a search for much more radical solutions. More and more confusingly, these entangled often very ill-defined and even contradictory notions of voluntary service with the need to 'do something' about the young unemployed.

Thus, despite opposition from the MSC itself, between 1981 and 1984 determined efforts were made to add a military option to the 'special measures' available to them. Resource and political constraints initially forced ambitious plans for a six-month course to be watered down, resulting instead in 1982 in a £1.5 million summer adventure training programme. However, the following year, though assurances had to be given that the plans were not a forerunner to compulsory national service, approval was given for the same basic training received by the armed forces' regular personnel to be offered to over 5,000 young men and 150 young women. Though organisations such as NAYCEO and BYC publicly opposed the scheme, in the end it was young people and the military which provided the most effective answers. Only 2,500 applications were received of which 80 per cent were rejected as unsuitable by the new high tech armed services not well disposed to taking on large numbers of semi-literate and unmotivated teenagers.

In many respects, however, even this was no more than a sideshow to much more determined, high-profile and often highly organised campaigns to get voluntary service established as a central, even compulsory, part of youth provision. In 1981 the Joseph Rowntree Social Services Fund provided Conservative MP Tony Marlow with a £5,000 grant for a feasibility report on the subject. During 1982 competing though supportive House of Commons' motions were tabled by leading Conservative and Labour MPs. In the run-up to the 1987 general election, the Social Democratic Party called for a £240 million investment in a national voluntary service scheme for young people. This got immediate and (in line with its long-standing stance) uncritical endorsement from one of the most influential national bodies in the field, Community Service Volunteers (CSV).

Most significantly, however, Youth Call, launched in May 1981, was by the middle of 1982 being strongly encouraged from within Parliament and was also attracting impressive backing from a much wider array of political and religious figures. One of its key source documents was a report prepared by Enrico Colombatto, *Nationwide Social Service: A Proposal for the 1980s*. This examined potential scheme numbers and financial implications, estimating that just to provide much needed but currently unaffordable extra services for the elderly could open up 250,000 placement opportunities for young volunteers each costing about £1,300 a year. It also recommended a compulsory residential element.

The Youth Call prospectus was also given articulate exposition by David Marsland, a leading academic exponent of Thatcherite ideas as applied to the youth service. He started from the proposition that, for dealing with youth unemployment, 'the established spokesmen (sic) for youth affairs' were putting forward 'old ideas which have failed before and will fail again'. Youth Call's proposals, on the other hand, he saw as 'radically innovative' because they faced up to the 'structural significance of youth unemployment'. In 1984 Marsland's Regional Youth Service Unit at Brunel University provided the back-up computer facilities for a £29,000 research project funded by the Carnegie

and Gulbenkian Foundations into how many volunteering opportunities could realistically be created. Its results once again offered optimistic estimates of the number of potential placement opportunities. These were underpinned by MORI poll findings suggesting that 28 per cent of 15 to 24-year-olds thought the Government should introduce a compulsory community service scheme, with three-quarters of the remainder favouring a voluntary scheme.

Though again supported by CSV, Youth Call nonetheless ran into strong opposition. The Thompson Review Group published its interim report in part to caution, albeit diplomatically, against any rapid acceptance of its ideas. More full frontally, Youth Choice was created – an alliance which included BYC, Youthaid, NAYCEO, CYSA, NYB, NAYC and NCVYS. The assessment of the NCVYS spokesperson, Fred Milson, was that the Youth Call 'voice is that of the educator but the hands are those of the recruiting officer'. This view was echoed by the National Working Party of Young Volunteer Organisers which saw Youth Call as in reality proposing 'a scheme into which all young people would be compelled, induced or "obliged" to enter'.

The opposition also contested the Youth Call spin on the MORI findings, pointing out that they also showed only 4 per cent of young people opting for a volunteer opportunity when positive alternatives – employment, staying on at school or college, joining the armed forces – were suggested. As NYB's Young Volunteer Resource Unit put it at a very early stage of the debate: 'If the problem is youth unemployment, community service won't solve it – jobs will.'

Community service – into the national policy agenda

Though Youth Call's intervention produced no quick or dramatic shift in provision for youth volunteering, interest in it persisted and indeed grew, often it seemed on an over-ambitious prospectus. In 1989, for example, The Prince's Trust announced plans for a Young Volunteers in the Community scheme to involve 7,000 young people by 1991 and 100,000 by 2001. A cost-benefit analysis carried out for CSV by the Henley Centre in 1993 recommended a scheme costing £773 million which over three years would recruit 250,000, mostly employed, participants – that is, around 10 per cent of the age group in any one year.

Meanwhile John Major's Conservative Government made determined efforts to seize the national policy initiative in this area of provision. While praising the role of community placements in training and unemployment programmes and in the rehabilitation of young offenders, his minister with responsibility for charities and the voluntary sector, Lady Blatch, saw the youth service as a 'natural vehicle' for achieving this outcome. In 1995 the Government launched its Youth Challenge which, as a high priority within a £20 million package to create 'a more neighbourly society', aimed within two years to give all 15 to 25-year-olds a volunteering opportunity. Though this programme never materialised, the Home

Office used the NYA as a funding and development vehicle to initiate 41 young volunteer development projects across the country staffed by full-time workers.

David Blunkett, shadow spokesperson on education, was working hard to set the Labour Party's own community service bandwagon rolling in time for the next general election. In 1993 he advocated that, with one million 16 to 25-year-olds 'without gainful employment', what was required was 'full-time community service for everyone between 16 and 21'. Two years later, his response to the Government scheme echoed these sentiments, accusing the Conservatives of 'failing to offer a new start to the 750,000 young people outside education, training and work'. Often his starting point was concern about a 'disconnected generation' – a 'nocturnal society where people get up at lunchtime, stay up to the early hours and make their neighbour's lives a misery' – which he saw as constituting an 'enormous ticking time-bomb'. At the same time, while moving away from notions of compulsion he was on occasions arguing, too, that community service was relevant to all young people and not just the disaffected.

Indeed by then the Labour Party was beginning to talk of citizens' service – a notion fed into the debate in 1994 by an Institute for Public Policy Research (IPPR) paper for the Commission on Social Justice written by James McCormick. Set up by the Labour Party in 1992 'to develop a new economic and social vision for the United Kingdom', the commission's report placed youth volunteering in the context of a 'something for something' society in which rights would be matched by responsibilities. As the time came to turn opposition rhetoric into costed and politically feasible policies, Blunkett slowly if, it seemed, somewhat reluctantly lowered his sights. In 1996 he still saw his £30 million Millennium Volunteers proposal as complementing the Labour Party's plans for tackling youth unemployment. This, however, was by then intended to build on existing programmes and, for 100,000 young people taking part, was to aim primarily at fostering personal development. (When the scheme was eventually launched in 1999 by the new Labour Government, the Prime Minister Tony Blair also declared that there was nothing wrong with people wishing to 'do good'.)

Yet, though the link between community service and youth unemployment was sometimes loosened as proposals diversified and became more detailed, it never disappeared completely. Liberal Democrat proposals in 1993, for example, while emphasising involvement in public service, also talked of helping the unemployed. Indeed often expectations were stretched to cover other 'youth problems' with the Henley Report for CSV providing a detailed calculation, not only of the 'opportunity costs' in relation to the unemployed, but also of potential crime reduction benefits.

On the other hand, compulsion – even strong persuasion – never gained significant political backing, not least perhaps because young people began to make it clear that they were none too

pleased at being put under pressure by top-down policy-makers. Black young people, for example, were often critical of the limited recognition given to their community activities as volunteering. An enquiry in 1995 commissioned by the Home Office's Voluntary Services Unit (VSU), though again revealing that many – though by no means all – young people were in principle sympathetic to serving their community, particularly in the context of community self-help, also contained some cautionary messages. Most were concerned that a national scheme could undermine personal choice and freedom while for young men from traditional working-class backgrounds, resorting to volunteering seemed tantamount to admitting that they had failed to find a paid job.

As David Howie, director of NYB had reminded those looking for quick, easy – and classless – political solutions very early in the 1980s debate:

> National community service will not respond to the needs and aspirations of young people, who want real jobs, income, status and choice.

From unemployment into poverty – and homelessness

As Thatcherite social policies bit deeper and deeper into their lives over the decade, it was precisely these issues rather than where and how to become a community volunteer which preoccupied more and more young people. Most directly and materially, the pressure came from the government's use of the social security system to discipline them and constrain their freedom of movement. By 1981 summer school-leavers were debarred from claiming benefit until the following September. The next year a campaign was needed to fend off proposals to withdraw benefit from YTS 'refusniks' – a temporary victory only since by 1988 all but a highly 'exceptional' minority of 16 to 18-year-olds had lost this right completely. The moves to contain – that is, reduce – young people's income were reinforced by the removal in 1985 of the minimum protection given to under 20-year-olds by wages councils.

During these years, too, changes in board and lodging and housing benefit rules virtually ruled out independent living for unemployed under 26-year-olds without children, in the process setting this as, de facto, a new age of majority for large numbers of young people. Towards the end of the decade, the National Association of Citizen's Advice Bureaux reported that 'significant numbers of destitute young people' were presenting themselves to its advisers while the Campaign for the Homeless and Rootless (CHAR) warned that many more young people were bound to end up sleeping rough.

On these issues some of the youth service's major national umbrella and servicing organisations did make their voices heard in more organised ways.

BYC, for example, put up some very public resistance to the proposed benefit changes. With its Youth Service Partner organisations, it also gave young people a chance in 1986 to present their experiences to MPs through the Parliamentary Youth Affairs Lobby. The previous year NYB had warned of the likely social costs of selling young people short and followed this up with a briefing paper for young people on the implications for them of the 1988 Social Security Act then being implemented. Some at least verbal backing was given, too, to groups like CHAR and Youthaid, the research and pressure group on youth unemployment whose creation in the 1970s had been backed by a number of youth service interests.

By the second half of the 1980s, the predicted rise in the number of homeless young people resulting from the squeeze on young people's benefits had duly materialised. In fact, according to the report of a National Enquiry commissioned by 10 youth charities by 1996, their numbers were considerably higher than had previously been acknowledged.

Over six issues in 1985 NYB's monthly periodical, *Youth in Society*, sought to raise youth workers' awareness of homelessness by running a series of six articles and providing support, information and resources. The following year NYB organised a seminar which brought together some 50 youth workers and officers from mainstream and specialist youth agencies, while in 1987 BYC helped to persuade a Labour MP to sponsor a private member's bill aimed at extending some of the existing housing legislation to young people. In 1993, a report by the Office for Standards in Education (OFSTED) on youth work with 'young people at risk' highlighted a number of local projects offering support to the homeless.

With the arrival of the Foyer movement from France and the establishment in 1992 of the Foyer Federation for Youth, youth service bodies like the YMCA were also being drawn into hostel developments which tied the provision of accommodation for young people to their agreement to undertake employment training. However, as it had in the 1970s, when young people's homelessness emerged as an early pointer to the dark underside of Britain's 'never-had-it-so-good' society, the service's levels of consciousness on the issue remained limited.

In 1995, for example, Andy Wiggans, previously coordinator of a homelessness project run by the Greater Manchester Youth Association, reminded the service of one Department of Health and Social Security working party proposal made 10 years earlier: that it should play a support role in work with homeless young people. Not only had little been done to implement this. According to Wiggans, the service had also responded poorly to conferences partly sponsored by NCVYS and by BYC as well as to a request for information from the field by NAYPCAS. Few youth workers or youth service managers, it seemed, were prioritising housing as a young people's issue.

Youth work meets law and order

Young people, youth workers and the police

During the 1980s and into the 1990s, youth service interests repeatedly expressed concerns over the way that the law and the police were dealing with young people. They campaigned, too, against emerging policies and legislation which risked unnecessarily criminalising many more of them. In published evidence to a Royal Commission on Criminal Procedure in 1979, for example, NYB had firmly rejected proposals to increase police powers in their dealings with young people. At NYB's AGM in 1980 its director, David Howie, publicly criticised the Government's White Paper on young offenders, as did an alliance of over 20 organisations that year at a Youth Affairs Lobby meeting with MPs.

Two years later Howie and others spoke out again against a Criminal Justice Act which contained plans to introduce curfews for young offenders – legislation which over the next two years helped to push up numbers of juvenile offenders in penal establishments by 21 per cent. The 1985 Police and Criminal Evidence Act also prompted some strong reactions from within the service, with both CYWU and NYB producing guidelines on its implications for young people and youth workers. NCVYS, calling the Bill 'a worrying development', expressed concerns that 'law and order ... (could) become the altar on which the freedom of young people, their confidence in the police and their trust in youth workers may be sacrificed'. Proposals in the 1992 Criminal Justice Bill and in the Criminal Justice and Public Order Act which, for example, specifically targeted youth 'raves', revived and reinforced such fears.

In a climate which was deeply affected by urban race riots in 1981 and again in 1985, the 1980s were also characterised by strains in young people's relations with the police which often spilled over into youth worker-police tensions. In stressing the levels of alienation which already existed among young people, the Thompson Report noted than even in the early 1980s 'relations between many young people and the police are difficult'. The 'sus' laws as applied particularly to young Black people on the streets of London were experienced as especially unjust and provocative, leading to a sustained campaign against them by, among others, BYC during Peter Mandelson's time as chair. (They were finally repealed in 1981.) Dissatisfaction with police harassment went much wider, however, including among Black young people. This showed up in some of the debates generated by the Scarman Report on the 1981 urban disturbances and in both the heated exchanges between delegates and senior police officers and the critical resolutions passed at NAYC's 1981 National Youth Conference.

From time to time youth workers, too, and again especially Black youth workers, found themselves at odds with the police, including standing trial for assaulting or obstructing police officers. On one occasion

they were even said by some sections of the national media to have fomented an anti-police riot among young people by supporting a demonstration against police harassment. With some schools' HMI urging closer liaison and joint training, for their part some youth service staff over the decade expressed growing unease at the police's own involvement in youth work. Police claims in Manchester in 1983, for example, to be working in 36 youth clubs in the city led to the formation of a youth workers' group to combat their influence. In 1987 NAYCEO went as far as to complain to the Home Office and the Metropolitan Police that police officers were hiding their identity by introducing themselves to young people as youth and community workers.

Against this background, in 1983 NYB undertook an investigation of youth work practice in relation to policing and young people. Though revealing a wide range of attitudes to the police among youth service personnel, from the highly cooperative to the deeply hostile, the enquiry also highlighted the fundamental imbalance of power in youth worker-police relations. Thus, while youth workers, lacking formal authority, could usually intervene in young people's encounters with the police only as 'concerned citizen', police officers were able to act from a position of considerable institutional power and authority. Nonetheless police penetration of youth service territory continued, and indeed increased, into the early 1990s as the service's core funding contracted and police authorities became yet another (short-term) way of providing youth work, especially through summer schemes and of supporting youth service programmes.

Dealing with offenders

Meanwhile, with the new Conservative Government deeply suspicion of 'soft' community-based approaches of all kinds, it initially gave little credence to long-standing expectations of youth work as an effective response to youthful law-breaking or as a way of guiding 'at risk' young people into safer habits. Its earliest move to deal decisively with young offenders – its 1980 White Paper – redefined intermediate treatment (IT) as an element of a hard-line 'law and order' strategy to be imple-mented mainly through custodial provision. It thus gave barely a sideways glance at the youth service's role in providing such diversionary facilities. For much of the rest of the decade, neither Thatcher herself nor ministers with relevant portfolios seemed much inclined to change their view.

Nonetheless, in usually taken-for-granted ways other policy-makers and indeed managers and youth workers continued to assume that the youth service could and should help young people avoid criminal activity. Since the 1960s at least, detached work had been seen as particularly useful for doing this – a view which persisted into the 1980s and beyond. Thompson certainly saw the service as having a role to play, including contributing to forms of intermediate treatment, while in the early 1980s NAYC conducted research and consultations specifically on how IT could be developed and sustained specifically through youth clubs.

Later in the decade, too, albeit often only out of financial necessity as they struggled to make up for lost mainstream budgets, some youth services were drawn into safer cities programmes. These often gave a high priority to reducing teenage delinquency and to dealing with young people's 'incivilities and unruliness, drug abuse, nuisance (and) assaults'. Youth work – especially again detached and outreach approaches – were thus in some areas seen as sufficiently credible for achieving such goals to get significant financial support and to enable some innovative work to be carried out.

By the early 1990s, this potential was getting some unexpected national recognition, including from the then Home Secretary, Kenneth Clarke. In 1992 he expressed concerns that, because most local authorities were not giving it the same priority as they were to other services, 'we are in trouble with the youth service'. More specific connections were made between new urban (and indeed sometimes rural) youth disturbances and the cuts in youth service budgets which by then seemed to be endemic. An inspector with the South Yorkshire force, convinced 'that there is a link between youth facilities and the levels of crime', offered to help set up or restart youth clubs. His views were later echoed by an assistant commissioner with the Metropolitan Police:

> Sustaining and enhancing youth provision provides an opportunity to reduce criminal opportunities by removing young people from situations where they are likely to commit, or become victims of, crime.

These views also began to get some more objective confirmation. A Home Office-funded research project carried out by Crime Concern suggested in 1993, for example, that youth workers 'can divert young people from the criminal justice system', especially by 'focusing resources on areas with high concentrations of young people at risk, rather than on specific or potential offenders'. A study carried out for The Prince's Trust and Coopers and Lybrand the following year, though able to find 'little objective evidence to demonstrate a causal relationship between youth work and crime diversion', also recorded 'a large body of subjective evidence' on such a linkage.

The absence of 'hard evidence' in the study left Michael Howard, by then Home Secretary, unconvinced. On the other hand, youth service personnel themselves were by now showing a greater readiness to consider such linkages – not least in order to go where the money was. The DES sought to encourage them in this line of thinking. Between 1987 and 1992 it invested £1 million annually in 19 projects designed to promote young people's 'social responsibility' which explicitly including helping them to avoid delinquency. In many respects, however, these projects were only trailers for a much larger and more ambitious GEST programme which, from 1993 to 1996, sought to test the effectiveness of youth work in responding to 'young people at risk of drifting into crime'. Worth in total £3.9 million in its first year and £2.9 million in each of its two subsequent years, every LEA in the country submitted a bid, with the successful 28 setting up in

total some 60 discrete pieces of work. Some – those in Bradford, for example – followed the social action approach being developed by the Centre for Social Action. By now established at De Montfort University in Leicester, this placed young people's control of developments at the heart of its planning and programmes.

The two evaluations of the Youth Action Projects – one by OFSTED, the other by an independent team of researchers at Sheffield University – listed a number of successes. The schemes, for example, were judged to have demonstrated that youth workers could work, and work innovatively, 'with some of the most at risk young people in our society', that such work could impact positively on the youth service's curriculum, especially locally, and that inter-agency partnerships could be successfully developed.

However, the evaluation reports also identified a number of striking weaknesses in their delivery, some of which were at least implied in The Prince's Trust study two years earlier. These also seemed to illuminate tensions in reconciling person-centred youth work methods with hard-line law and order expectations.

Thus, with considerable reliance again being placed on detached work approaches, the inexperience of staff and their unfamiliarity with key research findings on juvenile delinquency and its causes produced some poorly targeted and ineffective practice. Management, super-vision and monitoring and evaluation were often also weak while the evolving demands of multi-agency working, especially where projects were relying on referrals, often also produced strains. Even the more effective projects were shown to have had difficulty holding participants to the end of their programme, suggesting some significant differences in approach and even in basic premises between the schemes and the core youth service principle of voluntary attendance by young people.

Nonetheless, though seeking also to deal with young people as victims of crime, the schemes certainly drew the youth service further and more formally into crime prevention than had happened previously. In 1996 the highly influential Audit Commission report, *Misspent Youth* which focused on the use of resources for dealing with youth crime, added its general endorsement to this trend, suggesting that youth work and the youth service should become a valid component of anti-crime strategies. Noting that 40 per cent of young offenders had had some contact with youth workers and that 20 per cent saw them as important, it explored a number of ways in which the youth service might discourage 'juvenile nuisance and offending'.

Throughout these reports, however, the analysis on offer continued to perpetuate some linguistic and conceptual evasions, even sleights of hand. These had for long also characterised youth service responses to young people's (often inter-connected) experiences of unemployment, poverty and homelessness. Overwhelmingly the target group for the youth service anti-crime and anti-criminalisation initiatives were young people with little access to

power and material resources because of their place in the labour market. Yet where this, essentially class, dimension was not simply ignored, it was hidden in welfarist terminology which largely evacuated questions of power and money. It was certainly not seen or used as any kind of jumping off point for developmental practice with the young people – again, usually young men – concerned (see Chapter 6).

Promoting health to young people

Drugs: An everyday experience of youth?

One area of law breaking where concern came to be less concentrated on working-class young people was that of drug use and abuse. Evidence was accumulating that young people generally were trying illicit drugs at an earlier age. By the first half of the 1990s, a sharp rise in their use of soft drugs was particularly being recorded. During the 1980s 'recreational' drug-taking at discos, clubs and raves became something of a 'given' element of social life for a significant proportion of young people. Nor was it, according to one Joseph Rowntree Foundation study, the habit simply of 'losers'. By the second half of the 1990s, the use of harder drugs spread rapidly and among groups not previously perceived as touched by a drug culture. Overall levels of recorded drug abuse among young people in Britain emerged as higher than in any other European country.

Rising Government and media anxieties about these, sometimes over-interpreted, statistical trends were reflected in the attention paid to the issue within the youth service. Though often doubtful about, if not overtly critical of, what were seen as simplistic government-inspired anti-drugs campaigns, practitioners were in fact having increasingly to deal with the effects of drug-taking on the young people they were working with. Information and advice were thus more and more aimed directly at them and at their managers. Depending on what the current moral panic might be, during the 1980s and into the 1990s substance abuse ('glue-sniffing'), heroin and ecstasy were liable to get special, and cautionary, attention.

As (at an increasing rate) the demand for resources for public health programmes continued to exceed supply, policy-makers turned more and more to getting 'consumers' to stay healthy and even to deal with their illness themselves. Health promotion programmes thus gained momentum (and often offered some additional staff and financial resources). These included efforts to raise young people's awareness of the damage done by legal as well as illegal drugs – most notably smoking and alcohol – which thus came to be seen as yet another vital element of the youth work curriculum.

Though valid in themselves, youth service responses were largely piecemeal – as, for example, with NABC's publication of a *Young People and Drugs* pack in 1983. By

1986, however, local authorities were using ESG moneys allocated for 'action within the education service to combat drugs' to extend the drugs training available to youth workers. These youth service involvements were again endorsed by HMI reports, particularly in 1989 and again in 1993. Indeed the former concluded:

> The youth service plays an important role in combating drug abuse. It has developed models of good practice on ways of reaching out to and assisting young people who are using drugs, in educating young people on the risks associated with drug abuse; and in enabling young people to develop their own strategies to tackle misuse of drugs. There is scope for wide dissemination of such models.

Indeed, Government expectations that the youth service would contribute to its evolving anti-drugs strategy rose further during the 1990s. In 1991, youth service minister Robert Atkins, for example, emphasised the service's role in dealing with drugs as well as with other 'sensitive and complex' health issues. *Tackling Drugs Together*, a White Paper launched in 1995, was explicit about the need for youth workers to play their part in combating abuse, setting in motion an OFSTED study on how they were doing this. This preceded a DES review which, reporting just before the 1997 general election, showed that much of the service's funding was short-term and came from a variety of sources and that there was a heavy reliance on the commitment of individual workers rather than a coordinated service approach. Even so, much good work was going on in the youth service to help young people become aware of the risks of drug-taking.

The health of the young nation

As Atkins' 1991 statement made clear, over this period drugs education was usually treated within the youth service as part of the wider campaign to promote good health among young people. This broadening interest was reflected in the introduction from the middle of 1990 of a regular 'Health Now' section into *Young People Now*, the replacement from 1989 for both *Scene* and *Youth in Society*. This carried items of news and advice on health matters and was supplemented by feature articles and special reports on such topics as healthy eating and testicular cancer as well as on the dangers of smoking.

Once again HMI both examined and validated the new developments and a youth service/youth work style of dealing with them. As early as 1987 they examined the role of one local youth service in providing health education while a 1993 report provided examples of detached youth work approaches to health promotion. The Government's 1992 White Paper, *The Health of the Nation*, followed in 1995 by a campaign, *The Health of the Young Nation*, gave specific attention to health issues particularly affecting young people, including suicide, self-harm, smoking and alcohol.

Though many local services were issuing policy and curriculum guidelines on health issues, just how far into practice these priorities were reaching was far from clear. One report early in 1991 suggested

that, though having to deal with the effects of alcohol on the young people they were meeting, youth workers were doing little alcohol education work. Though more and more young people were self-harming, more and more young men were killing themselves and more and more young women were attempting suicide, a one-paragraph reference in an HMI report on youth counselling seemed to capture the still low overall priority being given within the service to young people's mental health needs.

Within the overall health curriculum, however, from the late 1980s onwards one specific health concern did get increasing coverage: HIV and AIDS. By then this was coming to be regarded as a major, indeed almost out-of-control problem, especially among the young. Basic information was increasingly targeted at them and at youth workers, often at some length, including on more than one occasion through *Scene*. In 1987 Kenneth Baker, then Secretary of State for Education, included the youth service in the educational institutions which, he said, had 'a crucial role to play in ensuring that young people know the facts about the disease'. Later that year, with local projects finding their own often ad hoc ways of responding, NYB sought to get workers to share their experiences of working with young people on the issue.

Given its overlap into sensitive areas of young people's sexual practice and sex education – to say nothing of its links, real or presumed, with homosexuality and drug-taking – responses could drag local youth services into difficult public controversies. These exploded most easily, it seemed, when youth workers proposed to distribute free condoms to young people, thereby masking the counselling and the more innovative developmental work a few were starting to develop, for example through theatre-in-education.

Responding to 'special needs'?

The confusions and internal contradictions of *Youth and Community Work in the '70s* and the disarray created by its rejection in 1972 left the youth service with blurred vision and uncertain direction. During the 1980s and early 1990s, the resultant vacuum was increasingly filled partly by a pragmatic need simply to 'follow the money'. This in turn usually reflected growing political pressures to deal with key items on the Government's wider social policy agenda, many of which found their way there in response to the latest moral panic about youth.

Indeed, through the 1980s and into the 1990s the category described as 'those in need' was further extended. In 1992, for example, the new youth service minister announced a new GEST programme focused specifically on 'young people at risk on large housing estates in inner cities and on the edge of our cities'. The following year his successor, Tim Boswell, refocused attention on young people who were 'vulnerable', including not just the disabled but (still) on those 'from ethnic and cultural minorities' – and went on to add for the first time young people in care and those leaving care.

More and more, the selectivity which had often been hidden within the youth service's repeated protestations about a 'universalist' provision which was 'open to all' was being made explicit. At the same time, some of its most committed practitioners and sometimes managers continued to struggle to pursue their own selective goals. These aimed at ensuring that, against worsening odds, particularly oppressed and neglected groups of young people whose needs had been forced into the service's consciousness during the 1970s also got greater attention – and resources.

Main references

Terry Cane, *Young People and Voluntary Action*, NYB, 1994

Department of Education and Science, *Young People in the '80s: A Survey*, HMSO, 1983

Alan France and Peter Wiles, *The Youth Action Scheme: A Report of the National Evaluation*, DfEE, 1996

Alan France and Peter Wiles, 'The Youth Action Scheme and the Future of Youth Work', *Youth and Policy*, No 57, Summer 1997

Henley Centre, *Establishing a National Community Service Programme for Young People: The Costs and Benefits*, 1993

HMI, *Youth Work Responses to Unemployment*, DES, 1988

HMI, *Survey of Youth Work Responses to Drug Misuse*, DES, 1989

HMI, *Youth Counselling Services*, DES, 1989

Labour Research, 'Council cuts spill young blood', February 1993

James McCormack, *Citizens' Service*, Institute for Public Policy Research, 1994

Mary Marken et al, *England's Youth Service – the 1998 Audit*, Youth Work Press, 1998

National Foundation for Educational Research, *Youth Service Provision in London*, Sir John Cass's Foundation, 1996

National Youth Bureau, *Young People and the Police: Written evidence to the Royal Commission on Criminal Procedure*, 1979

National Youth Bureau, *Citizenship and Community Service*, Conference Report, 1995

OFSTED, *Youth Work Responses to Young People at Risk*, OFSTED, 1993

Alec Oxford and Maureen Fair, *The Better Possibilities: A theory, practice model, and policy implications for Youth Service work with the unemployed*, Youth Clubs UK, 1987

Thompson Report, *Experience and Participation: Report of the Review Group on the Youth Service in England*, HMSO, 1982

James Wood, *Youth Clubs and Intermediate Treatment*, NAYC, 1983

6 Issue-based Work in a Thatcherite Climate

A new ideological context for the youth service

Though often experienced most keenly as a doctrine of financial cutbacks, Thatcherism's policy initiatives were run through with strongly held social attitudes and values. When encapsulated in the term Victorian values, for example, this moralism produced an uncompromising defence of individual responsibility and self-help and 'the traditional family' overseen by male breadwinner and housewife. When focused on 'Britishness' – as during the Falkands war in 1982 – it could easily tip over into a jingoism heavily tinged with racism. As such ideas became increasingly dominant, a sharp backlash developed against the 'liberation' ideologies of the 1970s. This came to constitute an uncomfortable, not to say hostile, environment in which to sustain and take further the issue-based youth work focused on the main social division within British society which the youth service had begun, albeit grudgingly and marginally, to incorporate during in the 1970s.

In general, the Thatcherite counter-attack – given unrelenting populist expression in much of the press – was embodied in the derision loaded onto 'loony left' Labour councils for their high-profile anti-discriminatory policies and practices and in the conversion of the notion of 'political correctness' into a term of abuse. More specifically, it led to the abolition of specialist women's and race equality units and posts within local authorities and to the infamous Section 28 of the 1988 Local Government Act which banned the 'promotion' or teaching of homosexuality. Conservative government resistance to equal opportunities advances continued into the 1990s with, for example, their active connivance at defeating private members' bills for tackling discrimination against the disabled.

During the 1980s and into the 1990s it was not always clear anyway which were the 'authentic' voices within the liberationist positions arguing for anti-oppressive and anti-discriminatory practice: Black, or Black and Asian; separatist or socialist feminist; gay and/or lesbian and/or bisexual; disabled people or people with disabilities? Nonetheless, the struggles which the 1970s had generated continued. The youth service's own commitment was probably expressed most assertively in November 1990 by the second of three ministerial conferences convened by the DES to clarify a core curriculum (see Chapter 7). This got as far as agreeing a statement of purpose which set the service the task of seeking 'to redress all forms of inequality and to ensure equality of opportunity for all young people'. It therefore saw youth work as in part needing to operate:

- *through the challenging of oppressions such as racism and sexism and all those which spring from differences of culture, race, language, sexual identity, gender, disability, age, religion and class; and*
- *through the celebration of the diversity and strengths which arise from those differences.*

The statement over time produced some healthy scepticism about the capacity of something as puny as the youth service to achieve such ambitious, not to say utopian, aspirations. This, however, needs to be distinguished from more traditional forms of resistance which, especially in the overall ideological climate of the times, the statement also provoked. As we shall see later in this chapter, this came particularly from some of the service's longest-established and most powerful interests as yet unready to contemplate the shifts in power and resources which the statement at least implied.

However, some of the statement's commitments were expressed in some less rhetorical and more grounded developments. Within young people's experience and in some practitioners' responses, there were no sharp dividing lines between the different issues. In their own right, however, these continued to provide important focuses for some of the youth service's activities and programmes.

Whatever happened to class?

One issue, one key indicator of significant social division especially within Britain, if it appeared at all usually did so only in token form. This was class. From a longer historical perspective, this might be seen as surprising. From its earliest days, even while claiming to be offering a provision open to all, youth work's sponsors had at least implicitly and often very explicitly been preoccupied with reaching working-class youth and countering their worst excesses.

However, as we have seen (Volume 1, Chapter 3), during the 1960s and even into the 1970s, the dominant perceptions of British society increasingly defined this as affluent, consensual and therefore as at least becoming *classless*. Within educational and social policy in particular, recognition of class characteristics and class differences were increasingly blocked or diverted. This was done particularly by policy-makers adopting forms of analysis and a supportive language which located needs and problems in the deficiencies of individuals and communities rather than in economic or political structures or even in supposedly 'helping' institutions and organisations.

Yet during the 1980s economic and social conditions had shifted yet again to the point where, by the middle of the 1990s, the gap between the disposable incomes of the richest and the poorest in Britain had widened by over 50 per cent. Claims to classlessness thus once more became hard to sustain as did, therefore, an absence of consideration of class from youth service debates on its curriculum and how this should be implemented.

Indeed, in this decade, the material world of large numbers of young people collapsed completely. Gone were the popular 1960s and early 1970s images of youth-equals-affluence-and-liberation. In their stead by the 1990s were grey socio-logical examinations and media accounts of teenage despair and extinguished prospects. Paul Willis, in his 1984 report on Wolverhampton's Youth Service, gave vivid expression to this 'new social condition'. Its roots, he concluded, lay in the loss of the wage – 'not simply an amount of money (but) … the means to and promise of a future'. As a result, for large numbers of young people 'transitions into what society defines as adulthood … have been frozen or broken', creating an 'extended period of relative poverty and dependency on the family and on the state'.

Though not focusing specifically on young people, in an influential analysis of the state Britain was in just prior to the Labour victory of 1997, Will Hutton refined Willis's picture. He saw 40 per cent of the population as 'privileged' by their 'market power', 30 per cent as 'disadvantaged' and 30 per cent as 'marginalised and insecure'. The latter were defined by some pretty stark characteristics: unemployment or mere 'scraps' of part-time work, wages below 50 per cent of the national average, jobs without protection or benefits, stressed family lives and poorly fed children.

A mid-1990s clarification of how young people were getting incorporated into Hutton's bottom-of-the-heap 30 per cent was provided in 1995 by Clive Wilkinson in an NYA publication, *The Drop-out Society*. Sub-titled *Young People on the Margin*, this drew on detailed research findings from a long-neglected area of Sunderland. It wove together evidence on the inter-connected effects on these young people's negotiation of their adolescence of home, school, vocational training, where they lived and how their family experienced the labour market. Wilkinson concluded that:

> *In some respects the structures that society has built that should ease young people through the transition from youth to adulthood often act more like obstacles than stepping stones, and operate in such a way as to create negative, hostile attitudes.*

This inter weaving of community, cultural and social markers with the economic facts of life was constructing personal and shared experiences which, even in the 1990s, continued to give the notion of class a considerable if often unarticulated resonance for such young people. For those policy-makers willing to read it out, other often incidental evidence supported this conclusion – for example, the unwilling-ness of working-class young men to participate in community service (noted in the last chapter) because, in their culture, this would be tantamount to admitting they could not get a job.

Though the youth service continued to restate its commitment to their social and (certainly during the 1980s) their political education, these class dimensions of their experience featured hardly at all as a planned focus for its issue-based work. This remained true even though research commissioned by the Thompson Review Group, broadly confirming the results of earlier research, revealed clear class biases in youth service take-up. Thus, though the figures for uniformed organisations were rather different, open youth clubs attendance by social class groupings C2DE was (at 34 per cent) nearly twice that of young people from groupings ABC1. The frequency of their attendance was also likely to be higher.

As we have seen, by the time these findings emerged some youth workers were trying to confront social divisions rooted in gender and race. By contrast, they rarely sought – or, more significantly perhaps, were never pushed by relevant liberationist interests – to construct a practice theory and ideology for responding to the class roots of the 'disadvantage' experienced by these young people.

Not that the expressions of such disadvantages were unknown or just ignored. During 1994, for example, NYA's monthly periodical *Young People Now* began to carry regular 'Money', 'Work' and 'Housing' sections. These often picked up on practitioners' concerns about young people's confusing and disempowering entanglements with 'the benefits jungle' and how they were often failing to overcome basic material problems in their lives. Two years later NYA's agreed work programme explicitly included a focus on poverty and debt.

An even more direct and consistent youth service brush with class issues seemed to

be promised by emerging, if again usually marginal, attempts from the late 1970s to focus on work with young men. This was, for example, explored in articles published in *Youth in Society* during the 1980s, one of which, by Tony Taylor, adopted a very explicit Marxist analysis of young men's situation. These were followed in 1985 by a NYB publication, *Work with Boys*. In this, Trefor Lloyd noted how the Albemarle Report's concerns over the emergence of teenage culture and rising levels of juvenile delinquency had put a spotlight on working-class young men. In reviewing how views on men and masculinity had changed over time, he also made passing references to other previous class perspectives on the 'problem'.

The initiatives being developed by these writers were at the time highly innovative – indeed, genuine breakthroughs in youth service thinking and, albeit still rarely, in some of its practice. Usually, however, they came as responses to the feminist demand, at least implicit in the work with girls' developments, that men – workers and users – 'do something' about their own attitudes and behaviour. Their main analytical and ideological reference points here, therefore, were sexism and men's oppression of women. Indeed, one of Lloyd's core aims was to challenge the popular notion that 'working-class and Black young men are "more sexist", "more macho" than other men' and so to assert that sexism is inherent to *all* men's experience and socialisation.

Yet, valid though such a proposition may be, it still made up only part of the truth. In particular, it failed to take account of wider analyses of youth which had gained ground during the 1970s. These treated young people's negotiation of adolescence as significantly differentiated by the crucial social divisions within society, including class. Indeed, one of the criticisms made of the work of the Centre for Contemporary Cultural Studies at Birmingham University, which took a leading role in developing these structural rather than primarily psychological perspectives on youth, was that it over-emphasised class, often to the exclusion of in particular race and gender.

In the more specialised work with boys which Taylor, Lloyd and others were urging on the youth service, the opposite seemed to be true, however. The reality of the work they were encouraging was that it was to be targeted mainly on working-class young men. Yet this key element of these young people's experience and condition was normally left out of the rationale and analysis underpinning such practice. This was true, too, of much of the work done with young women which took its main, indeed often overwhelming, inspiration from feminist ideas and initiatives.

One public document which received a great deal of national attention when it was published in 1988 seized on this intrinsic flaw in equal opportunities developments. The Macdonald enquiry investigated the circumstances of the murder of a 13-year-old Asian boy by a white pupil in the playground of Burnage High School in Manchester. This offered a harsh analysis of the 'doctrinaire application' of Manchester City Council's

and the school's anti-racist practices and policies. These, it concluded, had been 'totally divorced from the more complex reality of human relations in the classroom, playground or community' and in particular had failed to connect with 'issues of class, sex (and) age'. The 'unmitigated disaster' which resulted stemmed in part, the enquiry decided, from the deliberate omission from the council's equal opportunities policies of any reference to class. These weaknesses had arisen out of:

> ... an ostrich-like analysis of the complex of social relations (which left) white working-class males completely in the cold. They fit nowhere. They become all time losers. Their interests as a group are nowhere catered for.

At the start of the 1990s, two of the most critical commentators on the youth service, Tony Jeffs and Mark Smith, made one of the very few sustained attempts to locate youth work within a class perspective. They noted in particular how, in an effort to draw in sceptical and resistant working-class young people, forms of popular youth work had developed, involving 'a general move from improvement to containing entertainment'. And they ended their discussion by asking:

> Do (youth workers) ... seek to encourage working-class young people to reflect critically on their experiences of the labour market? Or do they simply seek to ameliorate the situation?

Such questions, run through as they are with a range of imponderables and contradictions, certainly set the service some hard challenges. Nonetheless, these absences had significant outcomes for both its practice and its policy. It resulted in a neglect of a potentially positive – developmental – focus for work on personal identity and collective action which could have paralleled what was being attempted by some workers and organisations with young Black people, young women and disabled and gay and lesbian young people. This in turn meant that the youth service's main messages to working-class young people on their class position, and especially to young men, were almost entirely negative. What was constantly picked out for attention was their sexism, their racism, their denial of sensitivity and their aggressive attitudes and behaviour. As a result, during the 1980s and 1990s working-class young people were offered few planned opportunities through the service to understand their class position better or to draw from it insights to aid their personal and indeed collective learning and development.

'I'm a feminist, but ... '

The New Right assault during the 1980s on the feminist gains of the previous decade was both full-frontal and indirect. Though the Equal Opportunities Commission survived, its approach was cautious to say the least. Other institutional expressions of public commitment to reducing women's inequalities and oppression, when they were not actually abolished, found themselves neutralised. One of the strongest Thatcherite arguments for ridding itself of the GLC and controlling local government expenditure generally was that local authorities were 'wasting' public money on such things as 'women's units'.

In addition, in the popular press but also through more academic publications, feminism was converted into a term of derision, to be associated only with women whose political correctness was now so extreme that they were putting men at a disadvantage. Filtered through these increasingly dominant conventional wisdoms, open adherence to arguments about continuing female oppression were dismissed as the rantings of small groups of extremists out of touch with the new realities. Important and searching debates which were taking place among feminists themselves (including sometimes among women youth workers) not only served to confuse non-feminists. They also opened up divisions which unsympathetic politicians (not all of them Conservative) and a largely hostile press were only too eager to exploit for their own ends.

Despite this climate, during the 1980s local projects continued to offer young women some separate space and opportunities to build up their individual and collective identities and confidence. New developments also occurred – the creation of a specialist girls' work post within a local authority here, the opening of a new girls-only building there. After a survey of its service in 1984, an ILEA report recommended more separate provision for young women and positive responses by all its workers to aggressive behaviour by boys. The Girl Guides, too, reasserted that its traditional aims and methods were to offer girls 'exciting activities ... to challenge sexism and the stereotyped images of men and women'.

To support and encourage this grassroots activity, out of what was to become its Girls' Work Unit, NAYC launched a *Working with Women* newsletter in 1980 which very quickly attracted sustained interest. This dissemination of the accumulating good practice in work with girls was reinforced by three editions between 1981 and 1985 of NYB's *Reader's Route Map* for working with girls, each edited by Kerry Young. After she joined NAYC's Girls Work Unit, Young also co-wrote with Val Carpenter *Coming in from the Margins*, aimed at all youth workers wanting to make youth service facilities more young women-friendly.

Women workers also continued to seek mutual support and affirmation with at least one regional grouping of women workers coming together early in the decade. More significantly, women workers won DES funding in 1984 and again in 1986 to appoint paid staff to develop the National Organisation for Work with Girls and Young Women (NOW). Formed originally in 1980, this provided information and resources, support and training for work with girls and to help develop more women-only residential and other facilities. By 1989 this was housed with five other women's organisations in the Pankhurst Centre in Manchester and had two full-time workers.

CYSA and then CYWU became another pressure point for collective action by women workers, especially though not only in relation to work with girls. A women's caucus was formed at the association's AGM in 1981 which quickly organised a national conference. This issued a statement of intent demanding full union support for challenging sexism and for developing positive initiatives in the work itself. The statement, which also put specific emphasis on the needs of Black and lesbian young people and workers, was the basis for considerable activity and campaigning over the next decade. The caucus also had some broader impact including acting as a route for women to gain key positions within the union itself. By the end of the decade, NAYCEO, too, sought to offer a response by sponsoring a meeting for women officers on issues of mutual concern.

However, familiar – even tired – debates, including still over whether such separatist work was needed and legitimate, continued to bubble beneath all this public organising and activity, sometimes vigorously and angrily. The work-with-girls cause was hardly helped by the Thompson Report's ultimately overriding concern that the service's mainstream provision must remain mixed. Apparently regarding sexism and women's equality as short-term problems, it thus gave a decidedly lukewarm endorsement to separate facilities for young women. Indeed, throughout the decade women workers and officers committed to such provision were required to go on making the basic case to the service's still mainly male power holders for more resources, and their more equal allocation to young women.

The deepening scepticism about – indeed hostility to – 'women's issues' in the wider environment made even defence of past gains increasingly difficult. This was demonstrated most dramatically by the NAYC's peremptory closure of the Girls' Work Unit in 1987. This had been set up only three years earlier after NAYC had commissioned research which demon-strated the need for a dedicated national resource for work with girls and young women. The main public explanation of the closure offered by NAYC was financial – an organisation-wide deficit of £140,000 needed to be eliminated. However, arguments were advanced, too, that a specialist facility was no longer required because work with girls was going on in other key association programmes. Opponents of the closure read into this 'gloss' on the action a more fundamental political rejection of the broader feminist underpinnings of most past developments, especially since no other section of the organisation suffered such an extreme fate.

Despite extended protests, the Unit stayed closed and the *Working with Girls* news-letter was never revived. NAYC chief executive, Jan Holt, tried to offer some reassurance:

> As a female I intend to ensure girls work will not disappear while its chairman (sic) assured its affiliated bodies that "the girls work dimension" is properly reflected in all its main activities.

She also promised that the organisation would help to establish 'a new national centre geared to the needs of people working with girls and young women'. By the end of 1987, NAYC's way of operationalising this was to expand the remits of its publications and information and development teams to give more attention to girls work.

This cause celebre was, however, only the tip of an iceberg which was also showing serious signs of crumbling below the water line. Two reports with a high national profile, both published in 1988 – one by HMI, the other by National Advisory Council for the Youth Service (NACYS) – revealed how far the struggles of the 1970s were still being fought, and often lost, by women workers. The HMI report, for example, concluded that, with only one girl participating in the service for every three boys, girls' work was 'under-developed'. Because it was 'still misunderstood (and) misinterpreted', it had had 'only limited impact on mainstream provision' with many authorities allocating too few resources to sustain or develop it.

The NACYS report reinforced these findings. Concluding that they 'deeply regret the mistrust with which girls' work is generally and unjustifiably regarded', the subcommittee set timescales for implementation of its recommendations. In addition to ones on staffing and training, these urged local authorities and relevant voluntary organisations to:
- formulate policies for work with girls;
- develop action programmes;
- undertake work to identify an appropriate allocation of resources; and
- state how they intend to meet the needs of specific groups, including Black and disabled young women and young lesbians.

The true prospects for such work were perhaps best summed up only months later, however. Despite the 'advice' offered to it by its own national council and an increased grant after the Girls' Work Unit was closed, one by-product of the new DES funding regime for voluntary organisations in the late 1980s was a serious financial crisis within NOW. This just survived – but only because staff members took a salary cut. Though managing to last long enough to produce a *Girls' Work into the '90s* resource pack, by 1994 it had, in the words of two of those involved, 'become impossible to meet the basic objectives necessary to run a national organisation' and the network was wound up.

Youth Clubs UK, the successor organisation to NAYC, continued to claim that it was as committed as ever to this area of work and was 'beginning to build up resources for work with young women'. Moreover, on the ground, determined work continued as a source book of good practice produced by Janet Batsleer in 1996 demonstrated. Women workers also still made opportunities for themselves to network, including for some through CYWU's Women's Caucus.

However, wider evidence accumulated to support NOW's conclusion that the idea was taking root that 'somehow girls' work has "been done" and, being rooted in universal good practice, can now drop from sight'. At the very moment that NOW was disappearing, the YWCA was complaining to the DES that support for work with young women was being squeezed by the increasing priority being given to work with young people at risk – that is, predominantly, with young men.

By the mid-1990s research carried out by Jean Spence in the north-east was revealing more complex dimensions to the struggle to maintain past gains. The women youth workers she interviewed not only saw themselves as continuing to operate 'within agendas which have been set elsewhere by a masculine establishment'. 'Constantly assailed by negative stereotyping around the image of feminism', they also now felt that, for the work even to survive, they must self-censor their aims and values. This was particularly true in relation to the feminist positions which had most influenced their work with girls and young women and to commitments to address Black or lesbian issues. Moreover:

> Despite the successes of practice, despite the hard won improved provision and consequent growth in numbers … despite pursuing a "safe" non-political stance in the public advocacy of female centred work, the women workers … received little, if any, organisational recognition for their achievements.

In a complex interaction, lowered aspirations and lowered morale among women workers themselves, it seemed, were as likely to limit the impact of the youth service's specialist work with girls and young women as were any of the more direct tactics adopted to curb it.

Work with Black young people

Over and above the damage inflicted on young people generally, for large numbers of Black and Asian young people the 1980s brought additional oppressive experiences of rejection, demoralisation and persistent racial violence. Even when, against heavy odds, more began to succeed in the education system, by almost every other measure – access to 'proper' jobs and training and to housing, treatment by the police, processing through the courts – they were liable to lose out. Early in the decade, their disenchantment was bubbling so close to the surface that, in *The Fire Next Time*, the Commission for Racial Equality offered the Government 'last chance' proposals for heading them off from violent rebellion.

Despite this kind of evidence, official reaction continued to deny that racism (or even deprivation) might be at the root of such discriminatory experiences. The tone for the debate had been set by Thatcher even before she became Prime Minister. In a speech in 1978 which carried strong echoes of Enoch Powell's 1960s 'rivers of blood' speech, she defined what came to be called 'the new racism':

> If we went on as we are, then by the end of the century there would be four million people of the New Commonwealth or Pakistan here. Now that is an awful lot and I think it means that people are really rather afraid that this country might be swamped by people with a different culture … There is a fear that … people are going to react and be rather hostile to those coming in.

Here too political correctness came under increasing and concerted attack. This insisted that, at worst, racism was an accumulation of individual prejudices, thereby denying it any structural or institutional basis. It also re-interpreted anti-racist programmes as a new form of intolerance perpetrated by so-called liberals. In 1986, David Marsland, as he did on a number of other policy issues, acted as the Trojan horse for such views within the youth service. His pretext was the presentation of a series of proposals for developing work with Black young people which were far less contentious even among (white) policy-makers than he seemed to think. However, Marsland's main purpose in writing the article seemed to be to castigate the service's 'home-grown apartheid' and its 'oceans of talk devoted to anti-racism'.

Three years later John Butcher, then junior minister at the DES with youth service responsibility, took up a similar, polemical theme. Shrewdly relying on a statement he attributed to Paul Boateng, a Black MP and later a Labour minister, he accused 'wishy-washy educationalists' of 'betraying' Black schoolchildren. He also detected:

> … early signs that Asian and African-Caribbean communities are fed up with being patronised by the possessors of an arrogant liberal conscience or the zealots of the race relations industry.

What was required, he asserted, was work 'with young people full stop – not young people and female, young people and Black, young people and unemployed, young people and middle-class'. It was a theme later taken up by one of his successors, Alan Haselhurst, as part of an effort to discredit a radical statement of purpose for the youth service agreed at a ministerial conference in 1990.

ISSUE-BASED WORK IN A THATCHERITE CLIMATE

As we shall see later, valid and urgent arguments could certainly be made for (mainly white) policy-makers to take a long hard look at what they were doing. These, however, would have had more credibility had the overall climate in which Conservative youth policy was being made not been soured by insistent official and media stereotyping of Black young people. This repeatedly portrayed African-Caribbean young men as would-be muggers, African-Caribbean young women as single mothers and Asian young women as passive daughters of oppressive male-dominated families.

These stereotypes gained renewed currency in the aftermath of the inner-city disturbances of 1981 and 1985. Because most of these occurred in multi-racial areas, they were immediately dubbed race riots, said to have been sparked and led by Black young people out of, as the Home Secretary at the time put it, 'greed not need'. Though the 'sus' laws were repealed early in the decade, much of the tough law-and-order legislation which the Thatcher governments introduced subsequently had, as one of its barely concealed aims, provided the police with the powers to stop, search and detain young Black men.

These wider developments inevitably limited the room for manoeuvre of a youth service which had emerged from the 1970s unclear, indeed often unconvinced, about its role in catering for Black young people or in countering the racism of users, workers and managers. At the start of the decade the Thompson Report made an unusually direct effort to break through

these doubts and confusions. It, for example, endorsed the need for a fully multi-cultural outlook and curriculum; for lobbying and campaigning for equal opportunities and appropriate community development; and for a measure of 'positive action in (the service's) management practices which would fully involve Black communities in policy-making'. It particularly argued for 'recruitment policies which would ensure a conspicuous presence of Black workers within the service as a whole – i.e. not just in Black areas, nor in the lower echelons of the service'.

On 'provision in multi-ethnic communities', the report was even blunter. It dismissed as 'naive' the integrationist doctrine of the Hunt Report which over 20 years before had insisted that Black and white must learn to love each other by always sharing the same youth service facilities. Instead Thompson started from the proposition that ethnic minority young people may need to meet separately in order:

> ... to enable the communities to preserve what they want to preserve and assimilate what they want to assimilate, and to help the young people concerned to resist the disintegrating experiences to which they may have been subjected.

It went on:

> A service which is dedicated to the principle of flexible response to the developmental needs of young people ... must orient itself towards the values and needs of the communities from which the young people come.

Many of the service's policy-makers, at best, reacted slowly and reluctantly to such advice. If the populations for which they were catering were predominantly white, their most likely response was to act as if all this talk about race and racism had nothing to do with them. A NCVYS report in 1984, for example, describing the national voluntary youth organisations as complacent, revealed that under 10 per cent of them were claiming to be in close contact with potential ethnic minority users – a finding which was likely to be equally true for the statutory service.

Yet the policies of some services did shift over the decade. For one thing, stated commitments to anti-racist policies and practices became increasingly common – indeed, almost a flavour of the time. This preoccupation was picked up directly in 1984 when, following requests for information from white workers, NYB published a resource pamphlet on *Anti-Racist Youth Work* mainly based on consultations with and aimed at white staff. It also supported the launch by the CRE of a set of race equality standards for the service.

Great commitment was made, too, to developing provision and practice which were race-sensitive and race-responsive. In 1983, for example, though criticised by Black staff, the ILEA commended for adoption throughout its youth service 'the practices of those establishments which have … prepared policy statements on multi-ethnic education, arranged in-service training for staff or designated specialists to coordinate multi-ethnic policy'. The Training Agencies Group (TAG) committed itself in 1985 to tackling the problems of inequality and

discrimination associated with race as well as gender and class.

Notwithstanding the minister's subsequent distancing of himself from such ideas, the second ministerial conference's statement of purpose, with its explicit endorsement of 'the celebration of diversity' and of the need to challenge racism, could be seen as an attempt to make this stance official service policy. Even NYA's Across our Differences project, also launched in 1990, though apparently reflecting an integrationist position by seeking in part to build alliances between Black and white young people, started from a presumption of significant and appropriate differences between the two groups.

As the decade progressed, separate provision thus became more established, including (even if often only just) within the mainstream. The survey of young people's leisure activities commissioned by the Thompson Committee thus reported that many chose to go to a youth club because 'my kind of person' attended. As a result, many clubs were 'race-specific' while 'a youth club on the border line of a mainly Caucasian and mainly West Indian area might become white or Black in its membership/usage pattern'. A 1987 HMI report on youth work in eight inner-city areas noted that 'much good practice in multi-racial areas is with single ethnic groups'. It also gave explicit support to 'the desirability of responding to the needs of different categories of young people, for instance those of different cultural groups'.

In recognising within this report that such work 'requires careful commitment of resources and, often, a higher level of these than may be necessary in homogeneous areas', HMI also signalled some tough policy dilemmas, especially locally. At a time of cuts, decisions to develop more separate facilities for Black young people almost inevitably meant shifting resources away from established (that is, white) groups and organisations. They also often required some delicate balancing acts to avoid threatening the autonomy of often fiercely independent community groups who, if only because they were new to the mysteries of even well-meaning public bureaucracies, could also very easily be set up to fail.

Against this background, Black groups and communities – though often starting from different analyses and defending some conflicting interests and aspirations – found themselves having to state and restate the case for more, and more appropriate and responsive, provision for Black young people. This happened even while the Thompson Committee was sitting when its only Black member, Jan McKenley, attended a conference organised by the Black Youth and Community Workers' Association. At this, participants complained about the lip-service being paid to their work and recommended more effective forms of consultation with Black workers as a way of ensuring that the service took on Black perspectives more effectively. Two years after the report appeared, following a conference of 200 Black young people organised by the CRE, moves were made to set up a national Black youth organisation to represent the views and demands of young people from all ethnic minorities.

By 1985 NYB was circulating a Black Youth and Community Workers' newsletter which in 1990 was expanded into *Shabaab*, a three-times-a-year magazine aimed at those working with Black young people. Nonetheless, these same concerns continued to be aired, and with equal passion, at the end of the decade and into the 1990s. The background paper for a national Black workers conference in 1990, for example, noted that there had been only 12 Black participants out of a total of 250 at the first ministerial conference on a core curriculum for the youth service. Though some Black workers had been consulted, most of them were seen as 'hand picked'. By setting up their own conference, the organisers sought to challenge the 'excuse' given in the past for the absence of more formal consultation procedures – that there was no 'recognised grouping … repre-senting the range of interests of diverse Black groups'. Their aim was thus not only to ensure that 'Black workers … make their voices heard'. In the longer term they hoped, too, 'to create a national constitu-ency to represent Black training interests and to set up a Standing Conference'.

At the end of the 1980s, therefore, the jury was still out on the youth service's responsiveness to Black and Asian young people's needs – or, more accurately perhaps, was divided on this according to position and perspective. This split was reflected in reports of two very different kinds of investigation into youth work with Black and Asian young people, both carried out in the late 1980s. One was by HMI, the other on behalf of NYB by Vipin Chauhan, one of its Black youth work advisers.

The HMI's criticisms of the service at the very least suggested an underlying malaise which, in their concern to encourage it in the progress it was making, they kept low key. Thus, of the 15 local authorities surveyed only a third had a policy related to 'ethnic diversity', some of which constituted no more than 'a passing reference'. HMI also found that links with community groups often needed strengthening, that many programmes were failing to differentiate adequately between different ethnic groups, that Black and Asian girls and young women were under-represented and that there were few Black and Asian officers. As much of the work was externally funded, it 'risked instability and marginalisation' and arrangements needed to be strengthened for ensuring Black voices were heard when policies were being decided and resources allocated.

Nonetheless, much of the HMI's report was up-beat about what was going on. They noted, for example, that Black voluntary organisations like the National Association of Muslim Youth were by then getting DES funding. In contrast to what NCVYS had found a few years earlier, they also concluded that other longer-established national voluntary bodies were 'seeking to adapt their programmes to make them more attractive and accessible to Black young people'. Most of the local authorities they examined were seeking to promote both equal opportunities in employing staff and delivering services and an awareness of ethnic diversity among their workers. They were also accepting that 'forms and styles of provision predicated exclusively on the

interests and values of the majority community may not be appropriate'.

Moreover, many of these positives seemed to be translating themselves into the work on the ground. Youth workers were found to be 'alert and responsive to the familial, cultural and racial conflicts to which young people are exposed' and by and large negotiating 'sensitive issues' between parents and elders and their young people with 'consummate skill and discretion'. With many local services taking special measures, detached and project work was seen as particularly effective in analysing community needs and opening up the service to Black and Asian young people, often in the process creating safe environments which young people valued and came to 'own'. The policy of training and recruiting more Black and Asian workers was judged to be working well, including for work as generalists within a service.

From his Black perspective, Chauhan was far more sceptical about the extent and impact of these advances. His enquiry, which concentrated on six urban areas with substantial Black and Asian populations, gathered its evidence through initial consultations with senior officers and visits to and interviews with the staff of 18 clubs, centres and other facilities used by significant numbers of Black and Asian young people.

Chauhan framed his picture in a demographic situation in which 40 per cent of Asians and 30 per cent of African-Caribbeans living in Britain were under 16 and over 50 per cent of Britain's Black population were under 25. Despite this, he judged that the changes which were occurring were sporadic rather than part of a strategic plan and depended heavily on Black pressure and on the commitment of individual workers. With Black staff remaining under-represented at all levels, he found that many services simply assumed that they knew what Black young people wanted or that they treated their needs as no different from those of white young people. Many local and central government-sponsored projects were 'hastily constructed, without sufficient running costs and sometimes run by inadequately supported and inexperienced staff'.

Though he acknowledged the gains it could bring, Chauhan also pointed out that anti-racist work was not the same as 'work with Black young people' and in fact often ended up marginalising the needs of Black young people and diverting attention and resources from them. His overall conclusion was therefore that 'very few initiatives are taking place to meet the needs of Black young people' and that, despite many earlier policy recommendations, there was 'very little evidence of any major, coherent initiative being undertaken by the youth service'.

One key blockage in the system which Chauhan identified was 'the monopoly of white men' in positions of power. These policy-makers and managers, he concluded, 'do not appear to have developed the consciousness necessary to understand the social, economic and political environment in which Black young people in contemporary Britain are growing up'. Another problem was

competing priorities, especially given the long-standing tradition of 'white young people and white youth organisations ... enjoy(ing) the patronage and support of the youth service'.

Chauhan's findings certainly threw into relief some of the outstanding gaps and flaws in the youth service's responses to race during the 1980s and indeed beyond. Nonetheless, in (recent) historical terms and when compared with much better resourced and more powerful education institutions such as the schools and further education colleges, the HMI's inclination to optimism was by then not altogether misplaced. Over 20 years, in its struggle to free itself from the constrained and constraining vision of the Hunt Report, the service had slowly cultivated some more culturally conscious and sensitive responses to Black and Asian young people.

Thus though often reacting only under pressure and though therefore usually only taking action where substantial Black and Asian communities existed, it had, for example, begun to support and even encourage separate facilities for a range of ethnic minorities. Using the wide variety of routes to qualification which CETYCW had opened up, more trained Black workers had entered the service with some of them even finding their way into managerial positions.

Notwithstanding Chauhan's doubts – nor the derisive reactions of right wing politicians and press to political correctness – anti-racist initiatives had helped to expose even some of the more subtle and masked types of racist arguments used to block development. Indeed, well before the 1998–99 enquiry into the murder of the Black teenager Stephen Lawrence had revealed the Metropolitan Police's refusal even to contemplate that institutional racism existed, this was being vigorously debated within the youth service and even occasionally conceded to be a problem. The result in many places was strategies and procedures for key areas of employment practice as well as for actual service delivery.

Nonetheless, with its historic (white) assumptions and ways of operating, the youth service remained unsure how to identify forms of 'Black youth work' which it wished to affirm and sponsor – and was often ham-handed in its attempts to do so. Over this period, the service's own Black constituency of workers and activist young people, though trying repeatedly and in the process generating some crucial thinking and pressure, had only limited success in putting together sustainable collective forums and alliances capable of representing its interests nationally. Despite many months of effort by a (Black-led) subcommittee, even NACYS – the body which came closest at the end of the 1980s to acting as a national policy-making body – failed to gather and then make public its agreed thoughts on work with Asian and African-Caribbean young people.

All of which – unsurprisingly perhaps – confirmed what was usually obvious to those working at the sharpest edges of policy and practice: that, within the parameters of a now largely state-sponsored service, the pursuit of shared strategic directions which credibly embodied Black perspectives on the work remained extremely contentious – and elusive.

Struggling towards integration: Work with disabled young people

The broader struggle for 'disability liberation' which had begun in the 1970s continued into the next two decades particularly through new and more activist organisations. The first umbrella body run by and for disabled people, the British Council of Disabled People, was set up in 1981, to be followed 10 years later by the much more militant and overtly political Direct Action Network. By the 1990s too, a number of the traditional voluntary organisations which had previously, in attitude and style, fully lived up to their 'charitable' label came more under the control of disabled people themselves. In the process they hardened their public stances against discrimination, including stepping up pressure on government.

A Disabled Persons Act passed in 1986 replaced the Chronically Sick and Disabled Person's Act of 1970. Though with some extended provisions, in particular disabled people's rights to be involved in their own affairs, this left untouched many of the disadvantages they faced. Its precise implementation also remained unclear even at the end of the decade. The increase in political campaigning during the 1990s did help to force through entirely new legislation, however – the 1995 Disabled Discrimination Act which, though deeply flawed, for the first time recognised that discrimination against disabled people actually existed. To get this on the statute book required a long struggle, particularly with a Government whose 'minister for the disabled' deliberately scuppered an earlier private member's bill even when his own daughter was a leading lobbyist for this. The new law was therefore only introduced with great ministerial reluctance.

Greater goodwill than this certainly existed within the youth service – something which was illustrated by the Thompson Review Group's concerned if somewhat platitudinous focus on this area of work. Specialist provision for those who wanted and needed it remained on offer. This continued to be made mainly through the National Federation of Gateway Clubs and PHAB which, for example, in 1984 was awarded a grant by the Royal Jubilee Trust towards the costs of a training officer. Advances were also made in the youth work provided for young people with hearing impairments. In 1987 the DES made a £26,000 grant to the British Deaf Association for a part-time certificate course for deaf youth workers in the north-west, to be developed jointly by the BDA, the Salford Youth Service and the Greater Manchester Youth Association. By 1990 the project was sharing information with the rest of the youth service through a newsletter.

However, with large numbers of disabled young people still isolated or ghettoised,

by the 1980s the goal of integrating them into the service's mainstream facilities was much more accepted. As it had done in the 1970s, in 1981 the National Youth Assembly, for example, focused on the issue at a one-day conference for disabled young people which set up a group to encourage integration, including in social activities. In a policy statement towards the end of the decade NAYCEO gave strong support to the principle of equal rights of access for all and in particular to integrated as well as specialist provision. So too did NCVYS in a detailed and thoughtful briefing paper. The Youth Leaders in the Inner City apprenticeship scheme based in Doncaster specifically targeted disabled young people for training as 'generic' youth workers.

However, on occasions these positive moves also offered up evidence of the service's lack of readiness for implementing its principled commitments. When looking at what was already happening, the 1981 National Youth Assembly conference, for example, concluded: 'Not much.' A national conference organised to bring together the apprentices on the Youth Leaders in the Inner City scheme found itself faced with a delegates' walk-out when it became clear that the venue could not cater adequately for those who were disabled.

As in the case of work with Black young people, it took two reports written quite independently by separate but authoritative groups to highlight just how much progress the service had to make as it went into the 1990s. The first was produced in 1989 by a NACYS working party which included three disabled people. This had as its remit 'to identify those measures which enable the youth service to serve the needs of young people with disabilities and to make proposals to secure their wider adoption'. In a cover letter to the NACYS chair, Trevor Owen who had chaired the working party, made clear the philosophy from which it had started:

> Disability may or may not constitute a handicap ... Handicap, in this context, is nothing to do with medical condition: indeed, it is not primarily about the disabled person – it is the environment in which he or she lives ... The greatest of these handicaps is ... the attitudes of those people who are not themselves disabled.

Some things in this environment were found to be encouraging. The report, for example, specifically recorded the 'pioneering role' of PHAB and Gateway, of some local authorities and of the Scouts and the contributions to thinking at the time of NAYCEO, NCVYS and NYB. It also reproduced snapshots of best practice throughout the text and included brief details of some cutting-edge organisations and projects in an appendix.

However, the NACYS working party was much more preoccupied with barriers and how to overcome them. These it located in the attitudes of young people with disabilities as well as of those who are not disabled; in inadequate flows of information to the young people; in insufficient direction from the centre – and in too few resources. The result was a service in which 'overall provision (was)

minimal', which 'as a whole had yet to come to terms with disability' and which 'in only relatively few instances ... (placed) the needs of young people with disabilities ... anywhere near the top of anyone's priority list'. In only 42 per cent of the 40 local authorities surveyed was there a clear policy for this area of work, with even this in some cases meaning 'no more than including PHAB or Gateway clubs in grant-aid allocations'. Some with no special provision simply assumed that 'young people are ... welcome to take part in all that the authority offers'.

The working party's 25 recommendations were therefore wide-ranging. Closely following the earlier Thompson recommendation, they stressed the need for local policies to encourage 'a continuum of provision' which would ensure complementary specialist and integrated facilities. They also made proposals for resource allocation, training (both initial and in-service), premises, transport and information dissemination. More specifically, they called, too, for pilot schemes to explore how to extend the service's reach, especially to young people with hearing and sight impairments.

The second report – again one written by HMI – was based on survey information and visits to 67 youth work units in England and Wales. Many of its findings confirmed or extended those of the NACYS report. Though some examples of 'excellent provision' were identified and described in some detail, both policy and practice were found to be under-developed including in many voluntary organisations. With many managers not giving enough attention to assessing need, the implications of integrating disabled young people into mainstream youth work were not always understood. Some authorities thus simply 'allowed young people, whatever their disability, into their centres and … then hoped for the best', leading sometimes to chaotic situations which involved 'neither integration nor youth work'. Practice was anyway often constrained by a lack of appropriate accommodation and equipment, including transport and, with few staff with disabilities being employed, by workers who lacked the necessary training, including in youth work skills.

The Thompson Report had started from the view that, though 'provision for handicapped young people (sic) has in a sense been part of the tradition of the youth service from its earliest days', this had only become 'systematic' in relation to the numbers in any particular area in the previous 10 to 15 years. These two key reports cast fundamental doubt on this proposition. As the HMI put it in the summary to their report, by the end of the 1980s:

> good work is more often the result of the drive and the flair of individuals than of systematic planning.

By 1992 at least 17 local authorities had started to fill this gap by issuing policy statements and curriculum guidelines. Other follow-up responses to the NACYS report also sought to inject more strategic thinking and cohesion into the work. Between 1990 and 1993, for example, this happened through a Changing Attitudes Project funded by the DES's successor, the

Department for Education and Employment (DfEE). The project's final report also promoted two further initiatives – a regional and national network for workers and a partnership of disabled and non-disabled trainers. In 1994, too, a network of Disabled Youth and Community Workers was also formed.

Even so, news of progress in this field could be scarce. In 1996 a national conference on the employment of disabled youth workers in the light of the new legislation had to be cancelled because there were too few takers. Meanwhile, yet another report released the year before – this time from the Jigsaw Youth Integration Project based in Lancashire and part-funded by the DfEE – concluded yet again that radical changes and considerable investment were going to be needed to open up the service to disabled young people.

Working with gay and lesbian young people

If historical absences tell us anything then, as it had done in previous periods, the youth service's (lack of) response to gay and lesbian (and indeed bisexual) young people during the 1980s and 1990s carried some particularly powerful messages. Over the decade and beyond, work with young women, young Black people and disabled young people were all subject to specific scrutiny, first by the Thompson Report and then by groups or individuals with some clout (HMI, NACYS working parties, NYB advisers). One HMI report with a wider remit did refer approvingly to work in progress with young gays. Nonetheless, even though the Thompson Review Group received substantial evidence on their plight, it had nothing at all to say to encourage or support work with one of the most submerged but consistently oppressed sections of the adolescent population. Nor over the decade did such key national youth service voices as HMI, NACYS or even most professional training courses effectively break this silence.

This remained true even though during the 1980s gay and lesbians were assaulted through public policy in ways which, by that stage, even a Thatcherite admini-stration did not feel able to adopt in its dealings with other marginalised groups. Though in part used quite cynically to bolster a wider strategy for attacking Labour local authorities, the Government's anti-gay campaign was also stoked by homophobic tabloid promotion of AIDS as 'the gay plague'. The Government's determination to get Clause 28 of the 1988 Local Government Act onto the statute book thus released public outbursts of prejudicial attitudes which, in discussions of other 'isms', were by then at least being muffled by a coded and more evasive language.

The youth service itself was very far from immune from the effects of such bigotry. The London Gay Teenage Group, for example, documented the hostile reception given to young gay people throughout society, including education and recreation. Its advertisement for two part-

time leaders in 1982 provoked the *Daily Telegraph* to advise that:

> The best counsel (the workers) could give the members of these "groups" would be to stop being groups, to stop being organised (for what dubious and possibly subversive purposes?) …

Nor did such hostility come only from without. At the very same time, the initial statement of intent of the CYSA's Women's Caucus included a reference to support for young lesbians. This produced a letter to its journal *Rapport* from one of its members which, following a homily on Christian teaching on sexuality, concluded with an appeal for recognition by all CYSA members of 'the right sort of relationships between males and females'.

Clause 28 itself explicitly prohibited the intentional promotion of homosexuality by local authorities and any teaching about its acceptability 'as a pretended family relationship'. By many in the youth service this was immediately seen as a threat to the, albeit tentative and marginalised, support to work with gay and lesbian young people which had begun to develop from the later 1970s. NCVYS lobbied against the clause, gaining support even from organisations which previously had had doubts about its and other youth service's bodies' proactive approach to work with gay and lesbian young people. CYWU, too, took a strongly oppositional stance. With *Rapport* stressing how the clause would constrain practice and legitimise discrimination against a section of the workforce, its 1988 annual conference sought ways of coordinating trade union resistance. Peter Kent-Baguley, an 'out' gay youth and community work tutor, also spelt out the clause's dangers for the service in the columns of *Youth in Society*.

Some overt and immediate effects flowed from Clause 28. One local authority, for example, banned an NYB resource pack on volunteering because it listed six gay and lesbian projects. The Conservative-led Borough of Kensington and Chelsea, after threatening to withdraw funding altogether from the Notting Hill Lesbian and Gay Youth Group, used the clause to force a split in its overall age group at 16. Well into the 1990s local authorities were still using it as the pretext for banning, or at least refusing to fund, youth work with gay and lesbian young people.

Clause 28 also had consequences which were often more subtle and hidden. As the development workers of NOW explained soon after the Act was passed:

> Some groups are less likely to get funds, and youth leaders who were worried about addressing sexuality in the first place are now even more cagey about discussing it.

As this statement indicated, even before Clause 28 youth workers had rarely fallen over themselves to cater for gay, lesbian or bisexual young people. According to a report published in 1985 by the London Gay Teenage Group, the way such potential users actually experienced the service directly contradicted its claims to be open and available to all young people.

Nonetheless, paradoxically, even as Clause 28 was being forced through signs of movement were detectable in the wider

environment. As early as 1980, a working party set up by the Church of England Diocesan Youth Officers' Conference advised that homosexual relationships should be judged by the same criteria as heterosexual ones. By mid-decade a Young Gay Christian Group was coming into existence while BYC, in spite of internal opposition, sustained its publicly proactive stance in support of gay and lesbian young people. Some local authorities maintained financial support for gay and lesbian youth groups even as the media campaigns against them grew in intensity while, not unconnected, more of these groups got established. Even the developing campaign to lower the age of consent for gay men to 16 attracted some youth service attention and support by the end of the decade and into the 1990s.

Clause 28 itself had one other longer term outcome. In the face of what was experienced as a major crisis, gays and lesbians, including within the service itself, were forced to overcome some long-standing divisions and find ways of building effective political alliances. A 'first' was achieved in March 1988 when, with Clause 28 high in their consciousness, lesbian and gay youth workers came together in a specially arranged conference. Later that year a new Lesbian Caucus began to form within CYWU while the following year a National Association of Lesbian and Gay Youth Workers was launched which was still operating well into the 1990s.

By then, the context for all this was a wider gay and lesbian movement which continued to raise its collective profile following the creation of a professional lobbying body Stonewall as well as through the more militant tactics of Outrage. These developments undoubtedly helped to shift the overall climate in which the struggle for gay rights was being conducted. However, as its continuing absences of mind (and occasionally more) demonstrated, the youth service still had a considerable distance to travel. Gay, lesbian and bisexual young people were still a long way from being able to assume that their access to the service would be developed in strategic ways or that their actual reception on the ground would be sensitive and welcoming.

Rural youth work: Escaping the shadow of the city

The urban rebellions of the first half of the 1980s may not have done much for urban young people. But, by concentrating youth policy-makers even more grimly on the inner cities, they did even less for young people living in the countryside. Any report on or investigation into their condition during the 1980s and into the 1990s invariably pointed to proportionately lower levels of resources for rural areas generally and for rural youth work in particular. As the Thompson Report pointed out, this was true even though, given the inescapable facts of rural life, per capita costs of services were bound to be higher.

Nor did the continuing popular 'fantasy' about rural life help. This, as described by Michael Akehurst, the coordinator of NAYC's Rural Youth Work Education

Project between 1980 and 1983:

> ... (had) something to do with sunshine and streams, harvests and cider, flowers, wild life and endless freedom – the summer image of the countryside.

During the 1990s, Prime Minister John Major's identification of things quint-essentially English with the village pub and village cricket only served to reinforce this image and bury still deeper out of political sight most of the hard realities of rural living.

As every 1980s analysis also showed, including that of the Thompson Report, where these realities were not actually worsening, there was little improvement to record. Still, rural young people were disadvantaged by basic poverty, lack of transport and inaccessible public and commercial provision, poorer educational opportunities and fewer job opportunities. As key resources were increasingly centralised, they were deprived, too, of local schools, leisure facilities – and youth clubs. Though they were much more likely than young people in cities to seek membership of a youth organisation, 67 per cent of rural parishes in 1997 had no youth club – a marginally worse figure than at the start of the decade.

By the 1990s what had previously been seen as urban problems – particularly drug use and abuse – had also invaded rural youth culture, again in a context where advice and support, both formal and informal, were likely to be even less accessible or available than in the city. The increasingly common 'solution' for individual young people to all such stresses – moving to live in the city – not only involved leaving family and friends: it also meant risking social isolation or, worse, homelessness or rooflessness.

Nor were the established power structures of rural life committed to shifting these imbalances, least of all in favour of young people. In 1980 Akehust, describing the countryside as 'a battlefield between a number of opposing factions', traced the continuing political dominance of landowning interests 'obsessed with the maintenance of low rates'. Yet, despite such an analysis, class was no more likely to appear in youth service calculations of what was going wrong within rural youth work and what needed to be done to develop it than it was in relation to urban 'disadvantage'.

Indeed, if young people in rural areas were to be targeted, something akin to a 'liberationist movement' was going to be required. Akehurst was able to quote the demands of 45 young people who, meeting at a European-wide conference in 1980, started by recognising their need 'to develop an awareness of their potential for power'. And at least one planned meeting of the Parliamentary Youth Affairs Lobby aimed to bring young people from rural areas face to face with MPs.

These, however, hardly amounted to concerted action by users or even by rural interests acting on their behalf, as the declining membership of Young Farmers' Clubs seemed to confirm. Long proclaimed as one of the best examples of a youth organisation based on members' self-programming and self-government –

and notwithstanding its efforts to offer an imaginative and often modernised programme – its numbers fell by nearly a quarter over the decade, from over 50,000 to 38,000 by 1989.

Though hardly comparable to the increasingly collective efforts of, say, women or Black groups within the youth service, during the 1980s and 1990s some significant pressure to advance rural youth work did develop. Early in the decade, a Rural Youth Clubs Association was created in north Lancashire to support voluntary workers running isolated rural clubs. At about this time, the NYB publication *Scene*, admitting that it rarely mentioned rural youth provision, expressed an intention (not noticeably realised subsequently) 'to devote more attention to this neglected area of work'. Though also somewhat tokenistic if perhaps in the long run more influential, the Thompson Report had five paragraphs devoted to the youth service's role in rural areas.

It was the Rural Youth Work Education project, however, which provided the beginnings of a broader and deeper analysis of what was needed and of the knowledge base required for responding appropriately to the rural situation. The project identified the outstanding characteristics of rural youth work as low esteem, under-resourcing, insufficient research and lack of an identifiable body of knowledge, methodology and support systems. With some justification, it claimed to have helped fill the last three gaps through its three publications. Together, these analysed the situation of young people and youth work in the countryside, proposed ways for supporting and servicing rural workers, and brought together examples of methods and ideas already being used in rural contexts. They were supplemented by *Shadows of Adolescence*, an NYB publication outlining strategies for working with rural young people which was written by a practising detached rural youth worker, Allan Kennedy.

Though the RYWE project's demise again illustrated the limitations of short-term funding, its messages were not allowed to dissipate entirely. By the middle of 1985 Kennedy and Ray Fabes, a long-time campaigner for rural youth work who taught a rural development option on the Leicester Polytechnic youth and community work course, worked with others to set up a three-day national symposium on rural youth work. With NYB's support this attracted 80 participants (and turned away another 50) and led to two further symposia attended by 80 and 130 people. Significantly, these were co-sponsored by Lancashire and Somerset County Councils – both local authorities with significant rural populations. At the third conference, at which the HMI with responsibility for rural youth work outlined a framework for developing the youth service in rural areas, plans were also made for a series of regional conferences to be held in 1989. One of these, in the Midlands, attracted over 100 full-time and part-time workers.

Another of the key focuses of the third symposium was the draft of a report then being prepared by a NACYS subcommittee. In rehearsing information and

arguments from previous work on youth work in rural areas, this, also published in 1988, particularly noted the existing 'background' evidence of 'deep-rooted economic problems'. It sought, too, to challenge the popular image of rural young people as less informed, less sophisticated and less open to educational opportunities than their urban counterparts. It was concerned, too, to see work with them located in the wider issues of race, gender and sexuality and disability.

Highlighting the absence of adequate curricular approaches the subcommittee tried to focus youth workers on issues specific to the rural experience – for example, the dilemmas involved in leaving home and what would constitute a relevant political education – as well as on sometimes less conventional methods for addressing these. Given the shortage of 'qualified full-time staff with suitable experience or sensitivity to the problems of rural youth work', it advocated, too, that new Starting from Strengths training initiatives for part-time workers and new (GRIST) in-service training funds (see Chapter 4) should include some rural priorities.

During the 1990s efforts continued to convert policy proposals into action on the ground. In 1993, for example, Youth Clubs UK won money from the Rural Development Commission for a three-year Rural Links Project, focused on enhancing the skills of volunteers. During this period, too, NYA mounted a project focused on Youth Work in Rural Areas which generated yet another new analysis of rural young people's situation and a training pack for rural youth workers. It also sponsored a series of conferences and other events. One of these, on rural realities, called (yet again) for urgent action to combat rural young people's isolation and deprivation. In 1997 a National Forum for the Development of Rural Youth Work was launched, serviced by the Federation of Young Farmers' Clubs.

With this kind of stimulus to encourage them, many rural authorities continued to look for innovative ways of reaching their young people and by 1998 the Rural Development Commission was able to gather together a number of best practice examples of rural youth work from across the country. In themselves these indicated that some real progress was being made – for example, in empowering young people including young women and through providing them with advice, information and counselling as well as extending mobility and facilities.

Whether such initiatives added up to a national strategy or any real shift in power or resources for youth work between town and country was much more doubtful. It is true that in 1994 Rural Challenge, the rural equivalent to the Government's competitive City Challenge scheme, required bids to specify proposed 'action to make rural areas more attractive to young people, including ... education ... and recreational facilities'. However, the following year the Government's White Paper on *Rural England* – which anyway was very much lighter on prescription than analysis – did little to suggest such concerns were a priority. Youth clubs and youth activities in the countryside, this

implied, were to be valued largely for what they could do to stop young people drifting into crime.

Main references

Michael Akehurst, *Until the Fire and the Rose*, Rural Youth Work Education Project, 1980

Michael Akehurst, *Rural Youth Work Education Project: Final Report*, NAYC, 1983

Karen Chouhan et al, 'Anti-racism and Black empowerment in Britain: Principles and case studies', in Anna Aluffi-Pentini and Walter Lorenz (eds), *Anti-Racist Work with Young People*, Russell House Publishing, 1996

Vipin Chauhan, *Beyond Steel Bands 'n' Samosas*, NYB, 1987

Department of Education and Science, *Young People in the '80s: A Survey*, HMSO, 1983

HMI, *Youth Work in Eight Inner City Areas*, DES, 1988

HMI, *Responses to the Needs of Young Women in Selected LEAs*, DES, 1988

HMI, *Youth Work with Black Young People*, DES, 1990

HMI, *Youth Work with Young People with Disabilities*, DES, 1991

Tony Jeffs and Mark Smith, 'Young People, Class Inequality and Youth Work', in Tony Jeffs and Mark Smith (eds), *Young People, Inequality and Youth Work*, MacMillan, 1990

Trefor Lloyd, *Work with Boys*, NYB, 1985

Macdonald Report, *The Burnage Enquiry: Extract of report for public use*,

Manchester City Council, 1988

David Marsland, 'Afro-Caribbean Youth: A Way Forward?', *Youth in Society*, October 1986

National Advisory Council for the Youth Service, *Youth Work in Rural Areas*, DES/Welsh Office, 1988

National Advisory Council for the Youth Service, *Changing Attitudes: The Youth Service and Young People with Disabilities*, DES/Welsh Office, 1989

National Advisory Council for the Youth Service, *Youth Work with Girls and Young Women*, DES/Welsh Office, 1989

National Council for Voluntary Youth Services, *Disability – A Youth Work Agenda*, Briefing No 8, NCVYS, 1988

Rural Development Commission, *Research findings: 1997 Survey of Rural Services*, RDC, 1997

Rural Development Commission, *Young People in Rural Areas: Making things happen*, RDC, 1998

Jean Spence, 'Feminism in Work with Girls and Young Women', *Youth and Policy*, Spring 1996

Tony Taylor, ' ... and rethinking a strategy', *Youth in Society*, October 1981

Thompson Report, *Experience and Participation: Report of the Review Group on the Youth Service in England*, HMSO, 1982

Clive Wilkinson, *The Drop Out Society: Young People on the Margin*, Youth Work Press, 1995

Paul Willis, *The Social Condition of Young People in Wolverhampton in 1984*, Wolverhampton Borough Council, 1985

7 'Accountability is the Watchword'

A curriculum without boundaries?

Pressure to target unemployment, homelessness, health and other governmental priorities and concerns together with its own determination to address some oppressive social divisions within British society increasingly stretched the youth service's vision – and resources. Even these focuses and activities, however, did not define the full extent of its curriculum, especially as some key interest groups urged that their speciality be given greater attention.

Adding to youth work's 'content'

Sport, long a youth service preoccupation (not to say obsession) was one of the curriculum areas given new respectability and resources by Conservative Governments intent on improving the health of the young nation as well as breaking the politically incorrect image of competitive games. Transformed into outdoor education, something similar happened to outdoor pursuits which during the 1990s, through a DES-funded ESG programme, were particularly targeted at inner-city young people from multi-ethnic communities.

Youth arts, too, demanded a higher profile in the early 1990s. Here the youth service was urged on by the creation in 1993 of a Youth Arts Network, jointly sponsored by Youth Clubs UK and the National Association of Youth Theatres and funded by the Arts Council and the Gulbenkian Foundation. The Gulbenkian Foundation also established a GAP project to develop ways of using the arts in issue-based youth work while in 1995 youth arts was made the focus of Youth Work Week – the national NYA-sponsored annual programme started in 1993 to encourage and support local youth services to showcase their achievements.

The youth service's overall remit broadly conceived was stretched in others ways, too. The 1989 Children Act at least implied that, as a local authority provision, the youth service should make its staff and resources available to support young people leaving care, for example. At the same time expectations remained, and in some respects were hardening, that the service would more systematically underpin formal education in schools and colleges. (In 1992, for example, HMI concluded that school-based youth work had considerable unfilled potential.)

In policy statements and circulars throughout the 1990s, the DfE explicitly sought to develop and release this potential. Increasingly, it looked to youth workers to provide young people with 'information and impartial advice'; to help re-engage disaffected, excluded and truanting pupils including through pupil referral units and study support centres; to accredit their informal educational experiences as complements to the records of achievement being developed in schools and colleges; and to support their volunteering. Following a consultative process prompted originally by DfE interest in the area in 1995, the NYA published a collection of case studies illustrating youth work's contribution to raising standards in schools. By 1997 it was collaborating in similar work within further education colleges.

Perhaps one of the most striking explicit additions to the youth service's curriculum during the early 1990s, however, was global youth work. International perspectives within youth work were of course far from new – indeed, they had been integral to the work of some organisations since their inception. After 1985, they had been given renewed emphasis and focus by the creation of the Youth Exchange Centre which reshaped the machinery for arranging international exchanges. However, the more organised and articulated expression of global perspectives within the service's programmes had brought with it a harder political edge. Quite overtly, the aim now became to develop young people's (and youth workers') awareness and understanding of economic and environmental realities across the world, how these were influencing everyday lives in Britain and how British young people might respond.

Launched in 1994 with youth groups as one of its priority targets, the Development Education Association quickly made its impact through conferences (for example, on an international curriculum for youth work), research and training and consultation. By 1997 it was running a Global Youth Work Advisory Service and circulating a newsletter. During the 1980s and 1990s, too, youth organisations and umbrella bodies – the Methodist Association of Youth Clubs, the Woodcraft Folk, the NYA – took their own initiatives while from September 1994 NYA's monthly *Young People Now* converted its established Environment section into a Global section.

Extending participation

Overlapping with the emergence of these forms of global youth work was a resurgence of interest during the 1980s and into the 1990s in empowering young people. By the late 1990s, for example, the Council for Environmental Education was sponsoring a National Young People's Environment Network of regional forums for 13 to 19-year-olds.

The roots of this commitment to participation also reached back to the service's earliest days. Indeed, of all the state sponsored institutions targeted at youth, the youth service was perhaps unique in making this a goal in its own right – essential to its raison d'etre – rather than seeing it merely as a valued but secondary by-product of other aims. It provided also one of the toughest tests of youth work's claim that *how* it practised (its 'process') was at least as much part of its curriculum as *what* it offered (its 'content').

Though often apparently stuck at the level of rhetoric, this commitment had been restated in different ways in each of the service's landmark reports. The 1942 report of the Youth Advisory Council of the Board of Education, for example, urged that 'some representation' be given to young people on the local authority youth committees they were recommending. Albemarle specifically designated young people as the service's 'fourth partner'. Milson-Fairbairn framed many of its recommendations, at least for young adults, around the notion of 'the active citizen'. Thompson strongly endorsed participation in general and political education in particular. Even the 1990s report produced by the independent business consultants Coopers and Lybrand Deloitte (see below), though focused specifically on the service's management needs, urged that less formal (and so more authentic) forms of participation by young people be adopted, even within bureaucratic local authority structures.

It was, however, the more formal machinery of the local youth council which most often and most publicly had expressed youth service attempts to draw young people into decision-making and the exercise of responsibility. Over its 60-year history, interest in and support for youth councils ebbed and flowed, illustrating particularly clearly the shifting fortunes of participation generally within the service. The post-war spread of youth parliaments barely survived into the 1950s. The youth councils created 30 years later in the wake of Thompson were again either gone or moribund within the decade.

By the mid-1990s, however, another revival was in progress, underpinned this time not just by BYC but also by NYA support or similar national sponsorship in the other three home countries. The 1998 audit of youth service provision by local authorities in England revealed that youth councils or forums were by then being supported or planned by over 60 per cent of local authorities. To back up what the audit report called this 'rapid growth', the financial backing from just 31 of these authorities totalled over £530,000. A joint NYA/BYC survey carried out in 1997–98 established that additional funding was coming from a variety of other sources including the National Lottery, Save the Children Fund, The Prince's Trust, the police authority and the European Union.

By then wider developments were building up pressure on the youth service to turn more of its participation rhetoric into action. The 1992 Earth Summit in Rio de Janeiro had agreed a global environment and development plan, Agenda 21. This encouraged local authorities to establish local partnerships with, among others, community and voluntary groups. As 'environment' in this context embraced people's immediate living surroundings and as the 'agendas' to be addressed specifically included youth issues, many local authorities in Britain used Agenda 21 to stimulate and support active youth participation.

At the same time, the move to a Single Regeneration Budget for the government's annual distribution of special needs funds to local authorities – particularly the 1994 'round' which had a specific focus on young people – also had its effects. It helped stimulate new expectations that the young would become more directly involved in developing and implementing local community projects. After 1997, the Blair Government's increased emphasis on community involvement in regeneration initiatives raised such expectations still further.

By the late 1990s, on behalf of the youth service's voluntary sector as well as for itself, NCVYS was thus restating its commitment to 'a participation strategy for young people'. Local authority youth services, too, were emphasising their commitment to what was by then being called 'active citizenship', with the youth service audit revealing that, in addition to their sponsorship of youth councils, they were using a wide range of methods to achieve this.

One of these – getting young people involved in centre or project decision-making particularly through members' committees or its equivalent – also had a long (and no less chequered) history. Other approaches included carrying out consultation exercises, adopting youth charters, statements of entitlement and complaints procedures, establishing forms of representation on council subcommittees and giving young people a role in inspecting facilities. The audit report was able to point to some 37 per cent of respondents who had offered convincing evidence of genuine participative activity through use of at least three such methods.

The audit report examined one other important participation approach: peer education. Though it was able to identify

only 21 local authority youth services stating an (albeit sometimes substantial) commitment to such projects, by 1991 they had become sufficiently fashionable for the NYA to initiate a survey to clarify their development and use within the youth service. During the 1990s, they were offered support and resources by Youth Clubs UK, culminating in 1997 in a national conference to launch five resource packs to complement earlier publications for workers and young people.

In fact, empowerment was often seen as only one – and sometimes only a subsidiary – aim of peer education work. Its main starting premise was usually that, on 'sensitive' issues affecting their lives, young people were more likely to listen to and be influenced by other young people than by 'out-of-touch' adults. Peer education projects were thus increasingly developed to pass on information and stimulate discussion on health matters such as drug abuse, AIDS and contraception. However, their scope was much wider. Among others, the Guides, the Woodcraft Folk and BYC all initiated peer-led projects focused on young people's rights and political participation. The British Red Cross began to develop its own specialist programmes in ways which gave prominence to peer education while one local project, in Lewisham, used the approach to respond specifically to young women's concerns, including those arising from experiences of abuse, racism and sexual harassment.

Despite these new – and usually well intentioned – initiatives, young people's authentic and sustainable participation in decision-making and indeed in actually delivering some services continued to prove an elusive goal. At least implicitly, the audit report echoed messages from earlier periods about (in perhaps 25 per cent of services) the rhetoric being more impressive than the reality. Evidence from further afield was illustrating even more vividly why this was so often the case.

Thus, research for the Joseph Rowntree Foundation into 12 regeneration area initiatives across the United Kingdom raised a number of fundamental questions. How, for example, were young people who were often deeply disillusioned with politics and with public services to be motivated? Within often tight deadlines laid down by planners with little time for 'process', how could they be provided with fast-track preparation and training in decision-making which would enable them to overcome their years of being sidelined as irrelevant and incapable? How could their agendas – for example, for reducing police harassment or changing adult perceptions of them – be reconciled with adult insistence that the top priority must be getting them better educated and properly trained for jobs? How could participative machinery be designed which, fitting young people's informal leisure styles for getting things done, was effectively 'bottom-up' – that is, which started from their grassroots concerns and involvements and ensured that those who rose to 'the top' of the participative youth structures remained accountable to their 'constituency'?

As it had throughout its history, at the end of the 1990s the youth service (no less than other state and even voluntary

institutions) continued to struggle to find workable answers to such questions.

Breaking the curricular taboos

This range of testing questions amounted in itself to a formidable agenda for under-resourced local youth services already trying to implement a highly ambitious array of other curricular commitments and methods. What is more, such diversification was happening at the very time that a government was in power which had no compunction about trampling all over educational terrain which for a century had been treated as out of bounds to legislators and Whitehall administrators. If such a government was prepared first to invade and then comprehensively to remodel 'the secret garden of the (school) curriculum', a youth service curriculum of such diversity and plurality of values could hardly expect to escape some similar attention. More than this, any service which was encouraging such diversity and plurality – and was disbursing public money to do so – was sooner rather than later going to be seen as in urgent need of overall rationalisation and sterner managerial control.

At the end of the 1980s and during the early 1990s, such restructuring was attempted in some very direct ways. Grants to the national voluntary youth organisations, for example, were much more carefully targeted on programmes identified by the DES rather than, as in the past, used to provide general funding support – a move which did little to increase their trust in the department's other plans. In the allocation of GEST monies, too, local authorities lost their freedom to spend on in-service training priorities which were locally determined.

However, three much more high-profile government-inspired initiatives also set out to achieve this kind of increased central control over the youth service. One involved consolidating the service's central information, support and training services into a single national agency – and then later concentrating its mind very sharply on priorities laid down by what was by then the Department for Education (DfE). The second sought to guide – some thought push – the service into agreeing a core curriculum of its own. The third subjected the service to another searching review, this time aimed explicitly at locking it into the much tighter approaches to managing public services overall on which the Conservative Governments of the late 1980s and 1990s were insisting.

From NYB to NYA – and beyond

A change of director in 1988, from David Howie who had been in the post for 10 years to Janet Paraskeva, brought a distinct change of 'political' style to NYB. More fundamental, however, was its major re-organisation by the Government in April 1991. This was always justified publicly by Secretary of State for Education John MacGregor as essential for developing:

A strong, comprehensive national body which can effectively provide, for the whole

youth service, the range and quality of support necessary to assist it in meeting the challenges of the 1990s.

However, the origins of the changes lay in the appointment in 1989 of an 'efficiency scrutineer', an R. P. Norton, as part of a wider review of voluntary sector funding then in progress. Norton's task was to examine DES funding for the five specially designated and centrally funded youth service bodies: NCVYS, BYC, NAYPCAS, CETYCW and NYB. The review's remit also provided for an examination of the functions of these quite separate and autonomous organisations, their operational relationships and management mechanisms and how their use of funds, public and private, could be made more effective and efficient.

What had happened during the 1980s to related public bodies – for example, to the Health Education Council and the Community Projects Foundation – acted as warnings to the service on what might lie behind the review. Suspicion of its motives were sown from the start by the lack of consultation prior to MacGregor's announcement that it was to take place and by his repeated refusal to publish the Norton review report. Nor was its credibility helped by its being sprung on the service at the very moment that the DES, with proactive NYB support, announced that it would push ahead with ministerial conferences briefed to agree a core youth service curriculum. It was thus widely assumed that the review's 'real' aims were to cut costs and increase the Government's ideological and political control over the bodies under review by collapsing all five of them into one super-agency.

Out of the review came offers to the five organisations which the key DES civil servants (in close consultation with Paraskeva) assumed and hoped they would be unable to refuse. The two under the Department's most direct control, NYB and CETYCW, were to be merged into a National Youth Agency (NYA) – though clearly with NYB as the very senior partner. The others were told: join this new body or re-form as voluntary sector organisations. If they took the latter option, they were warned that they would have to take their chance on funding alongside all the other national voluntary youth organisations – though they could then expect no more than 50 per cent of their costs to be met. Nor could they look for funding for areas of work falling within NYA's remit – which, DES officials made clear, was to include voluntary sector development and youth advice and counselling.

In the event, NAYPCAS, NCVYS and BYC did decide to go their own way, though in attenuated form and in reduced circumstances. With Janet Paraskeva's appointment as director of the NYA and NYB's chair taking up the same position with the new body, merger for CETYCW turned out to be something much closer to takeover. Initially, this seemed to be confirmed by the relatively poor resourcing and low status apparently being allocated to former CETYCW tasks, and especially to its field-led structures for validating and monitoring qualifying courses. However, after pressure from key field organisations, the work of the NYA's

Education and Training Subcommittee (ETS), supported by one of its four youth work development teams, did go some way to retrieving the situation. By 1992 a Wales Youth Agency had also been created with functions largely parallel to those of the NYA.

Through its three other youth work development teams, the agency was also committed to what DES officials saw as its key functions. One was to monitor and evaluate wider forms of training provision and practice throughout the service. A second was to undertake curriculum development, especially in the context of the anticipated core curriculum. The third was to encourage and help define organisational strategies, systems and structures for effective delivery of the curriculum.

The new agency was provided with an Advisory Council, one-third of whose 24 members were to be Government appointees with the rest coming as representatives of the unions, employers and training groups and of the voluntary sector via electoral colleges. (These arrangements were meant to ensure the inclusion of key marginalised and less fashionable 'voluntary' interests as well as of the traditional voluntary sector.) However, all the members of its manage-ment committee, which was much smaller, were appointed by the DES, though again with provision for different sectors of the field to be given 'representation'.

The scepticism, not to say cynicism, generated by the manner of NYA's rapid invention continued to dog the organisation when it finally got down to work in April 1991. Jeffs and Smith, for example, commented at the time:

> The unnatural haste with which NYA has progressed from being a glint in the eye of the DES to the advertisement appearing for a director has restricted the opportunities for public debate regarding its role and function ... It will be designated a Non-Departmental Government Body; overwhelmingly dependent upon central government funding and, therefore, like its predecessor the NYB, safe and docile.

In an article announcing its arrival, even the new agency's house journal, *Young People Now*, felt bound to acknowledge 'two contrasting canine metaphors' being used in youth work circles to describe its role. Was it to be, asked Tim Burke the journal's youth service editor, Government poodle or field rottweiler? Paraskeva's answer was that it was to be neither since the Agency would have no views of its own. By some wholly objective process, it seems, it was to act as the conduit to ministers for the *service's* views. She did not actually deny that, alongside the talk of a core curriculum, its creation might provide an example of creeping centralisation. Nonetheless, she argued, the flip-side of this was a unified service – and that unity was strength.

Within three years what was by then the newly created DfE was back for a further major shake-up of the agency. In 1995 its youth service civil servants decided that a new review was needed of NYA's functions, 'the effectiveness with which they have been carried out, value for money, and the likely need in the future

for these function'. The trigger was the service's effective subversion of what from 1989 to at least 1993 had been *the* DfE agenda for the service – getting it to agree to a core curriculum. For newly appointed departmental officials much less well disposed towards Paraskeva and the NYA, the argument now seemed to run: 'No core curriculum – no need for a National Youth Agency with multiple developmental functions.'

Though involving consultations with some 84 interested bodies, the DfE sought to keep maximum control over this new review by carrying it out internally. In ways which did little to displease DfE officials, it nonetheless acted as a release valve for the kinds of, albeit often contradictory, critical comment which a central resourcing body like NYA was always liable to attract. The process thus provided ample 'evidence' for unconvinced central government officials to interpret unfavourably if they so chose.

Thus, the agency's information and library services, its promotion of equal opportunities, its coordination of Youth Work Week and its response to individual enquiries were all well regarded. Somewhat contradictorily, however, it was seen as 'remote from the field'. It was also judged to be offering inadequate support to the voluntary-statutory partnership and 'not sufficiently committed to the ethos of the voluntary sector'. As the NYA carried a brief for voluntary sector development (though with limited resources for fulfilling it), it was wide open to such complaints, notably from NCVYS which itself had suffered at NYA's expense in the 1990–91 reorganisation.

Criticism came, too, from the Training Agencies Group (TAG). Its most explicit argument against NYA's endorsement role was that this was not reflecting 'the needs of a broader occupational sector' which was now using youth workers to deal, for example, with young offenders, health issues and playwork. Here, however, there were wider pressures at work. For one thing, host institutions were looking to free themselves from external validating bodies of all kinds. For economic as well as educational reasons, they were also driving through much more integrated course arrangements based on modular structures. NYA's peer-led validation processes and the distinctive – indeed, in the new climate idiosyncratic – style of youth and community work courses approved by the NYA fitted ill with such expectations.

It quickly became apparent that, however valid their specific criticisms, many of the review's respondents had – somewhat naively even in this post-Thatcher period – offered up some tempting hostages to fortune. In response to TAG's comments, for example, the DfE did not hesitate to point out that 'the voluntary sector favour the introduction of NVQs' for qualifying youth and community workers – an approach which in the long run could have put the training agencies out of a job. More fundamentally, however, it in effect used the comments it had received at least to trail proposals for dismantling the NYA as a unified national body.

Thus, in its first phase report, though it conceded that the NYA should be able to continue to look for funds from other government departments, the DfE made it clear that it was looking to reduce substantially its own role and resourcing commitment. It proposed that its own financial support should be restricted to one-off national initiatives and – at a reduced 50 per cent level – to specific publications and information services which could not be provided locally. The report also recommended – though without specifying how this would be funded – that a new independent body for endorsing a range of 'informal education' courses should be set up, perhaps as a subcommittee of the Joint Negotiating Committee (JNC). For meeting local and voluntary sector needs, it proposed that the relevant DfE resources within NYA be redirected either through the GEST programme or to the local authority associations through the Government's Revenue Support Grant.

The way the review was moving did not just shock Janet Paraskeva and her NYA colleagues. CYWU labelled the proposals 'ill-considered' while NYA's own Advisory Council, representing a wide range of youth service interests (including, for example, TAG), called unanimously for existing structures to be maintained, albeit with appropriate adaptation. The secretary to the staff side of JNC saw what was being recommended as 'totally without merit'. Indeed, by claiming that 'a gap' existed between the evidence submitted to the review and that cited in the report, he seemed also to support a widely held view that the DfE had 'cooked' the findings in order to get the result it wanted.

In the face of these reactions, which were reinforced by questions in the Lords, the Department rapidly backtracked, claiming that it 'did not envisage under any circumstances the dissolution of the National Youth Agency'. In the event this did not happen and the NYA retained all its major functions including course endorsement. However, by reducing its financial responsibility largely (and on a declining budget) to supporting the agency's publishing activities, the DfE was able in effect to return its own role merely to sponsoring a 'youth service information centre' – the narrowly focused agency created in the 1960s out of which NYB and the NYA had emerged in the 1970s and 1980s.

The management of NYA's other functions was taken over by the Council for Local Education Authorities (CLEA). It took these on partly because, despite all the setbacks of the past two decades, many local authorities had retained a genuine commitment to their youth services. Less nobly it also welcomed the return of some powers from central to local government. From April 1996 the relevant funding was transferred to CLEA from the DfE by 'top-slicing' the Revenue Support Grant. To the extent that CLEA was now responsible for agreeing the major elements of NYA's work programme, at least the DfE's pressure to get its services to become more responsive to local and voluntary sector needs had paid off.

Though born out of anxiety and frustration, particularly over the Government's perceived indifference to young people and its continuing misunderstanding of the youth service, the outcome of the review brought some important changes for the NYA. These were underpinned by a change of director which also took place at this

moment (1995). While the DfE review process was in full flow, Janet Paraskeva had announced that she was leaving the NYA. She was replaced by Tom Wylie who, as well as having worked for the Scout Association, had set up INSTEP in 1976 and was a former senior youth service HMI.

Clearly the 'new' NYA was going to need to be vigilant about meeting the expectations of its new local authority paymasters and mistresses. However, by the mid-1990s the youth service's national resource – and potential national voice – was rid of the oppressive and often obsessive political and managerial control over its work which had characterised the long DES/DfE's oversight. Like the constituencies it served, it of course remained constrained by – indeed sucked into servicing – central government priorities. This became even clearer after 1997 as the Labour Government, placing young people at the heart of many of its most high-profile policies, pushed ever harder to get the youth service to conform to its sharply targeted policy initiatives for excluded and disaffected young people.

Nonetheless, in the late 1990s the NYA involved itself, and with a new vigour and outspokenness, in more or less overtly campaigning interventions into national policy-making. This represented something of a return to a style and role which it and its predecessor organisation, NYB, had adopted before the Thatcherite assault on 'enemies within' had forced it increasingly to self-censor – or be censored. It sought, for example, to record and affirm progressive local developments, especially where these might have national significance. It began, too, not only to advocate on behalf of young people but also to press with others for a stronger legislative base for the service – something which the DfE had explicitly vetoed in 1994. Under Labour, it also worked hard to explain the need for a youth service which, if it was to avoid being converted into just another state safety net, must at its core remain demand-led and non-stigmatising.

Whose core curriculum?

Janet Paraskeva – described by the *Times Educational Supplement* in 1990 as 'once a radical figure in the youth movement' – remained at the NYA long enough to have a major influence on another of the DfE's attempts to tighten its grip on the youth service: putting in place an agreed core curriculum. Working on the principle that 'you've got to be inside the system now', Paraskeva (with others within the NYA) acted as the willing public voice of equally proactive Departmental officials to convince the service that this had become essential. It would, she argued, 'put the service further up the educational agenda' and demonstrate 'the need for proper resourcing'. Fanciful though this turned out to be under successive Conservative administrations, she also saw it and the three ministerial conferences mandated to bring it into being as the vehicles for finally getting the service to its holy grail: a stronger legislative base.

NYB quoted its own 1987 review of post-Thompson local developments, *Reshaping the Youth Service*, as providing the evidence that a core (national) curriculum was needed. Yet the NYB report could be read in a different way. It, for example, showed that a number of local services had produced or were in the process of developing their own articulate statements of curricular intent. With subsequent NACYS and HMI reports adding at least partial confirmation of this interpretation, it suggested that little if any of the energy driving the ministerial conferences initiative was coming 'from below'.

In fact, the whole notion of a youth service or youth work curriculum was a relatively new one which had taken root within the service only slowly and shallowly. According to Bernard Davies, for example, until the mid-1970s, as youth workers 'had largely assumed that it applied only to schools', the concept had evoked for them 'images of school subjects, rigid timetables, exam requirements and the rote learning of facts, dates and formulas'. Only in 1975 had a NYB pamphlet written by its director, John Ewen, *Curriculum Development in the Youth Club*, endorsed the term as a credible way of grappling with the question: 'What are we doing in this club?' The result, according to Davies, was that:

> From our Cinderella position, we then managed to convince ourselves that we could magically convert this pumpkin term into the beautiful coach for conveying youth work's values and methods to the DES ball.

With the concept suddenly being embraced in such influential Departmental circles, 'midnight now seems to be about

129

to strike'. For a practice in which, as we have seen, the medium (*how* the 'teaching' was done) had always been conceived as integral to the message – *what* was 'taught' – the term's lack of substance was, it seemed, about to be exposed.

Mark Jackson, the *Times Educational Supplement's* youth correspondent had a more cynical view of the whole project:

> A national youth curriculum? It sounds like a bizarre extension of Whitehall rule, conjuring up images of the regimented youth of totalitarian regimes. Britain's youth workers, the guerrillas of the education system, who mainly work with youngsters alienated from conventional learning, are not noted for their readiness to take orders.

This scepticism was widely shared within the service. Nonetheless, as we saw earlier, the range of issues and content areas which the youth service had by now taken on left it open to criticisms of being over-stretched and even of curricular self-indulgence. HMI reports noted how often local youth services lacked policy guidelines for directing and checking this burgeoning flow of commitments and concerns and asked who was establishing what was valid and essential. They also commented regularly on how often developments – innovatory and relevant though they may have been – were the result of individual flair and interest rather than service-wide decisions on priority responses to identified need.

A top-down move to clarify a core curriculum thus posed the service with some uncomfortable dilemmas. Ever since, two decades before, Margaret Thatcher, as

Secretary of State for Education, had rejected the Fairbairn-Milson Report, it had complained that it was getting no central direction. What if this was what was now being offered – but if the service did not like what was being proposed? In any case, so soon after the Government's invasion of the teachers' previously sacred curricular territory, could Departmental motives really be trusted? Or had the moment in fact finally come – especially at a time when resources were so tight – for minds to be fiercely concentrated on what could and should be at the core of the service's work?

Such complications were, however, to be further compounded. Ministers and especially civil servants may have been convinced that a core curriculum was a good idea. Yet, despite the coincidental appearance at that very moment of an independent (and substantial) contribution to the debate by the Further Education Unit (FEU), they seemed to have no very clear notion of what such a curriculum should look like. Nor were they getting full-hearted encouragement in their search from HMI who, at the very least, had deep doubts about the need for and viability of the whole project.

Even though officials and professionals were providing the main driving force, the effort to generate a core curriculum was further weakened by the speed with which, yet again, ministerial responsibility for the service changed. During the nearly three years between the build-up to the first ministerial conference in December 1989 and the third and last of the conferences in June 1992, three junior ministers held the brief, each of whom had some significantly different concerns and priorities. Key changes in the DES's own staffing also brought significant behind-the-scenes shifts in commitment and alliances – especially between the Department and the NYA – which further undermined the process. As a result, ample gaps and flaws existed in the NYA's and the Department's positions through which the service could – and eventually did – make its escape.

The whole initiative can notionally be traced back to the promise to develop alternative ways of getting advice to ministers on youth service policy made when the DES decided early in 1989 to wind up NACYS. Even so, in an interview for *Young People Now* only six months before the first ministerial conference in December 1989, the then minister with responsibility for the service John Butcher made no mention of the new initiative. Indeed, nor did *Young People Now* itself – which was, after all, the NYA's house journal – until, a month before this opening conference, a one-page article appeared. Significantly entitled *Accountability is the Watchword*, it was written by a member of the NYB Curriculum Development Team which by then was well into the initial consultation process. His key message to the service was that it should support the development of a core curriculum if only on the grounds that it was 'getting the message to tighten up … to define itself and measure its achievements'.

The first official word that something was afoot came in a letter from Alan Howarth to all chief education officers (CEOs) and

senior representatives of the national voluntary organisations in England and Wales. Howarth had taken over from Butcher weeks after the latter's *Young People Now* interview and thus became the first of the ministerial fall-guys in the core curriculum saga. Headed 'First National Youth Service Conference: A Core Curriculum for the Youth Service?', his letter invited a senior member of the local authority or voluntary organisation to attend the first of a series of three such 'consultations'.

The overall purpose of these, it was explained, was to 'deal with the idea of a core curriculum for the youth service' – 'a broad, analytical framework, for use and adaptation locally'. The minister's hope was that this would produce 'some common understanding and agreement about the unique role and contribution of the youth service' including priority groups among young people and 'the target skills, experience and opportunities it should help them to achieve'. All this was to be done 'in the light of all the resources, statutory, voluntary and private, which might be available' – and which, the minister did not fail to point out, were 'limited'. None of these platitudes, however, came close to addressing some much harder questions. What, for example, could reasonably be expected of the local authorities and the national voluntary youth organisations? How could they play complementary roles in delivering such a curriculum? And how could the latter be assured that their autonomy was not about to be undermined?

Advice on mounting the conferences, it emerged, was being given by a small steering group, established initially for two years. In addition to Janet Paraskeva, this was made up of HMI and DES officials and five individuals appointed 'in a personal capacity, from the voluntary and statutory youth sectors in England and Wales'. It was chaired by a former Director of Education for the Wirral, Mike Nichol, with Linbert Spencer, chief executive of Fullemploy, acting as consultant.

Resourced by the NYB Curriculum Development Team, consultations were held in the run-up to the first conference at eight national and 80 field events. These involved nearly 1,500 people working in management, field and training roles and representing women's, Black, disabled and lesbian and gay groups. A description and analysis of these discussions together with a background paper containing historical and current information on the service was circulated prior to the conference.

Even with this extensive consultation and preparation, this first conference and what was being proposed still seemed remote from many in the field, especially given the 'elite' nature of the 200 people who attended. To add to the continuing doubts about why a core curriculum was needed at all, participants were greeted by a keynote address by Howarth in which he adopted some very hard-line positions. He certainly worked hard to reassure his audience that, by seeking a core curriculum for the service, he had something very different in mind from that which 'ministers had just introduced for schools'. He also stressed that he 'was not proposing a strait-jacket, but a spotlight' – a means of redressing the service's 'unwarranted and unfair' marginalisation.

At the same time, the minister was blunt about his expectation that in future the youth service would be education-based and therefore would use DES resources, including those focused on the voluntary sector, for clearly educational purposes and programmes. In a follow-up letter to the conference, he also gave advance notice of a circular in which he came as close as he dared to instructing local authorities to keep the youth service as an education department responsibility. Many at the conference would have been representing services which had diversified well beyond such boundaries, including some which were located outside education. These messages could therefore have brought them little reassurance about the shape and direction of this nascent curriculum development initiative.

All this left the conference with, at best, a somewhat doubtful mandate: indeed, as the report on the pre-conference consultations acknowledged, 'some people, groups and organisations (already felt) "less consulted with" than they would have wished'. It also found itself operating in an uncertain and somewhat demotivated atmosphere for completing its demanding tasks. For, over just two days, participants were expected 'to achieve positive and practical outcomes and to produce a realistic basis for future planning'. In particular, they were asked to identify the main elements of a curriculum planning document which the DES could recommend to local authorities and voluntary organisations and, somewhat optimistically, to approve a draft mission statement tucked away at the very end of the background papers.

With only limited progress made on this ambitious agenda, the most concrete outcome of this first conference thus turned out to be a somewhat scaled-down and cautious commitment to 'a process of further consultation with the field which might itself lead to an agreed national statement'. Indeed, the steering group seems to have emerged from the experience somewhat chastened. As a brief piece in *Young People Now* on 'the next stage' put it: 'the need for ownership by the field of any core curriculum and set of outcomes for the youth service emerged as an issue of central importance'.

To give time for the new consultation exercise, the second conference was delayed until November 1990. An invitation for written submissions produced 165 responses – 79 from local authorities and 86 from a variety of 'voluntary' and other organisations. Their analysis generated a 30-page document which constituted the main background paper for the second ministerial conference. This offered a revealing insight into the youth service's collective and highly pluralistic view of itself, its mission and its methods. With their strong emphasis on the need for local decision-making on priorities and the importance of equality of access, empowering young people and challenging oppression, the consultations also gave notice to the would-be centralisers of some tricky problems ahead.

By the time the conference convened, again over two days, these reactions had encouraged the steering group to, in effect, refine the remit of the whole exercise. The original mission statement, which it now described as 'cumbersome and repetitive', was replaced by a draft of 'a short, clear statement of purpose'. This gave greater emphasis to current youth service preoccupations such as equal opportunities and environmental and international awareness and sought to illustrate 'the importance of spontaneity' within the youth service's unique contribution to young people's education.

However, with a DES-sponsored review of the management of the service under way, the steering group's interpretation of 'curriculum' was also acquiring a distinctively managerial flavour. For the second consultation exercise, which had been initiated in March 1990, respondents had had their attention focused on targets (age range, priority groups and priority issues), outcomes or learning gains, methods and provision. By the time the conference discussion groups got their remits nine months later, these had been reconstituted simply as an 'outcomes matrix', 'performance indicators' and 'other key areas of curriculum design'.

The 225 people who came together for the second conference were still made up mainly of principal youth officers and chief executives of national voluntary organisations. Again, a gathering as large, and still as varied as this, found it difficult to generate a consensus of ideas and grounded proposals which were not just lowest common denominator. And again, too, Howarth's contribution had something of a dampening effect, not just for its heavy emphasis on Thatcherite 'family values' but also because, rather than appearing personally, his speech was delivered via a video.

The five steering group recommendations put to the conference were the outcome of what Mike Nichol, the conference chair, called 'the authentic voice of the service' – the pre-conference consultation exercise. Somewhat optimistically he and his colleagues therefore assumed that they would be non-contentious. In the event, two of them dominated proceedings.

The draft statement of purpose had to be redrafted twice, not least because of pressure from a Black working group for a clearer recognition of Black young people's oppression. The result was an ambitious (perhaps over-ambitious) and, in historical terms, radical 'official' declaration of intent which gave explicit recognition to young people's collective and cultural identities.

Thus, the new statement did not only see youth work as offering young people opportunities which were educative. It committed it, too, to promoting equality of opportunity and participative and empowering forms of practice. In applying these broad purposes, it also set the service the task of challenging oppressions such as racism and sexism and supporting young people to act on the political and other issues affecting their lives.

Extra conference time was also needed to deal with a proposal that, within an overall target group of 11 to 25-year-olds, the service should give priority to the 13 to 19 age group. This raised fears among a range of organisations that they might not get funding for work with both younger and older young people. As a result, with little progress being made on what the steering group had seen as other key issues such as identifying nationally agreed learning outcomes and performance indicators, it was left with considerable follow-up work before the final conference.

Much was to happen in what turned out to be the 18 months before this took place – including, once again, a postponement of the conference itself. For some powerful interests in the service, especially those in the traditional voluntary sector, the statement of purpose was over-ambitious, if not downright subversive. Behind-the-scenes lobbying could not alter what had been agreed by a national conference, ostensibly unanimously. Perhaps, however, the minister could be persuaded to distance himself and the Government sufficiently from the statement to undermine its credibility and its take-up?

In relation to its most significant values, this within two months is precisely what Howarth did, clearly and quite comprehensively. In a response which described the statement as 'a challenging document', he asserted that 'not everyone ... will be at ease with some of the language used in it, particularly some of the politically charged terms'. He also encouraged the service as a whole to 'rightly insist on their own freedom to accept or reject the statement' - a comment which lead one steering group member to suggest that he might as well have said: 'Don't bother using it'. Howarth also warned the service that it would be 'less strongly placed' to play its part in the education system 'if it is embroiled in political controversy'. And, noting that 'idealism is not the same as ideology', he sought to return workers to their traditional value position by counselling them to 'relate to young people first and foremost as individuals, rather than as representatives of types, classes, races and so forth'.

The response also came close to admitting that Howarth and his advisers had yet to win – perhaps were close to losing – the central argument on which the whole ministerial conference initiative had rested: that the service needed an agreed core curriculum. The notion, his statement acknowledged, 'still seems to some people to be an alien one in relation to the youth service'. Though those who had been converted knew how the term was being used, there were 'others – including participants in youth work – (who) remain mystified and anxious about it'.

Though such communication failure was hardly surprising, it sprang from much deeper misunderstandings than the minister – or indeed key actors within the DES and NYA – were prepared (or perhaps able) to acknowledge. For them, curriculum was largely synonymous with 'outcomes'. For the youth service by and large, in so far as the term had any operational value, it was inseparable from (perhaps even the same as) 'process'. This barrier, which was conceptual rather than merely linguistic, was never bridged, and probably could not have been given the contrasting (even conflicting) models of learning being applied by both sides.

With the ministerial project clearly running out of steam, momentum was further lost when Howarth was moved from the DES to be succeeded by Robert Atkins. Though

Atkins agreed to take part in a third national conference, he announced that this would be run as a seminar to review progress on the detailed work on values, goals and priorities which was now to be done at local level and in individual organisations. In October 1991 a paper was circulated to guide nine regional and three national consultation seminars, including one in Wales which by then had produced its own version of the statement of purpose. These, which again focused attention on learning outcomes for young people and performance indicators for the service, would provide the basis for the background material for the third conference.

Nearly a year after the second conference, dates and venues for this third one were 'still being investigated for Spring 92'. In the event it took place in June 1992 and, though attracting over 330 participants, proved to be the final resting place for the ministerial bandwagon. It laid plans for further work on performance indicators with the NYA being mandated to produce curriculum guidelines to help local authorities and voluntary organisations plan and evaluate their work. However, over and above the statement of purpose which had so displeased one of his predecessors, the most Nigel Forman, the latest minister, could point to after three years of intensive debate was a greater sense of common educational purpose within the service – and an acceptance that it was determined to settle its fate locally.

The final moment was perhaps best captured by the *Times Educational Supplement*. Under a headline 'No change for the youth service', it drew the conclusion that, for youth workers, the whole exercise 'left them where they had started'. Within the year, though trying to make the most of the failure, Janet Paraskeva herself was concurring with this. There was to be, she acknowledged no 'national core curriculum, nor indeed published common learning outcomes'. Far from going out with a bang, the youth service's conference season, it was clear, had ended with a ministerial whimper.

Not that the effort had been wholly without effect: far from it. In a broad and often elusive way, it had changed self-perceptions and self-expectations, leaving the service open to examine some previously unconsidered possibilities. Internally, it initiated a rare national debate on its value base. This in turn produced a statement of purpose which – though the rhetoric may often have been more impressive than the action flowing from it – began to appear regularly in the policy and curriculum documents of statutory and voluntary agencies across the country. An OFSTED report on the youth work curriculum confirmed that this was happening as early as 1991–92. The results included local descriptions of the principles and values on which statements of purpose rested, wide internal consultation processes and clear guidance on 'the areas of experience which might be included and the methods of social education to be used'.

As Janet Paraskeva pointed out, even the national statement of purpose was not a core curriculum. It did, however, provide a public and a collective affirmation of where the youth service now stood on

some key principled issues. In effect it replaced the definition of aims which – with its overriding concern for individual development and self-realisation – civil servant Sir John Maud had first enunciated in 1951 at a national conference of senior youth service personnel. This (largely uncritically) had been wholly or partly endorsed since by every significant state paper on the service, including Albemarle, Fairbairn-Milson and Thompson.

By the 1990s, however, not just Maud's vision but also his at least implicit social analysis had long been overtaken by events – in particular by the liberating effects of the 'youth revolution' of the 1960s and by the conversion of Britain into a multi-racial and multi-cultural society. Crucially therefore the new statement of purpose moved the service on to a commitment to values which acknowledged that such a thing as society did exist and that this, and not least its collective and institutional practices and ideologies, did much to shape the lives of the service's clientele.

The statement did not appear, nor did it start to take root, in a vacuum. Though the service had proved far too stroppy to agree to a national curriculum, it paid a price for its resistance. In part this showed itself in a neglect which left it exposed to further financial attrition. However, from the start the undisguised interest of the DES, and especially of its civil servants, in the whole curriculum project had been to make the service more accountable within the new education structures created by the Thatcher Governments. Not surprisingly therefore, the managerial ideas and concepts towards which the ministerial conferences increasingly pointed the service also acquired a wider currency and credibility.

A review for the 1990s

Ultimately, the main central government instrument for embedding these ideas turned out to be, not ministerial conferences or a core curriculum, but a new review of the service. Over the six decades of proactive state involvement, such government-inspired examinations had occurred at regular intervals, including three between 1959 and 1982. All had resulted in reports which were thorough, wide-ranging and, certainly in the case of Albemarle, imaginative and politically 'sussed'. All were undertaken by 'public' committees which often included figures of some stature, many with insider knowledge. All provided philosophical as well as organisational markers against which, albeit with varying degrees of enthusiasm, the service could and did measure itself, at least until the next review.

A clear indication of the changed political and ideological circumstances in which the youth service was by then operating was the DES's decision to commission this review for the 1990s from Coopers and Lybrand Deloitte, one of a number of high-profile private business consultancy firms which had gained increasing credibility and influence. Carried out in 1990–91, its remit was deliberately narrowed – to an examination of how best the service could be managed in the new local authority

conditions of the early 1990s. Though ostensibly answering to a four-person steering committee, this met only three times (and then merely to monitor progress and read draft reports). Only one member of the group had a youth service background and all, broadly speaking, were administrators. Moreover, though one of the consultants was Mike Nichol, the chair of the ministerial conference steering group, the perspectives and language of the (all white, all male) field work team were private business rather than public education and welfare. Finally, though expounding with clarity and some insight the strategic and structural implications for the service of the shift in its local education authority environment, the report's impact was instrumental rather than inspirational.

The timing of the review was also significant. Whether by accident or design, it was in effect part of a package of interconnected DES initiatives which also included the creation of the NYA out of NYB and CETYCW and the sponsorship of the ministerial conferences. The effect of these was to draw the youth service ever more tightly into wider policy strategies which during the late 1980s and into the early 1990s were radically reshaping public education. As a result, the service's space for risking critical and less orthodox action was, it seemed, being deliberately targeted by a government which, in direct contradiction of its libertarian rhetoric, was demonstrating unmistakably centralising (and indeed authoritarian) tendencies.

To some extent, these were masked in this case by the stated reason for the review:

the need to clarify the implications for the service of the 1988 Education Reform Act. By introducing local management of schools (LMS), this had seemed to threaten resources – especially premises – previously available to the service (see Chapter 2). To cope with the significant reallocation of responsibilities and indeed of power resulting from LMS, LEAs had also been required to fundamentally restructure themselves. This raised questions about the youth service's location within what was left of the LEA as an institution and about the appropriate style and machinery for managing it.

These features of the remit the Coopers and Lybrand report addressed in very direct and probing ways. However, its sub-sections if not its sub-text suggested that the DES might have some additional expectations. In considering strategic planning, for example, the consultants were asked to recommend, not just on the coordination of the maintained (statutory) and voluntary sectors, but also on 'the critical determinants of effective youth service planning'. They were asked, too, to consider whether the LMS 'formula funding' arrangements for resourcing schools had anything to teach the youth service and to examine processes for delegation, monitoring and managing information.

The Coopers and Lybrand team liberated themselves impressively from these constraints in a number of ways. They noted, and endorsed, the strength of the service's educational commitment even when it had been placed in a local authority department other then education. It is true that they had not caught up with

the shift to more 'political' perspectives emerging from the ministerial conferences' debates on purpose. Nonetheless, they specifically recommended that the service's 'underlying philosophical values' as expressed through 'a commitment to social education and personal development' should normally be decisive in determining where it was located organisationally.

In unpacking the options for its funding and internal management, the consultants also displayed considerable sensitivity to the service's distinctiveness and indeed to how idiosyncratic and complex some of the factors were affecting its planning and operation. They returned more than once, for example, to the voluntary nature of young people's engagement with its practitioners and facilities and their rapid 'turnover'. When considering how the service could provide methods of 'quality assurance', they highlighted 'the problems for the youth service (of) ... the timescales over which changes in young people need to be measured to become discernible'. They also saw that if young people were to participate in authentic ways in the kinds of management processes they were discussing, whatever more formal structures were set up, informal approaches were essential.

The consultant team acknowledged anyway that, because the youth service worked partially through the voluntary sector, it could expect to have only limited information and influence on what was going on. This the team saw as particularly true of its relations with the 'independent sector' – those newer often innovative groups which, though doing as much work with young people as the traditional voluntary sector (often with priority and especially Black groups), saw themselves as outside both the established voluntary and the maintained sectors.

About such statutory-voluntary relationships generally, the report was extremely clear-sighted. 'These structures are not working effectively', they declared. Indeed, they offered a linguistic litmus test of their condition: 'whether the phrase "youth service" is used subconsciously by managers to include both sectors, or whether it is taken to refer only to one'. LEAs were said to be paying lip-service to voluntary organisations, at times giving the impression that, if they had enough resources they would dispense with them altogether. For their part, voluntary organisations were in many cases regarded as unrepresentative and less than committed. The consultants' conclusion was therefore that 'all sides are disappointed with the results'.

The report went on to recommend in some detail a 'model for effective planning through partnership'. This reappeared repeatedly in some form as the consultants picked their way through a variety of options for allocating funding and delegating responsibilities (including for 'quality assurance') down the structures. Recognising the risks of clubs being 'pushed into a numbers game', they strove to identify not just mechanisms but also appropriate levels in departmental and service structures at which these should operate. They also explored how these could be developed and implemented with sufficient sensitivity to cope with the service's messiness – its unreliable and

difficult-to-measure outcomes, elusive 'mission' and a set of funding processes which were still largely historic in the way they operated.

Overall, in fact, the report adopted a positive and optimistic view of the service and its potential for dealing with the upheavals flowing from the Education Reform Act, treating this at least as much as an opportunity as a challenge for the service. It pointed out, for example, that, as a result of the Act, the youth service had become 'one of the most significant educational services to remain under direct local authority management'. It was impressed too that, as local authorities moved to being enabling rather than just providing organisations, the service's experience of supporting and facilitating services through the voluntary sector was to some extent placing it 'ahead of the game'.

Advantages could accrue to the youth service, too, closer to the points of the delivery. With the schools' national curriculum placing greater emphasis on pupils' personal development, openings were being created, the report suggested, for 'youth workers to become more involved in school-based work'. This in turn would help enhance 'the complementary role of the youth service to schools', especially, the consultants concluded, if wherever feasible it was located in a 'client services' rather than an 'institutional services' division. For a report intentionally focused on strategic questions and explicitly geared to offering managerial solutions co-opted from a profit-making rather than people-oriented world, it succeeded in retaining and displaying considerable heart and humane insight.

Nonetheless, the Coopers and Lybrand exercise had some significant limitations, not all of them of its own making. As further major education legislation was laid on top of the 1988 Act, the balance of (especially financial) advantage tipped decisively against the youth service. Increasingly LEAs came to use their budgets as in effect a reserve fund for resourcing new statutory requirements and for funding the financial inducements needed to persuade potentially recalcitrant schools not to opt out of local authority control (see Chapter 2).

Some of the weaknesses of the Coopers and Lybrand report had much more deep-seated origins, however. At first sight these seemed to be traceable to the consultants' strange, not to say alien, language and core concepts – their talk of business plans, resource models and performance indica-tors composed of inputs, processes and outputs. Beneath the semantics, however, lay an even greater risk. Such mechanistic terms and the 'systems' to which they pointed had a potentially seductive simplicity. To a service which at that very moment was struggling – and, other than at a very broad ideological level, failing – to reach agreement on its essential mission and key priorities, they were therefore likely to promise relatively instant and straightforward solutions to its complex unresolved problems.

The consultants were clear in a number of places that, if their work was to take root,

the DES, HMI and the NYA would need to continue to research and resource the application of their recommendations; and that the ministerial conferences would need to complete their work – and complete it well. However, their references to the ministerial conferences revealed some surprising blind-spots. Certainly, their affirming references to the youth service's 'given' commitment to an educational philosophy were welcome to a service under increasing pressure to target special needs. However, these took too much for granted since, beyond a broad 'lowest common denominator' consensus, much about this stance remained contentious and indeed undebated.

Much more serious, however, was their failure to notice the significance of the main outcome of the second ministerial conference: a statement of purpose agreed at least six months before they reported which was radical enough to stir the minister responsible into issuing a sharp rebuke. Though, as noted earlier, one of the consultants, Mike Nichol, was throughout at the centre of the core curriculum debates, he and his colleagues offered no comment on this major shift in the service's declared ideological position nor on the implications for their own proposals of the value conflicts which this had again exposed.

In fact, the consultants seemed to make the debate on values and purpose which was still needed even less likely. Again perhaps unintentionally, the effect of their analysis and recommendations was to give the continuing ministerial conferences discussion a firm nudge away from philosophy and priorities (and indeed methods, too) and in the direction of organisational forms, processes and procedures. They noted, for example, that a shift in 'the focus of the conferences ... from curriculum to management issues' had already – and appropriately – taken place. Reinforcement was thus given to a long-standing youth service preference for action prior to (even instead of) reflection and analysis – that is, to a pragmatic tradition which anyway, in the face of the tensions and contradictions released by the core curriculum debates, was once again asserting itself.

It is true that, in the middle and later years of the 1990s, the ministerial conferences' statement of purpose was to be found cropping up all over the place in youth service self-presentations. So too, however, were the managerial concepts of the Coopers and Lybrand report. Sometimes they arose out of a confident under-standing of *why* the service existed and for whom and were used with the kind of analytical insight and qualifications which the Coopers and Lybrand consultants brought to them. In these circumstances, they undoubtedly helped the service to a sharper sense of itself and to a greater credibility with crucial 'others', especially local politicians and other funders.

However, though the search for a core curriculum may always have been a contradiction in terms for the youth service, its debate on its overall mission nationally and usually also locally was far from complete. The Coopers and Lybrand prescriptions were thus liable to be superimposed from above, sometimes it

seemed gratuitously, on a workforce which was unprepared for them and so had little understanding or ownership of them. In these circumstances they could act as escapes from, rather than as tools for resolving, the service's uncertainties and confusions about its direction and priorities – that is, about what it should be using such concepts for.

OFSTED takes a hand

One of the clearest signs of the increasing pressure on the service to tighten up its managerial act was the publication of a 'framework' for inspecting youth work. This was first issued by OFSTED after consultation in 1994 and revised in 1997 and, for example, gave strong prominence to the accountability of staff and systematic monitoring and evaluation of the use of resources.

By now the numbers of the youth service inspectors were much reduced after their conversion from HMI. Though (at least at first) technically more independent than their predecessors, they also found themselves having to give due weight to much of the 'new' educational thinking and many of the expectations of the post-Thatcher era. Like all their inspectorial colleagues, they were therefore being pressed to give even greater priority than in the past to 'value-for-money' questions – where value, certainly according the dominant Government and DfE credo, would give little credence to the youth service's person-centred criteria.

In fact the youth service's inspection document again sought to steer a careful course between the contradictory pressures of these governmental expectations and the youth service's adherence to a more liberal education tradition. Thus the framework continued to endorse evaluation criteria concerned with young people's growth in confidence, self-esteem and a sense of empowerment and with differentiated responses to young people according to, for example, their gender, ethnic origin and – despite Clause 28 and all that – sexual orientation.

Nonetheless, for political as well as educational reasons, HMI clearly felt it essential to give some detailed attention to how resources were being deployed and used. It thus specifically sought calculation of units costs of provision – for example, of youth worker contact hours, for each young person reached and for each registered attendance. More broadly, the efficiency of the service as well as the quality of the experience it provided for young people were among the framework's most significant features.

Indeed, though necessarily (and not before time) it concentrated the service on questions crucial to its development, its application was usually experienced by all staff as, in its own right, a major additional exercise in self-justification and managerial oversight. By the end of the 1990s, for example, the North West Regional Youth Service Unit was offering senior managers – of whom over 50 responded – a one-day conference on 'OFSTED made easy'. For all its relative liberalism therefore, the OFSTED

framework and the inspection system it underpinned represented as clearly as anything the new ethos to which the youth service was being required to respond.

Main references

Tim Burke, 'NYA: A new breed of agency', *Young People Now*, April 1991

Coopers and Lybrand Deloitte, *Managing the Youth Service in the 1990s: Report*, DES, 1991

Suzanne Fitzpatrick et al, 'Including young people in urban regeneration', *Findings*, Joseph Rowntree Foundation, 1998

HMI, *Survey of School-based Youth and Community Work*, DES, 1991

Tony Jeffs and Mark Smith, 'Youth Work, Youth Service and the Next Few Years', *Youth and Policy*, November 1990

Hugh Matthews et al, 'Local Places and Political Engagement: youth councils as participatory structures', *Youth and Policy*, Winter 1998–99

Mary Marken et al, *England's Youth Service – the 1998 Audit*, Youth Work Press, 1998

National Youth Bureau, 'Towards a Core Curriculum for the Youth Service?: Background papers for the First Ministerial Conference', NYB, 1989

National Youth Bureau, 'A Core Curriculum for the Youth Service?: An Analysis of the Youth Work Dynamic – a summary of the National Youth Bureau's consultations with the youth work field, NYB, 1989

National Youth Bureau, 'Towards a Core

Curriculum for the Youth Service?: Report of the First Ministerial Conference', NYB, 1990

National Youth Bureau, 'Towards a Core Curriculum for the Youth Service?: Second Ministerial Conference Steering Committee Consultation Document', NYB, 1990

National Youth Bureau, 'Towards a Core Curriculum for the Youth Service?: Report of the Responses to the Ministerial Conferences Steering Committee Consultation Document', NYB, 1990

National Youth Bureau, 'Towards a Core Curriculum for the Youth Service?: Comments on the Recommendations of the Ministerial Conferences Steering Committee Consultation Document', NYB, 1990

National Youth Bureau, 'Consultation seminars: Towards the Third Ministerial Conference', NYB, 1991

Office for Standards in Education, *Inspecting Youth Work: A revised inspection schedule*, OFSTED, 1997

Tom Wylie, 'Those that guard I do not love: A memoir of HM Inspectorate and youth work in the Thatcher era', (pending)

8   The 1990s: Cuts, Bills and Political Promises

Take-up: The 20 per cent threshold

At the end of 1993 and early in 1994 youth service 'take-up' in England was again tested – this time by the Office of Populations Censuses and Surveys (OPCS). It questioned some 3,700 11 to 25-year-olds, giving particular attention to the service's priority age group, 13 to 19-year-olds.

Unsurprisingly, most of those responding thought of a youth organisation as somewhere you went to have fun and meet friends. Many, however, particularly young women, were wanting other things: opportunities to 'play a part in the community' and to 'become more confident', 'supportive youth leaders', 'interesting activities'. Though most eventually left the service because they felt they had 'grown out of it', 25 per cent were put off by poor facilities. Half of those who had never attended said that was because they 'preferred other things' or that it was just not 'their scene' – though 25 per cent were not sure what it had to offer.

However, in spite of all the Government pressure and the national and local effort of the previous five years, its bottom lines were hardly any different from previous such studies. About two-thirds of all young people – some 2.7 million – had engaged at some time with the service. However, for its target age group, current attendance at a 'youth organisation' (quite narrowly defined) was 20 per cent – a total of 840,000 young people. For 16 and 17-year-olds, this figure fell to about 15 per cent, slightly more of whom were boys, and for 18 to 21-year-olds to 5 per cent. Within the full 11 to 25-year-old age group, some 82 per cent, about 1.13 million, used the service at least once a week and another 10 per cent once a month.

Baselines and definitions for establishing youth service participation varied over time. By the mid-1990s, too, because demarcation lines between the youth service and other providers, especially of detached work, were more difficult to define, 'returns' on usage were likely to have become even less reliable. Nonetheless by then figures suggested that, over the half century since it was established, the proportion of the teenage population being 'touched' by the service at some point during their teenage years had remained more or less constant. However, its current usage, it seemed, had dropped – from about a third to about a fifth of the 13 to 19-year-old age group. With the problem of holding on to older young people still unsolved, it was also still widely seen as 'for kids'.

In the end, it seemed, statements of purpose and a stronger managerial framework could not compensate for reducing resources.

Resources: Increasing or declining?

A threadbare network

Clearly, it is not possible to establish a straightforward causal connection between this fall in take-up and the service's reduced funding and staffing over approximately the same period. A variety of factors will have been at work, many of them wholly outside the youth service's control – or indeed government's.

Nonetheless the OPCS findings at least implied at some points that resources were a factor – for example, in the service's limited ability to 'sell' itself. A survey carried out for CYWU at the same time also suggested that by then the service was 'a threadbare patchwork' with areas of greatest need having few if any youth workers. Using the recommendations of the 1944 McNair Report on staffing levels – one full-time equivalent qualified worker for every 300 13 to 19-year-olds – the CYWU calculated that on average every authority, regardless of type, was short of 50 such staff.

At the time the OPCS survey results were released, the DES claimed that spending per participant each year was some £208 – and that this represented ('broadly

speaking') a 50 per cent rise in local authority expenditure between 1981 and 1994, to a total of £291.1 million. In so far as this growth was real, a significant proportion of it may well have been accounted for by non-mainstream funding – that is, moneys coming into the youth service from outside local authority budgets. Much of this would have been provided by special government programmes and external grants. After 1996 such income was further and very substantially increased by National Lottery grants, with the Charities Board's first round Youth Issues awards alone injecting nearly £67 million into youth projects of all kinds.

The special funding coming from government, however, was not immune to cuts. In 1989 the DES's contribution to GEST funding was reduced from 70 to 60 per cent while in 1991 the complete abolition of the scheme's local priority allocation meant an effective cut of 50 per cent for local authority training for youth and community workers. This funding was cut further in 1996–97. In 1992, at least 12 local authority youth services had had applications for the renewal of Section 11 grants turned down.

Surviving as a voluntary organisation

One voluntary youth organisation which emerged from these years, not just unscathed but with substantial (and extra) resources was the military Cadet Forces. Just prior to the 1997 general election, defence secretary Michael Portillo announced that, to enable every young person to participate in their activities, their £68 million budget was to be increased. The new Labour Government not only confirmed this increase but, as part of its own defence review in 1998, increased it yet again.

One of the much more recent arrivals on the voluntary youth sector stage, The Prince's Trust, also flourished impressively through the 1990s. (By the end of the 1990s, its turnover had reached £40 million, a significant proportion of which was being raised from industry and business sources.) Its earlier embodiments – for example, the King George Jubilee Trust – had had a record of funding youth work and voluntary youth service projects dating back to the 1930s. From its foundation in 1976, The Prince's Trust had extended this tradition. By the late 1990s, in addition to its direct grant-giving role, it was supporting a range of its own initiatives, often started by groups of volunteers and professionals as small experiments, which concentrated on reaching and helping 'the disadvantaged'.

Until the Blair Government followed its lead by announcing in 1998 that it would be using £180 million of Lottery money to extend state provision, the Trust had, for example, been instrumental in developing out-of-school study and homework clubs across the country. It was also enabling the young unemployed to become self-employed by sponsoring business start-ups. Its voluntary service scheme, The Prince's Trust Volunteers, with its emphasis on personal development training for young people through community-based team work activity, represented one of the 1990s' better

thought-out examples of such developments. Following a radical review of its work in 1999, as well as focusing its grant-giving to individuals much more precisely, the Trust decisively shifted its priority towards becoming a developer and deliverer of these kinds of programme.

These examples of expansion were the exception rather than the rule, however. For most of the voluntary youth sector the dominant experience was one of actual or threatened contraction of (especially state) support. The DES did continue to grant-aid the headquarters of over 60 national voluntary bodies, an arrangement which OFSTED commended on two separate occasions as 'good value for money'. Over time, however, though the total fund was marginally increased, it had to be spread more thinly among a larger number of organisations, leaving many of them struggling to make ends meet.

Many still managed to make their mark nationally, as in all previous decades seeking to adapt to survive and develop. The National Association of Boys' Clubs, for example, formally acknowledged the participation of girls in its affiliated clubs in 1993 – something which had been a reality on the ground for decades – and, adding Clubs for Young People to its title, relaunched itself in 1994. The Scout Association too, after a survey suggesting that scouting was seen by many as outdated, also took further steps to make itself more accessible to girls. With 40 per cent of its membership without any connections with agriculture or land industries, the National Federation of Young Farmers' Clubs by 1997 was also seeking to remake its image and to re-position itself in the search for members as 'the youth service of the countryside'.

More basic and long-standing worries remained for these organisations, however, and were sometimes dominant. Thus during 1996 the Guide Association, though increasing its number of young leaders, saw its overall uniformed membership fall by nearly 2.6 per cent. The following year, after months of internal community debate, the Association for Jewish Youth's financial crisis forced it to merge with a long-established social work organisation, Norwood Child Care, in order to safeguard its basic commitments to affiliated clubs. As it had for many years, the Boys' Brigade continued to search for ways of retaining older young people.

As the Coopers and Lybrand report noted, the voluntary youth sector locally now had a significant independent element made up of 'alternative' groups and organisations, often small and community-based, often assertively holding the youth service at bay. Even so, many of the pressures experienced by voluntary organisations nationally were strongly reflected at local level with London-based agencies suffering particularly following the demise of the ILEA.

The DES did agree to the continuation of the Youth Work Development Grants scheme, though from 1993 the NYA took over the administration of the funding which now came from local government rather than the DES itself. This offered a small number of local or regional voluntary organisations – in 1993, eight, in 1996 eleven – up to £50,000 a year for three years to undertake innovatory work. However, the increasing emphasis by government on funding such time-limited special projects contained its own longer-term costs. Because such grants rarely contributed to their ongoing overheads and similar core expenses, they could actually put, especially smaller, local voluntary organisations under even greater pressure. Moves by local authorities to replace grant-aid based on historic patterns of allocation with contracting arrangements or service-level agreements, though often long overdue as a way of getting resources to where they were now most needed, nonetheless placed new and extra pressures on the local voluntary sector.

Local authority youth services: Budget-led restructuring

None of this was helped by the fact that, in spite of a half century of rhetoric and not inconsiderable effort nationally and especially locally, 'partnership' still did not seem to be working very effectively. As we have seen, in its own dry way the Coopers and Lybrand report had some pretty tart things to say about both parties to the arrangement and their lack of commitment to and trust in it. In 1996, in London at least, the research carried out by the Sir John Cass 's Foundation related a familiar, 50-year tale:

> The views emerging of these two sectors were in sharp contrast. There was a feeling among local authority interviewees that in the last five years partnerships with the voluntary sector had been greatly strengthened. However, these views differed

to those encountered in the voluntary sector who felt that their relationships with local authorities had changed very little in the last few years.

The relationship was not helped, of course, by the effects on local authorities of the unrelenting Thatcherite (and post-Thatcher) clamp on their spending throughout the 1980s and most of the 1990s. During these years, the majority of local authority services experienced direct cuts of their own or at best standstill budgets, with in the early 1990s nearly half of them having their mainstream resources reduced by up to 11 per cent. *Labour Research*, which monitored local authority activity for the labour movement, reported that, for 1993–94, 32 of the 55 local authorities it surveyed were cutting to the tune of over £4.8 million. Two years later research done by the National Foundation for Educational Research (NFER) found that, in most of 14 sample local authorities where it carried out in-depth interviews with key staff, an overall decline in mainstream resources had occurred.

London Youth Matters (LYM), a watchdog for the service after the ILEA was wound up, logged a substantial decline in borough allocations throughout the decade. By 1993 its was claiming that 325 full-time equivalent posts had been lost in the previous four years and that spending had been cut across London by £2 million, or 27 per cent after inflation had been taken into account.

Later in the 1990s there were fears – not always unfounded – that the ILEA scenario was about to be replayed nationwide many times over. A major

re-organisation of local government produced a large number of new, often small, unitary authorities whose lack of budgetary manoeuvre, to say nothing of their ignorance of what youth workers were trying to do, did not bode well for the youth services they took over. These changes also had some serious knock-on effects for voluntary organisations, especially those operating regionally across local authority boundaries, who thus found themselves having to carry the begging bowl to a strange new array of purse-holders.

Though the DfE resisted any direct comment by Inspectors on 'sufficiency', while their relative independence lasted HMI were liable to make unmistakable links between, on the one hand, poor quality local provision and, on the other, cash and staff 'starvation'. Press reports of cuts to local services also continued to grab newspaper headlines, including year by year in the *Times Educational Supplement*. Not surprisingly in the light of such, often authoritative, evidence of repeated and accelerating reductions local authorities' spending on the youth service, the Government's claims about overall growth were often vigorously challenged.

What is more, well before the Lottery came on stream, it was also becoming clear that the balance in youth service budgets was tipping away from mainstream and towards external (and short-term) funding. Between 1992–93 and 1993–94, for example, though some 35 per cent of services got extra resources when only mainstream funding was included, this proportion rose to 47 per cent when total funding – that is, including external and other income – was taken into account. This trend was confirmed in 1995 by the NFER survey. In all its 14 sample local authorities, it concluded, 'the service was becoming increasingly reliant on external sources of funding'.

Some councils were able to offer their service protection, even sometimes increasing spending on it. Others such as Bury went for more radical reorganisations, often incorporating it into broader youth affairs structures. Though some like Manchester were again choosing the leisure option, according to an NYA survey of 69 local authority services in 1992 a renewed trend to locating the service in a community education structure was developing. Still others – Bexley, Bromley, Westminster, Warwickshire – whether forced by financial pressure or simply taking pride in pioneering a solution for their times, sought to contract out their services to other, sometimes independent, agencies.

The NYA survey also revealed that, while most authorities had no plans to take this contracting out option, most of the 69 surveyed had moved to contracts with voluntary sector organisations negotiated against agreed specifications and criteria. Encouraging such arrangements had been one of the main aims of the Coopers and Lybrand report as one of a range of ways in which youth services could deal with their new financial situation within radically restructured education departments.

Despite such advice, for most of those working in the service, the dominant – and cumulatively debilitating – experience

of the decade-and-a-half up to the 1997 general election was once again that of cuts. Indeed, some of these were so big (sometimes 'massive') that they amounted locally to wiping out the service altogether – or at best, as we have seen, to 'selling it off'. On at least two occasions this led to patience snapping – and specifically to workers mounting legal challenges to local authority proposals.

In 1995, for example, workers in Walsall served a writ on the council for breach of contract when it threatened to make them redundant and cut their wages. It was Warwickshire, however, which – at least in youth service terms – provided the cause célebre. In 1992, needing to save £6 million overall, it chose initially to take £1.7 million out of its £2.1 million youth service budget and then hand over responsibility for what was left of the service to schools, parish councils and voluntary agencies. CYWU promptly took the council to the High Court, arguing that its action placed it in breach of its statutory duties under the 1944 Act.

Statutory duty?
What statutory duty?

The Warwickshire case, though certainly important in its own right, was also the most overt eruption of an underlying frustration which, with varying degrees of strength, had been rumbling throughout the youth service for at least two decades. Indeed, the ambiguities surrounding the service's legislative status had from time to time attracted comment almost since it emerged as a state provision in the 1940s. However, it was only when the assault on its resource base became acute, perhaps life-threatening, that the muttering and grumbling was converted into an articulated set of arguments – and into overt political action. With public spending plans feeling the chill winds of oil and International Monetary Fund crises, this occurred in the 1970s, most noticeably in the four attempts to get private member's bills through the Commons. It then reappeared in a number of guises in the late 1980s and the 1990s as the accumulated effects of Thatcherite cuts threatened dismemberment by attrition.

Though revised by later education acts, throughout its existence the clearest legislative commitment to the youth service remained Sections 41 and 53 of the 1944 Education Act. These placed on local authorities a responsibility to provide 'organised leisure-time occupation' within further education and 'facilities for recreation and social and physical training'. In more general ways, non-education legislation had reinforced these duties. Under the 1969 Children Act, for example, local authorities were required to 'provide care and supervised activities for schoolchildren in need outside school hours'. They also had powers under the 1976 Local Government Act to provide 'clubs or societies having athletic, social or recreational objects'. However, only in Northern Ireland, and even then only after 1986, was the relevant local government body explicitly required 'to secure adequate facilities for *youth service* activities' (emphasis added).

Local authority youth services were not specifically embodied in law, therefore. Nowhere, either in the legislation or in government guidelines, was a minimum level or standard for their provision indicated, still less laid down. At least in theory, this left an LEA free to claim that, because it was paying expenses to one volunteer, it was meeting its statutory duty.

In fact barely three years before the Warwickshire case, NACYS had attempted to fill this gap. Its subcommittee report *Resourcing the Youth Service* was in part a response to cuts. More positively, however, it sought to make links between 'what constitutes an effective service and levels of resourcing'. It commissioned its own research in five local authorities to test out a model for working out what was usually the most resource-hungry element of local youth service budgets – staffing levels. This it described as:

> ... a set of calculational (sic) relationships which reflect the way in which the service is delivered and which can be used to estimate empirically the amount of youth worker-time required to provide particular levels and types of service.

Directly and indirectly, the model had much to say about what constituted youth work as well as about what was meant by youth work resources. It took account of users' ages, the kinds of localities in which they lived, the social divisions within the local teenage population and the specific issues or conditions affecting their lives. It also assumed judgments within a local authority and a youth service on, for example, the size of service target groups, the number of users one worker could work with in one session and the proportion of worker time to be allocated to face-to-face work.

The NACYS report went on to offer some illustrations of how many worker sessions would be required by some notional youth services. Overall, its aim was to 'help managers to secure and, indeed, expand resources available to the service and to obtain realistic effective levels of youth provision'. In a policy statement issued in 1992, CYWU called for NACYS's work to be extended to the construction of agreed models for capital programme development and for grant allocation to the voluntary sector.

Whatever impact the somewhat complex NACYS resourcing formula had within individual local authorities, at the level of national policy-making it caused hardly a ripple. Throughout much of the 1980s and into the 1990s, Whitehall might insist on indulging in hugely complex assessments of local need in order to calculate local authorities' grant related expenditure or standard spending. However, Conservative governments repeatedly denied all responsibility for influencing, still less trying positively to shape, local decisions on youth service budgets – a position reiterated by the Labour Government in 1999.

The main official line against the need for new legislation – restated by different ministers between 1991 and 1993 and in a 1993 DES circular – was that the appropriate sections of the 1944 Act as subsequently amended were still perfectly

adequate. Indeed, in the context of a Further and Higher Education Bill going through Parliament in 1993, the Government went further, arguing that the service's legal base:

> ... rests on the necessary cross fertilisation of provisions in the Education Acts which together cover the provisions made by the youth service for those of school age and above.

That year, too, Tim Boswell, another of the many Conservative youth service ministers who came and (usually very quickly) went, put a further gloss on the Government's case. In an exchange of correspondence with the director of the NYA Janet Paraskeva, he used the service's failure to agree a core curriculum with common learning outcomes or performance indicators as grounds for concluding that:

> The diversity and disparity of the youth service make it difficult to conceive of a funding mechanism which would adequately cover the service's complexity.

Boswell could also have reminded his wider youth service audience that this was far from an original view. It had been expressed, too, by the Thompson Committee. One of Boswell's recent predecessors, Neil MacFarlane, had talked in 1979 of agreed standards for youth service spending being 'light years away'. And as far back as 1957, a spokesperson for what had then been the Ministry of Education had insisted that, as there were no national standards of provision, it was very difficult to 'apply anything in the way of a fairly vigorous prod to a local authority'.

Even so, albeit with caveats, the Thompson Report had made the only serious case during most of the 1980s for a stronger statutory base for the service. Not only had it recommended that additional legislation was needed: it had offered a 'proposed clause for inclusion in a Bill' which would have made it a duty for LEAs to ensure that provision existed for a defined age range. Inevitably the proposal broke on the rock of Thatcherite resistance to any such extension of state power.

What ministers did not acknowledge, however, was that by the end of the decade and certainly by the early 1990s the terms of the debate had changed dramatically. Indeed, despite its care and thoroughness, even the Coopers and Lybrand report, with its optimism about the implications for the service of the 1988 Education Reform Act, failed to spot how unstable the ground beneath the service was becoming. The disaster of the poll tax for local government finance generally provided an overall destabilising context. More directly, the very legislation which ministers were quoting in support of their arguments was exposing anew – indeed, was substantially increasing – the youth service's weakness within local authority power structures and especially within their budget-making processes.

Indeed the new legislative landscape had some major and inter-connected new features with far-reaching consequences for local youth services.

- Local management of schools, including of budgets, had given school heads and their governors greater control over school facilities used by youth groups and organisations. It had also left them feeling much more independent of their local authority.
- Most of them now also had a route for making this independence all but complete – opting out of local authority control altogether. Such grant maintained status (GMS) was also seen as potentially threatening to youth service use of school facilities, though an NYA survey in 1992 showed that in only a minority of authorities was the threat felt to be real or serious. In fact, GMS had a more indirect but much more damaging consequence for the service. Having already 'lost' control of further education, most local authorities were anxious, often desperate, to reassure their schools that they were their very top financial priority. This became a promise they became increasingly determined to deliver even if it meant cutting, and cutting again, non-statutory provision such as the youth service.
- By detailing much more precisely the local authorities' statutory responsibilities for providing schooling for 5 to 16-year-olds, particularly through a national schools curriculum, the new legislation tied their purse strings even more tightly.

During a Lords debate on the effects of youth service cuts on the voluntary sector, one of its most vocal Parliamentary advocates, Baroness David, summed up the outcome of this new political and financial relationship between local authorities and their schools. 'When an LEA is short of cash', she concluded, 'it plunders the youth service.' It was a view which was confirmed by other evidence including that collected by the NFER from its interviews with LEA officers during 1994 and 1995.

The regularity and extent of this plundering galvanised key youth service interests from the late 1980s onwards into renewed efforts to underpin the youth service with a much clearer legal definition and recognition within LEA structures and provision. This goal certainly lay behind CYWU's decision in 1992 to take out its High Court action against Warwickshire County Council's proposals to, in effect, close down its maintained (that is statutory) youth service.

The judge eventually refused the application – though largely, it seemed, because neither the government nor the council could provide him with a usable definition of what constituted an 'adequate' youth service. Much of his reasoning was therefore negative, almost it seemed reluctant. He felt unable to accept, for example, that 'the figures which Warwickshire regard as adequate are in fact inadequate' or that 'a court would hold the level of expenditure contemplated involves a breach of statutory duty'. The CYWU case would, he acknowledged, have been stronger (though not conclusive) 'if the government itself had indicated that a certain per capita expenditure was in the government's view adequate'.

The judge made it clear too, that, in interpreting the key sections of the 1944 Act, he felt bound to attach importance to 'the *general* terms in which the (local authority's) duty is expressed' (emphasis

added). Indirectly he appeared intent on exposing the flabbiness (at the very least) at the heart of the legislation and of past and current government policy on the youth service. As adequacy could not be defined he was unable, it seemed, to find against Warwickshire.

In the end case law failed to give the youth service a stronger legal standing. Attention therefore turned again to strengthening the legislation itself. Post-Thompson, one effort had already been to do this: in 1988 NCVYS proposed amendments to the Education Reform Bill then going through Parliament. These were supported by, among others, two former youth and community workers, Paddy Ashdown and Hilary Armstrong (who later became a minister in the 1997 Labour Government). However, like all such previous efforts, the tactic failed.

Under pressure from within the service, three further (and again unsuccessful) attempts were made to take the legislative path.
- Amendments to the 1992 Further and Higher Education Bill were presented and re-presented three times in the Lords (on one occasion failing by only 16 votes) and once in the Commons. These sought to ensure 'organised informal part-time and leisure educational activities and experiences suitable to the requirements of young people from the ages of 11 to 25 and tending to their spiritual, mental, physical, cultural and social development'.
- For the first time ever, in 1993 a Labour MP, Tony Lloyd, tabled a youth service

bill. Among other provisions, this proposed that LEAs should have the duty 'to assess the need for and secure the provision of a youth service … whereby all young people may be assisted to discover their own resources of mind and body (and) to understand … society'.

- Two years later another Labour MP, Peter Kilfoyle, another former youth worker, presented a very similar bill. Among its supporters was future Labour Secretary of State for Education, David Blunkett.

Between these more high-profile efforts, Parliament found itself contemplating the state of the youth service on a number of other occasions. In the Lords, where the voluntary sector could usually rely on vocal and influential support, a 1991 debate on young people in Europe was used to raise concerns about the service's insecure financial condition (as well as to press proposals for a Minister for Youth). So too was the debate on the deterioration of the London Service early in 1993 while in June, when the Lords were considering yet another education bill, an amendment was put to safeguard youth service use of school premises and facilities. After the failure of their youth service bills, both Tony Lloyd and Peter Kilfoyle used Parliamentary procedures in the Commons to highlight the service's value and its diminishing resources.

Parliamentary attention of this kind was not achieved by accident or absence of mind: to a considerable degree, it resulted from a build-up of pressure from within the service itself. Somewhat in the

tradition of the earlier Youth Affairs Lobby, BYC – which was also still working hard to get young people to use their vote – brought MPs face-to-face with up to 1,000 young people through annual Parliament Days. NCVYS, too, often backed by individual voluntary organisations, lobbied actively. It was, as we have seen, behind the youth service amendments to the 1988 Education Bill while from 1996 a Lottery grant enabled it to appoint a parliamentary affairs information officer to give 'early warning' on legislation and policy initiatives which might affect the voluntary sector.

Meanwhile CYWU, having committed £150,000 in 1993 to its campaigning activities, organised a series of lobbies of Parliament. Usually timed to support one of the attempts to get youth service legislation passed, these too attracted up to 1,000 people (in this case workers as well as young people). It also gained support from the wider trade union movement: in 1996, for example, it got unanimous backing at the TUC's annual conference for a motion which, among other things, noted the youth service's 'unique role' in work with young people.

By this stage the NYA was arranging receptions at the TUC conference and all three of the main party conferences in which a range of other youth service organisations participated. In 1996 these included the Scout and the Guide Associations, NAYCEO and a new body, the Standing Conference of Principal Youth and Community Officers (SCPYCO). Quickly adopting an influential lobbying role, within a year of being formed in 1995,

SCPYCO had drafted a position statement 'in favour of securing a clear statutory base for the youth service'.

This, however, was far from the only policy analysis and development generated by the service in this period in order to underpin its political activities. Following up CYWU's 1992 policy statement and an NYA conference on adequacy held in 1993, an ad hoc Sufficiency Working Group brought together individuals from a range of professional interests in the service. Its consultative paper in 1994, *Planning for a Sufficient Youth Service*, suggested that the youth service should have its eye on something more ambitious than adequacy. The goal, it was argued, should be sufficiency which was seen as requiring at least two million places for 10 to 19-year-olds – one in three young people – each of whom would be funded for 10 hours of informal social and political education a year.

Planning for a Sufficient Youth Service provoked a determined containment response from the DfE which vetoed NYA's involvement in the sufficiency campaign until after it was released from its Departmental shackles in 1995 and came under new, local government management. Nonetheless, it was followed in 1996 by *Agenda for a Generation*, produced by a United Kingdom Youth Work Alliance – 15 youth work bodies which included BYC, CYWU, NCVYS, NYA and SCPYCO. Though prefigured by the work of earlier alliances such as the Partners Group in the 1980s and its successor, the National Youth and Community Work Alliance, the pamphlet nonetheless represented an important

breakthrough for collective action within the service. It also provided another 'hard' set of propositions on the scope and needs of the service.

Thus, it did not just advocate that youth work be given 'an unequivocal statutory base', 'consistent public funding' and 'a recognised distinctive place in delivering national programmes'. Via a linked NYA leaflet, it in effect also proposed a set of minimum standards for such provision. These included 'a safe, warm, well equipped meeting place within a bus ride for every young person'; easy access to reliable information; an opportunity to participate every month in drama, music, sport and voluntary action; and planned opportunities to develop personal skills.

After having had its fingers burnt (as it saw it) by the ministerial conferences and their push for a core youth service curriculum, the DfE remained largely unmoved by all this political pressure. It again unambiguously distanced itself from the demand for new legislation when in 1995 DfE minister Robin Squire asked: 'What would the (Kilfoyle) Bill achieve for the youth service?' His answer was 'very little,' adding:

> The legislative basis for the youth service if it was in doubt, is not in doubt now. The Education Acts of 1944 and 1992 already place a duty on local education authorities … to secure the provision of a youth service. This was relatively recently confirmed by the courts.

The two other main parties, however, were unconvinced by these arguments – something which gained growing significance as, in the run-up to a general election, opinion polls continued to predict a Conservative defeat. From as early as 1991, Liberal Democrat MP Simon Hughes, yet another ex-youth worker, used a Commons debate he had initiated to attack some of the cuts in youth service spending as 'deeply shaming'. Seeing these as the result of the Government 's failure 'to provide a sufficiently, and statutorily, funded service', by 1996 he had firmly committed his party to new legislation.

The Labour Party also entered the 1997 general election having made such a commitment. The roots of this could be found in a conference on youth in 1989, held in Jack Straw's Blackburn constituency. At this, Straw, the party's education spokesperson at the time, announced that he and his front bench education team were preparing a paper on the service. This, he suggested, would include consideration of how to strengthen its statutory base. In 1994 Straw's successor, David Blunkett launched the Party's Youth Task Group with what was in effect a broad youth affairs remit. Almost a year into its work, its chair Peter Kilfoyle was insisting in Parliament that:

> The youth service was one of the few agencies actively engaging young people in a debate around their interests and that it deserved all the support MPs could give it.

By 1996 the Task Group's draft report, as well as favouring appointing a Minister for Youth, was proposing that Labour commit itself to new legislation on the youth service. In public statements in the run-up to the 1997 general election, Kilfoyle seemed determined to firm up

this promise. Thus less than two months before Labour came to power he argued that constructing a youth policy framework 'which is coherent and geared towards service delivery' implied:

> … a clear statutory basis for the youth service, with targets set and expectations of a quality service at local level. That cannot be achieved if it is left up to local authorities to decide what is, or is not, the appropriate level and style of provision.

Or, as the former chair of BYC, radical 1970s campaigner on behalf of young people and New Labour political guru, Peter Mandelson, put it:

> The youth service has a proven track record in innovation and in responding to the different needs and circumstances of young people … We are signed up to support you.

In the early morning of 2 May 1997, the flow of results to Labour built up into a landslide while even the Liberal Democrats made significant gains. Was the youth service at last going to get some real political recognition? In particular, was it finally going to be given the firm legislative base for which it had been struggling since, 60 years before, a war-time circular had, almost accidentally, brought it into existence?

Main references

Community and Youth Workers' Union, *Youth Work and Community Work into the Twenty-First Century: Policy Statement*, CYWU, 1992

General Federation of Trade Unions Research Services, *Data for the Youth Service in England and Wales*, GFTU, 1994

Government Statistical Service, 'Statistical Bulletin: Young People's Participation in the Youth Service', DfE, 1995

Sally Hollerman, *All Our Futures: The impact of public expenditure and fiscal policies on Britain's children and young people*, Barnados, 1995

Karen Maychell et al, *Providing for Young People: Local Authority Youth Services in the 1990s*, NFER, 1996

National Advisory Council for the Youth Service, *Resourcing the Youth Service*, DES/Welsh Office, 1989

National Foundation for Educational Research, *Youth Service Provision in London*, Sir John Cass's Foundation, 1996

Sufficiency Working Party, *Planning for a Sufficient Youth Service: Legislation and funding for the Youth Service – a consultative paper*, Sufficiency Working Party, 1994

United Kingdom Youth Work Alliance, *'Agenda for a Generation' – building effective youth work*, Scottish Community Education Council, 1996

9 New Start with New Labour?

Towards a national youth policy

The significance of the 1997 Labour election victory went far beyond the mere size of its majority. As David Marquand, a leading political scientist, put it in October 1998, what had been played out on the nation's television screens that May night was an 'electoral earthquake' whose scale was difficult to grasp. In achieving such an outcome, Labour had made 'Education, Education, Education' its top priority – its 'big idea'. Though without even mentioning the youth service in its manifestoes, it had particularly stressed the role of education in overcoming social exclusion – by then *the* buzz word for individual deficiency and societal imperfection. Tying its image to 'Cool Britannia', it had also promised to create a 'young country'.

Once in office, Labour 'hit the ground running' – in relation to youth policy, very fast indeed. For the first time in perhaps a quarter of a century, here was a government which sought to place young people at the heart of its educational and welfare strategies. Not all of its starting assumptions were appreciated, least of all by those working within the youth service. Too often it seemed to be operating on the same deficiency model of youth which

had shaped most Conservative (and indeed some previous Labour) policies since the mid-1970s.

This continuity in policy-making was most vividly – and for young people most materially – demonstrated by a refusal even to contemplate restoring benefit entitlement to 16 and 17-year-olds. On the argument that young unskilled workers should not be priced out of jobs, it was displayed, too, in the decision that the minimum wage for under 25-year-olds was to be set at some 17 per cent below that set for other adults. On this, the Government's kite was most publicly flown months before the announcement was due by Peter Mandelson who two decades earlier, in the second of two angry open letters to Conservative ministers, had called for 'a coherent policy … for all young working people'.

Nor did the Government's tactics and style always win approval. It courted business interest in and even sponsorship for some core areas of provision where previously it had been assumed the profit motive had no place. Driving the New Labour strategy, too, was a confidence in the correctness of its own analysis of what was wrong and a faith in its top-down solutions which – as Thatcherism itself had shown – were rarely borne out in practice.

Nonetheless, within its first two years, the new Government had made some, often substantial, responses to almost every major youth issue.

- An *Excellence on Schools* White Paper, published 10 weeks after the election, promised action on such long running concerns as truancy and pupil exclusions, support for pupils with behaviour difficulties and out-of-school study support. By the summer of 1998, in pursuit of a rapid raising of educational achievement in disadvantaged areas, new partnerships between schools and other public and commercial bodies had been launched through 25 education action zones. The urgency driving these proposals was reinforced in April 1998 by a Commons Select Committee report, *Disaffected Children*.

- The notion of lifelong learning acquired a new and taken-for-granted currency with three major reports on higher and adult education being published during the Government's first year in office. In February 1998, the DfEE released its own Green Paper response, *The Learning Age: A Renaissance for a New Britain*.

- Perhaps the centrepiece of the new Government's youth policies was its New Deal initiative – a £3.5 million programme set within a much broader welfare to work strategy. One of its key aims was to get young people who had been unemployed for more than six months through a variety of forms of 'high-quality' work preparation and training and into jobs. It encountered many of the doubts and criticisms stoked up by 20 years of such 'special measures', especially about the threat of compulsory participation which it contained. Nonetheless, it was presented positively, even passionately, by David Blunkett, the Secretary of State for Education, as 'not just another Government scheme. It is a national crusade.'

- Youth justice, too, though injected with renewed and highly energetic attention, gave free rein to some of Labour's more negative perceptions of young people. The 1996 report *Misspent Youth*, which the Audit Commission revisited in a 1998 survey of local services for young offenders, proved to be something of a seminal document. It, for example, underpinned new legislation (the 1998 Crime and Disorder Act) designed to speed up the judicial process, produce local youth justice plans and establish youth offending teams comprising a range of local providers with a remit to coordinate programmes and activities with strong preventative intentions. Other measures with unmistakable law and order echoes included parenting orders, child safety orders and – particularly controversial – local child curfew orders.

- Youth volunteering, too, received the boost promised in Labour's build up to the general election. Along the way Blunkett, a long-time supporter of Community Service Volunteers (CSV), had to be headed off simply reproducing its model of working which many young people found constraining. Nonetheless, by early 1999 the Millennium Volunteers scheme had been launched with a £48 million budget – four times the sum originally announced. This assumed sponsorship by local community-based organisations and commitments to helping young people themselves to identify and respond to community need.

- In April 1998 a 10-year government strategy for tackling drug misuse was launched under the direction of a drugs tsar. Based on a vision of 'a healthy and confident society', its development had included some consultation with young people and gave significant emphasis to their needs. Its suggested approaches shifted away from mere coercion to providing information, education and support. Though weakened by a controversy over the Government's response to ending the tobacco companies' sponsorship of motor racing, controls of sales of cigarettes to children were also tightened.

- Though the rhetoric could seem more striking than the action – or the resources on offer – other important youth issues came under the New Labour microscope. These included unintended teenage pregnancies; the age of consent for gay men (though not initially the repeal of Clause 28); through a 'rough sleepers' initiative, homelessness among young people; young people's mental health needs and especially the rising levels of teenage suicides and attempted suicides; and young people's often devastating experience of being in care.

Within such a limited timescale, these initiatives constituted a formidable youth programme, much of it targeted at the main losers of the Thatcherite revolution. What is more, without ever conceding that it had

worked out an explicit national youth policy, the Government was claiming, too, to be striving for 'joined-up' responses across Whitehall – and was demanding that local authorities did the same.

Here much was riding on its newly created (though not unprecedented) piece of machinery for social engineering solutions to previously intractable social problems: a Social Exclusion Unit. In September 1998, again following some consultation with young people about living on 'sink estates' and sleeping rough, the unit produced a major report, *Bringing Britain Together: A National Strategy for Neighbourhood Renewal*. This set in motion a three-year, £800 million programme, 'New Deal for Communities', which laid great stress on investing in people and not just buildings, and on local community participation. One of the programme's 18 cross-cutting action teams focusing on young people was to be coordinated closely with other key Social Exclusion Unit projects. These included those on teenage pregnancies and 16 to 18-year-olds neither in school nor in employment as well as, in due course, how (perhaps if) the pre-election commitments made to the youth service were to be delivered.

This flurry of major youth policies initiatives seemed to hold out the promise that the youth service was finally to get some serious governmental attention and support – more, perhaps, than it had had since the 1960s post Albemarle period. However, a warning about over-optimism came early. In his allocation of ministerial posts, the new Prime Minister Tony Blair sent Peter Kilfoyle to the Office of the

Duchy of Lancaster. He thus summarily dispensed with Kilfoyle's experience of youth issues which, as chair of the party's Youth Task Force, he had painstakingly accumulated in the run-up to the election.

Instead, responsibility for the youth service was given to Kim Howells, as part of his brief as junior minister for lifelong learning. The NYA's house journal *Young People Now* was barely able to suppress its doubts about the appointment. Its editor Mary Durkin, reported:

> Kim Howells … visited the National Youth Agency in June (1997). Was he part of Labour's Task Force? No … Had he ever heard of the youth service before he got the job? Hardly. Does it matter? Quite possibly not.

On the other hand Howells had made the visit only six weeks after the election, something his Conservative predecessor had never managed in his two years in office. He had by then briefed himself on the Task Force's work. He was insisting, too, that the youth service was 'central to the (Government's) new deal with young people' and that 'no service had better links with disaffected young people: those who have slipped through the net'.

Nor were these offered merely as private, throw-away remarks. In an interview with the *Times Educational Supplement* in the same week he stated:

> Often the only people who know where disaffected youth are … are youth workers … The service … has got a mainline to young people who can't see the future for themselves … It can help with … re-entry.

His conclusion therefore was that:

> The youth service must not be reduced to a mechanistic system for getting kids off the streets.

Business as usual

Though encouraging, the material and local political context in which all this was happening remained for the youth service largely unchanged. Across the country, reports persisted of continuing cuts in planned youth service expenditure. More broadly and authoritatively, the figures produced by the Chartered Institute for Public Finance and Accounting (CIPFA), though not adjusted for inflation, showed a 3 per cent (£8 million) decrease in actual spending for 1995–96 – the first such annual fall for five years. A year later CIPFA recorded a further 1 per cent drop. Moreover, in answer to a Commons question, Howells provided figures which showed that since 1988–89 youth service budgets had in real terms fallen by nearly £50 million or some 16 per cent. As if to highlight this shift away from mainstream funding, at the end of 1997 the National Lottery Charities Board which in 1997 alone awarded £27 million to youth projects had, via the range of its programmes, fed some £60 million into work with young people.

Clearly these returns related to periods before Labour came to power. However, the first of the new Government's provisional Standard Spending Assessments (SSAs) offered little comfort to the youth service. By reducing by 6.7 per cent the SSAs' notional allocation to 'Other Education' (the category which covered the service), they were seen as indirectly legitimating further local cuts in youth service spending. More generally, the new Government also launched pilot 'Best Value' projects aimed at stimulating systematic and simultaneous consideration of cost and quality.

As in the past, separately and jointly, youth service interests tried to fight back. In particular, the United Kingdom Youth Work Alliance, which brought together most of the key national bodies, continued to meet, arguing the case for a youth service role in most of the Government's policy initiatives. Shortly after the general election, the NYA also sponsored a UK youth work conference attended by 440 delegates designed to stimulate movement on the *Agenda for a Generation* manifesto published by the Alliance in 1996 (see Chapter 8). However, the Secretary of State for Education, David Blunkett, as well as other ministers showed little knowledge of and, it seemed, even less interest in the youth service. All the organisations involved, including the NYA, the unions and the voluntary bodies, thus found it difficult to get more than reassuring noises and some teasing promises out of the Government.

Auditing the youth service

In fact, in Labour's first two years, in only one way was its often effusive statements of faith converted into positive action: through the completion of an audit of

youth service provision in England. After being trailered throughout the summer, this was formally announced by Howells in September 1997. When its findings appeared a year later, Tom Wylie, chief executive of the NYA, described its detailed report as the service's Doomsday Book.

Certainly, in the history of the service, this was a unique exercise and a unique document. Previous attempts had been made to gather together material on local youth service resourcing. The Albemarle Committee, for example, as well as collecting statistical information from government departments, sought responses to a questionnaire sent to all LEAs in England and Wales. Both the Milson-Fairbairn Committee in 1969 and the Thompson Committee in 1982 offered some breakdown of local authorities' expenditure on and staffing for the service. The former also helped prompt a survey of young people's usage of the service while Thompson commissioned research on young people's leisure attitudes from a commercial market research organisation. Subsequently, year by year, both the NYA itself and CIPFA published breakdowns of local authority expenditure figures while one-off analyses of spending – for example, by NCVYS in 1984 – also appeared from time to time.

Very largely, however, these analyses were based on existing local authority statistics produced for other purposes. They therefore required the (often speculative) extrapolation by the authorities themselves of specifically youth service data, including those often deliberately buried deep within wider community service budgets and plans. The 1998 audit on the other hand was undertaken in its own right, on the basis of a very detailed questionnaire drawn up in consultation with the NYA, the Local Government Association and the Standing Conference of Principal Youth and Community Officers (SCPYCO). It achieved a 100 per cent return from the 127 English local authorities. Its stated purpose was to clarify both the existing level and nature of provision and the authorities' strategic development plans in the following few years. It was determinedly focused on the youth service elements of local authority activity (and not just spending). It thus asked for and usually got, not just statistical information, but descriptive material backed up by policy documents, committee papers, practice guidelines and codes of practice, local monitoring reports and similar papers.

Though lacking any reference to its distinctive methods and process, the audit report did attempt a definition of the service, describing it as:

> ... a diverse range of opportunities – youth clubs, information centres, specialist projects, street-based work – which is intended to support young people in their transition from childhood to responsible adulthood, encourage their social development and individual fulfilment, and help them engage fully in society.

In an authoritative way, it also filled in some important factual gaps. It, for example, revealed that:

- 90 per cent of services were located in an education department.
- Most services prioritised 13 to 19-year-

olds though within a wider 11 to 25-year-old age group.

- Total spending on the service in 1996–97 was £239 million, over 90 per cent of which still came from local authorities' mainstream budgets.
- This amounted to 1.29 per cent of total education spending in England.
- Other significant sources of income included Single Regeneration Budgets (£4.9 million) and Training and Enterprise Councils (£2.7 million).
- For 1996–97, 42 local authorities said they had increased their youth service spending while 50 reported decreases.
- Local authority support to the voluntary sector added up to over £36 million.
- Over the whole country the paid work-force was made up of 750 full-time youth officers, nearly 3,200 full-time workers and nearly 24,000 part-timers (equivalent to 8,000 full-timers).
- In a typical week, over 600,000 11 to 25-year-olds and 400,000 13 to 19-year-olds were said to be making use of local authority provision.

The bare statistics, however, told only part of the story – perhaps even hid more than they revealed. One of the most telling of the audit's findings was picked up instantly by the newly appointed junior minister with responsibility for the service, George Mudie, in his foreword to the report. Albeit indirectly, he used it to underscore key messages already emerging from the DfEE (see below). This was 'the great variation in youth service provision in the country' which he saw as:

> ... not simply a matter of expenditure, although that is undoubtedly one of the

determining factors, but also of the quality of provision and the relationship and interaction with other services for young people.

These discrepancies showed up startlingly and in a number of ways:

- While 12 authorities were spending £100 or more per head on 13 to 19-year-olds (with the maximum reaching £292), seven were spending under £30 per head with the lowest falling to £18.
- In the 13 highest spending authorities, youth service budgets were 2 per cent or more of the total education budget with the biggest spender reaching 4.5 per cent. At the other end of the scale, three authorities were spending 0.5 per cent or less while 36 authorities spent less than 1 per cent.
- Spending on staff training ranged from 0.4 per cent to 6.4 per cent of total youth service budgets.
- Between authorities, ratios of workers to young people in the 11 to 25-year-old age bracket ranged from 1:266 to 1:4,900.
- Though only 10 per cent of local authorities were using specific indicators of disadvantage to allocate resources, nearly 90 per cent of them (113 out of 127) claimed to be targeting particular groups for priority attention.

Barely hidden within this latter finding, too, was an insight into how the priorities and indeed approaches of the service had been changed, not just by real cuts in resources, but also by the appearance of some radically different funding regimes. The evidence of the audit confirmed that, for the youth service, the almost too

familiar term 'partnership' had taken on a whole new meaning. As it had found itself, more or less enthusiastically, working with other services, notably social services, health and the police, it also had come to rely increasingly on some £17 million-worth of external support a year. Welcome though the money clearly was, it of course assumed pre-set curricular priorities – and short-term funding. For a service looking for the most optimistic interpretation of its future prospects, it could perhaps hope that the growing ministerial pressure on it to target more precisely socially excluded young people might also bring longer-term funding allocations built into mainstream local authority budgets.

The new funding mechanisms also had implications for the voluntary sector. One of the audit's major weaknesses was that – no doubt for pragmatic and logistical reasons – it implicitly reinforced the often undeclared power differentials within the service's much-trumpeted voluntary-statutory partnership. Voluntary organisations were not involved in the prior consultations on the audit process while its data on the voluntary sector came not from the voluntary organisations themselves but via the local authorities. Yet some of the audit's own evidence suggested that, not just the statutory sector but the voluntary sector too was getting access to new external sources of finance. As this enabled individual voluntary organisations to become more financially independent of the local authority, it re-emphasised the need for genuine partnership working if overall local strategic planning was to be achieved.

In addition to clarifying such broad trends, the audit report also offered an in-depth focus on two specific aspects of service delivery. One looked at how the service was contributing to the development of active citizenship and young people's participation in decision-making (see Chapter 7). The other examined its work with schools and its role in helping to raise educational achievement. This revealed that 83 authorities were claiming some specific youth service involvement, either by using youth work approaches to complement what schools were doing themselves or by targeting their youth work on poor attenders, excluded pupils or those in danger of exclusion.

However, because of the 'extensive youth work provision closely linked to educational goals', the report concluded that this kind of analysis was liable to underestimate the amount and range of the service's overall educational contribution. Its more detailed case studies from 12 areas, included to illustrate this point, also provided further evidence of how here too curricula and resources were being targeted, especially on disaffected young people.

Indeed, though harder to pin down statistically, the more qualitative findings of the audit contained probably the most important lessons for the service. Mary Marken who carried out this major element of analysis subsequently offered her own personal commentary on what she called the five Cs – the five challenges – confronting the service:

- *Clarification* was needed, particularly to answer the basic question: 'Does the service really know who it aims to work with and what it can offer?' This was true even though most services were claiming to have mission statements and written curricula, to be recording usage and/or attendance, to be monitoring and evaluating delivery and evaluating value for money and standards and to be consulting young people on effectiveness. It was a need which was confirmed by OFSTED's annual report for 1996–97 which talked about 'the evaluation of achievement, as an integral part of youth work practice, (still) being under-developed'.

- A need existed, too, for the service 'to sustain or develop *coherence* in the face of the fragmenting pressures of short-term policies and funding' which in turn were generating 'confusion and fragmentation' in the way it was describing its curriculum. This particularly meant articulating 'what is achievable with whom and to deliver consistent positive outcomes across the range', especially given its own and others' expectations of the range of young people it should engage.

- Thirdly the service needed to assert the *centrality* of young people in its work so that this 'runs through every aspect of organisational life – like the lettering in a stick of rock'. This was required particularly to reduce the mismatch between the service's rhetoric about citizen empowerment and its practice.

- In the context of 'a relatively small local authority service coping with major and sometimes unpredictable outcomes' – as well as of increasing expectations of partnership working – the service also needed to embrace *change* undefensively, particularly if it was to remain 'responsive and innovative in the interests of young people'.

• Finally *'consistency* of performance was required within and across youth services'. Here the audit material offered an opportunity to 'read out' benchmarks from the qualitative characteristics, not of the average but of the best performing local authorities. Though the report had sought to identify these, it had also noted that, for such a description to be complete, quantitative descriptors would be needed, especially in the continuing absence of any nationally agreed definition of adequacy.

The clear overall message of the audit in fact was that, though much of quality was going on, the youth service's distinctive contribution to young people's development remained unreliably embedded in its practice and delivery nationally. Much internal work was thus still required – reflective as well as action-oriented – to convince politicians with a hardening agenda for the service that its own definition of role within and input to their burgeoning youth policy were both valid and achievable.

Promises postponed

A quarter of a century after Margaret Thatcher, as Secretary of State for Education, had rejected the Fairbairn-Milson Report's (albeit deeply flawed) proposals for a strategic way forward for

the youth service, this kind of central state endorsement was long overdue. In opposition, New Labour had promised to provide this. Now it was so securely in office and so energetically committed to a youth policy, surely it would act – and act quickly and decisively?

Initially, it seemed that it would. As early as July 1997 Howells was assuring the service that:

> *Further details about ... (our) proposals for legislation to place the youth service on a clearer and more specific statutory footing will be included in the White Paper on* Lifelong Learning *in the autumn.*

Later in the year he repeated the commitment in equally clear terms:

> *At the end of the day I am convinced that we shall be left with legislation which clearly explains the duty of local authorities to provide for a youth service – everyone in the field, whether voluntarily or as a profession, will know where they stand.*

At some point during the next few months, however, momentum drained away, with Howells himself seeming to become personally disillusioned with the youth service and how it was presenting itself. By early 1998 – that is, well before the audit's findings were known – though still promising legislation, his tone had changed completely. In a series of off-the-cuff remarks at a conference in Devon he told a youth service audience:

> *It's the patchiest, most unsatisfactory of all the services I've come across. I've never met such down-at-heart, "can't do" representatives as I've met of youth services throughout Britain.*

Somewhat more soberly in June, not unreasonably but by now, it seemed, rather more threateningly, he was again reminding the service that 'some of the work lacks focus'. Nor, when the audit report was published in the September, did his successor miss the opportunity of reminding the service that, given the huge variations in its practice, it was going to need to look to the authorities which were performing well in order to build on its strengths.

By that stage, however, the service was clearly being shunted into a siding, as ever awaiting the signal for higher priority policy initiatives to proceed. Firstly, as the Government faced up to the financial implications of some of its grander aspirations, the colour of its promised discussion paper on lifelong learning changed, from White to Green. With this shift, deadlines for the release of the paper also slipped, to February 1998. When it finally came, it contained just two brief paragraphs on the youth service which, though again not ruling out new legislation, focused mainly on how it should be supporting the work of formal education, the welfare to work programme and the youth justice system. That this renewed marginalisation of the service might reflect particular ministers' perceptions and evaluations of it seemed to be confirmed by the rather fuller and much more positive attention it got in the Green Paper for Wales. Here, for example, recognition was given to what, in its own right, a youth service might contribute to young people's learning beyond school.

As if to drive home its slippage down the policy ladder, in the first Government reshuffle the youth service again lost its junior minister. With Howells transferred out of the DfEE, he was replaced by George Mudie. He was a former leader of Leeds City Council which, while maintaining a significant youth work presence, had reorganised its youth service into a client-contractor structure involving both the Education Department and the Community Benefits and Rights Department.

Both Howells before he moved and then Mudie continued to restate the commitment to legislation. Increasingly, however, the service was being told that, in the light of the audit's findings and of wider Government priorities, this was going to have to wait. Meanwhile the service was urged to in effect 'get on with it' – with, in this context, 'it' being described as:

> … play(ing) a more central role in education and training

and also as:

> (targeting) teenage mothers, young people caring for sick and elderly relations, those working in the black economy (sic) and school and college drop-outs.

Indeed by now the core message the service was getting was unambiguous:

> Youth service workers and authorities … know the task that the Government have placed at the top of the agenda: ending social exclusion.

Given these emphases, it was perhaps hardly surprising that, by late 1998, Mudie was reporting that the Government was:

> … broadening the debate on the youth service and bringing on board other players like the Social Exclusion Unit to ensure we include the full range of learning and services to young people.

As a result deadlines slipped again, and then once more, from shortly after the publication of the audit report to 'in the New Year' (1999) to (in January 1999) the seemingly even more distant and fluid 'soon'.

Historical crossroads?

Despite the prevarication, by early 1999 the broad lines of the Government approach were becoming clearer. If it chose, the service could simply get on with its 'traditional tasks'. However, if the Government was to deliver its promises to bolster its statutory base and its resourcing, local authority youth services were going to have to meet two additional, and stringent, conditions. One was that they focus their efforts much more – perhaps primarily – on those young people who were pre-defined as excluded, disaffected or disadvantaged. Secondly, in order to do this effectively, they must increasingly work in partnership with other youth-serving agencies. As these would invariably be much bigger players in the relevant fields, this expectation meant in effect turning the service increasingly into the instrument of other services' needs, intentions and priorities.

As decision-time approached, the youth service tried hard to tread a middle path between its traditional role and the new political realities. On the one hand – for example through SCPYCO and the NYA – it mounted a defence of core youth service provision which was as demand-led and

non-stigmatising as possible, based on young people's voluntary attendance. At the same time, it staked a strong claim to being able to contact, and then engage constructively with, the parts of the adolescent population which other services either could not reach or had rejected.

One of it most articulate and committed commentators, Howard Williamson – part-time youth worker, academic researcher and from the end of 1997 member of the Government's Advisory Group to the New Deal Task Force – vividly captured the dilemmas facing the service. The new policy agendas being urged on it, he pointed out, carried the risk that:

> The young people who are creating social policy concern will simply draw the line at a different point. Where they previously avoided contact with the careers service or the police, they will now steer clear of such so-called youth workers.

To counter this danger, Williamson argued that:

> The youth service must be ready for engagement with the broad social agendas around health, training, crime and volunteering while, simultaneously, arguing forcefully for the first step requirement of open access traditional youth work.

Assuming that the Government did in due course get round to giving the youth service some specific attention, 1999 therefore seemed likely to be the year in which a series of core policy questions with long historical antecedents might finally be addressed – and perhaps even answered.

Main references

Kim Howells, 'Speech to the Standing Conference of Principal Youth and Community Officers', SCPYCO, 1997

David Marquand, *Must Labour Win?*, Ninth ESRC annual lecture, Economic and Social Research Council, 1998

Mary Marken et al, *England's Youth Service – The 1998 Audit*, Youth Work Press, 1998

Mary Marken, 'Message from the Audit: draft presentation to the Standing Conference of Principal Youth and Community Officers', SCPYCO, 1998

Mary Marken, 'From the Wings to Centre Stage', *Rapport*, January 1999

George Mudie, *The Principal Youth and Community Officer as a Curriculum Manager*, SCPYCO, 1998

Howard Williamson, *Quo Vadis the Youth Service – whither or wither?*, NYA, 1998

Retrospection

Tensions and dilemmas in the history of the English youth service

Though not exhaustive, four key areas of tension and dilemma – of choice and contention – were identified in the *Introduction* as running through the history of the youth service in England. Somewhat oversimply, and in ways deliberately intended to emphasise the element of struggle within them, these were defined as:

- universalism vs selectivity;
- education vs rescue;
- professionalism vs volunteerism; and
- voluntary vs state sponsorship.

Both how the service has understood and described its role and tasks, and how it has then actually carried these out, have been significantly shaped by how it has responded to each of these dimensions of its collective experience. At times the debates have been conducted with such subtle and diversionary hair-splitting that they have allowed policy pragmatists to drive their own solutions virtually unimpeded through the resultant confusions, gaps and divisions. Nonetheless, with roots in some of the service's most testing material realities, all retain a strong contemporary resonance. They therefore provide one potential

framework for attempting a critical retrospective review of the service's 60-year development.

To draw out these 'lessons', it is necessary to extend the approach adopted throughout this book. This has assumed that historical development is in significant ways constructed out of differences, even conflicts, of values and interest among the key 'actors'. What at any moment is or has been seen as 'the youth service', therefore, has been examined as the 'unfinished' product of struggle, negotiation and active human decision-making involving a range of individuals, groups and institutions. Each of the four themes is examined through just such a lens, clouded and even distorted though the images sometimes are.

Universalism vs selectivity

Voluntary participation by young people

A, perhaps *the*, defining feature of youth work throughout its history has been the insistence that young people's engagement with it must be voluntary – that they must be able to *choose* whether to take part, or not. On occasion this principle has had to be vigorously defended. This happened in

FROM THATCHERISM TO NEW LABOUR

the 1970s, for example, when the service was pressed to take on young offenders required by the courts to join intermediate treatment schemes. It again became necessary in the 1990s as demands built up that the service reach and draw in the socially excluded. Nevertheless, it survived, at times despite the state's tightening grip on youth work and the youth service.

In the context of provision for young people, the combination of being non-compulsory *and* state sponsored is unusual, if not unique. True, for the youth service it has proved a flawed asset. It has offered state policy-makers none of the guarantees (sometimes more apparent than real) of a direct and certain engagement with and impact on captive audiences. In part this explains why solid state recognition has been withheld from the youth service, particularly in the form of stronger legislative underpinning and more reliable state funding.

Nonetheless, for defining what is distinctive and most effective about youth work, young people's voluntary participation has remained central. So too has the existence of a youth service. With its explicit mandate endorsing practice delivered on these voluntaristic terms, this has provided an ultimate safety-net for the survival and even development and diversification of this form of practice with young people.

'Take-up, leakage and unattachment'

This commitment to voluntary attendance by young people has often been treated as proving the presence of another core feature of youth work: that the service is open to all and therefore a universalist provision. Such a claim, however, requires close critical scrutiny.

On the ground, for many voluntary sector groups this in more recent years has barely been an issue. While perhaps stating some general aspiration to cater for the more vulnerable, they have long been more than happy to welcome in extra members regardless of who they are or what their social origins.

The early pioneers of these voluntary movements, however, were much more concentrated and up-front in their intentions. Their target was quite explicitly those 'who had to spend their lives in the (city's) mean and sordid districts and slums'. Later generations of providers, especially once the secular and profession-alised welfare state became dominant, tended to use rather more circumspect language. Nonetheless, even allowing for very different social conditions, their primary focus was very similar – indeed, on the questions of who and how many they were reaching, they could rarely afford to be as relaxed as their voluntary sector counterparts. Hence their efforts to hold on as long as possible to those who were coming through the door. And, even more revealing, hence their anxious pursuit of some selected sections of that majority of young people who, in every period, chose to exercise their freedom of choice by *not* becoming 'joiners'.

Indeed, two related questions have constantly preoccupied, some might say obsessed, the service's policy-makers: what proportion of the designated youth

172

RETROSPECTION

population is using its facilities; and how long do these young people stay? Within these, some sub-questions have also attracted anxious attention – for example, at what age are young people starting and then ending their participation; and how does the involvement of boys and girls differ over time?

Answers to these questions have never come easily. Definitions have been elusive: how, for example, do you define and delineate, not just youth club or youth project, but a youth service which some-times might, sometimes might not, be taken to include whole forms of sport or the arts or community service? Information-gathering has been tricky, too: who does the counting, when and with what reliability (even trustworthiness)? Baselines have varied as the size of the youth population has risen and fallen and as the service's own target age-group(s) have altered. Snap-shots of the number of young people using the service at any one time have given significantly different results from more panoramic pictures of who has been an attender at some time during their teenage years.

However, cumulative evidence over 60 years has offered some tentative answers:

- Overall take-up at best remained steady at around 30 per cent of the age group – though by the 1990s it may well have fallen, perhaps to 20 per cent or even lower.
- Certainly after the push to mixed work in the 1960s, young women's usage fell, dropping below that of young men and ending at an earlier age.
- Though this may have been less true of

Black and Asian young people, older teenagers – the 16-plusses – have probably always been in a minority and came to use the service in even fewer numbers in later decades.

- With some important exceptions, the voluntary sector – especially the uniformed organisations – while also losing membership overall, kept up its numbers by catering for pre-teens.

Whatever the precise statistical facts, however, the service repeatedly acted on the perception that it was not attracting enough, or a wide enough cross-section, of the designated age group. This aspiration was revealed most obviously in an anxiety to reach and draw in 'the unclubbables' who, post-Albemarle, became the unattached and then, in the 1990s, the disaffected and the socially excluded.

Absences – of mind and of action

Paradoxically, some highly revealing absences illuminate how far such definitions were social, even political, constructs. For one thing, state and other policies aimed at understanding and responding to those not using the service invariably ignored one potentially vital feature of their experience and identity: their class position. Despite evidence to the contrary, from the 1960s onwards the dominant assumption within official policy-making was that greater affluence and equality of opportunity had turned Britain into a virtually classless society. By the 1980s, this meant that even those deeply committed to tackling other deep social divisions made little use of class analysis for understanding the young people with whom they were working. Still less did they see such a perspective as a basis for identifying potential strengths and resources among these young people on which the work might draw.

This, however, was not the only significant absence. Unattached and excluded groups not officially labelled as such often remained deeply hidden from the service's attention. Only when they themselves and/or adults (including workers and officers) who shared a crucial identity with them pressed for their recognition and inclusion did they (eventually) get a hearing and receive an (often grudging) service. Most prominent here were Black and Asian young people and young women. However, their ranks also included disabled young people, gay, lesbian and bisexual young people and young people living in rural areas.

Some progress was made in providing for these groups – more for some than for others. Sometimes these responses came because they overlapped with existing state priorities – for example, to contain the perceived threat of Black and Asian young men on inner-city streets or to stop unmarried young women getting pregnant. What, however, did most to secure their often finger-tip hold within the youth service were the concessions they (including again many who became paid or unpaid workers) won through their organising and campaigning. For them, positive spontaneous advances were rare and knee-jerk reactions usually dismissive or even damaging. Indeed, nowhere was policy formation via political pressure and struggle illustrated more

clearly and often more uncomfortably than in the processes which were required to open up the service to these segments of the unattached and excluded youth population.

Targeting special needs

Ultimately, however, these terms carried very different connotations, not least because they came with handed-down (usually state) definitions. As always these were liable to be deeply contradictory. Often, for example, they contained strong elements of compassion and concern for social justice. At the same time, though again labels changed, an often predominant emphasis was given to targeting the service's expertise and other resources on young people seen as potential or actual threats to good order – most specifically 'juvenile delinquents' and 'those at risk of breaking the law'.

With some coming and perhaps going, the list was then steadily extended. From the 1970s onwards, the unemployed, the homeless and the drug-taker made a decisive appearance. By the early 1980s, young people in care and young people leaving care were being drawn in, and in the 1990s, teenage mothers, school and college drop-outs and those working in the 'informal' economy.

State policy-makers did not always demand that the youth service's approach to selectivity be so explicit and specific. During and immediately after the Second World War, the threat of totalitarianism abroad concentrated the earliest official pronouncements – for example, in the 1942 report of the Youth Advisory Council – on how the service could help reinforce the country's democratic traditions. This gave its rhetoric as strong a universalist flavour as at any time during the service's history.

In its commitment to an expansive educational perspective, the Albemarle Report – given instant endorsement by a (Conservative) Government – provided further indirect support for such relatively open access. It never assumed the service's reach should be universal – it, for example, took it for granted that university students would look elsewhere for their social education. Nonetheless, unambiguously it asserted that 'the service is not negative, a means of "keeping them off the streets" or "out of trouble"'. Moreover, even post-Thatcher, within the inherently contradictory pulls and pushes of state policy-making this liberal tradition survived. Some thus continued to argue that, on the grounds of social justice, some targeting of scarce resources was essential and that this need not involve any breach of young people's voluntary participation.

It was during Margaret Thatcher's time as Secretary of State for Education that the state's pressure on the youth service to target its energies first acquired a harder edge. Reflecting tightening economic conditions as well as a growing fear of youth, in 1971 she decreed that the service should concentrate on 'areas of high social need'. From this point on, the balance of state expectation tipped overtly and in due course decisively towards more precise forms of selectivity. Though particularly true of the way the central state directed its own resources to local authorities – for

example, via the mechanisms for allocating local government rate support grant – indirectly the voluntary sector, too, was drawn into the net.

Thus, in 1975 a Labour Government urged the youth service to focus more on young people 'who are demonstrably disadvantaged'. By 1982 Conservative Secretary of State Sir Keith Joseph – not known for his interest in, still less passion for, the youth service – was telling it to get more involved with the young unemployed by 'incorporating its resources and skills into the Youth Training scheme'. Two years later, in his response to the Thompson Committee, he went further. Under a telling sub-heading 'special needs', he suggested to local authorities that, in catering for these, they should allocate 'relatively fewer resources (to) other groups'. From 1989 the DES was also insisting that its headquarters grants to national voluntary organisations be allocated according to very similar 'ministerial objectives for the youth service'.

By the time New Labour came to decide its policy, the youth service, it seemed, was about to be made an offer it dare hardly refuse: target the disaffected and the socially excluded or give up all hope of extra funding or a clearer legislative definition. Youth work might never have been the open-to-all provision which some of its more enthusiastic and idealistic proponents had often claimed. By the late 1990s, however, it seemed possible that the leverage of state sponsors could produce still more demanding versions of, and procedures for achieving, selectivity. As these contained the potential for weakening if not undermining young people's right to choose whether to be involved or not, albeit unintentionally they threatened to jeopardise the distinctiveness of the service's contribution to practice with young people – and indeed of youth work itself.

Education vs rescue

Youth work as liberal education

As this universalism vs selectivity debate reveals, from its inception one of youth work's earliest core concerns was to rescue an underclass of the younger generation living, working and playing in conditions of poverty, neglect and often great cruelty and exploitation. In this sense, its pioneers belonged to the wider 'child-saving' movement spawned by 19th century philanthropists. Within this, too, implicitly or explicitly, contradictory motivations lurked, with, for example, a 'deficiency model' of youth and of human nature more generally often interacting with a sharp awareness of the wider social and economic conditions shaping young people's lives and opportunities.

Adherence to this model, however, was much weaker – indeed was often barely discernible – among those who initiated youth work, and also among later state policy-makers. They might be gloomy about where many young people were starting and coming from. In the early

days, they might even encourage them to wash or change their socks more often and, in one way or another, they continued to urge the boys to 'stay out of trouble' and the girls to remain 'pure'. Yet, rather than assuming simply that these young people had in-built and irredeemable personal defects, most of the planning for and delivery of youth work relied on a model of youth which emphasised *potentiality*. Whether the providers' impetus came from religious belief, political commitment or, later, professional ethics – and often in defiance of constraining material conditions – their primary focus was on young people's possibilities and the untapped capacities and talents which youth work and later a youth service might help to liberate.

From this notion, too, stemmed the youth service's (albeit often rhetorical) commitments to participation and later empowerment. These made explicit the conviction that, far from being instruments of others' intentions – even perhaps mere victims – young people's potential carried within it a capacity for them to do what needed to be done *for themselves*.

In due course, the tug of some strong state expectations, especially locally, was often towards perspectives and responses which emphasised deficiency over potentiality. Here again the pressures on the service to make its contribution to intermediate treatment seemed to risk significantly tipping balances in this direction. In this same early 1970s period there was some talk, too, of the youth service finding a more congenial home in the newly-created social service depart-ments. Even this argument, however, started from an expectation (over-optimistic though it turned out) that these new unified social work agencies would have a strong community development ethos.

Such proposals anyway never made any significant political or professional headway. Indeed the nearest the youth service came to losing its essentially educational mission was when, from the 1970s onwards, it faced usually idio-syncratic and certainly uncoordinated takeover bids by local recreation and leisure departments. Even where these were successful, however – and the 1998 youth service audit showed this had by then happened in only 10 per cent of local authorities – the case for a change was often argued in terms of young people's individual development.

Though here too the language changed over time, throughout its history the youth service thus continued to be defined within national and largely local policies as an educational provision. In 1940, though in far from original terms, *Circular 1516* set the tone by concentrating on 'developing the whole personality'. The 1944 Education Act – overall designed to provide educational opportunities 'according to age, aptitude and ability' – mandated the youth service to provide these through 'social and physical training'. With his focus on individual young people's discovery and develop-ment of 'their personal resources of body, mind and spirit', Sir John Maud, a senior civil servant at the Ministry of Education,

offered an eloquent restatement of such purposes in 1951. The Ministry's decision in 1958 to institute an (Albemarle) review of the service was very deliberately intended to ensure it retained responsibility for the service and so to de-emphasise 'welfare' objectives and concerns.

Because Maud chose to propound his definition of youth service aims at a major national youth service conference, intentionally or not he got a collective endorsement which reverberated well beyond this one-off event. His statement became the benchmark against which for at least 30 years, usually uncritically, all major state papers and expressions of policy on the youth service measured themselves, including Albemarle, Fairbairn-Milson and Thompson.

Assuming an essentially unified and consensual society, Maud kept his focus unwaveringly on *individual* young people, on their *personal* resources and on opportunities for them to equip *themselves* for given civic duties. He thus started from and also sought to reinforce a strongly entrenched British tradition of liberal educational thinking. Buried (often deep) within this too, was the service's commit-ment to young people's participation in and empowerment for shaping their own destinies: an 'up by your bootstraps' expectation that ultimately individuals must make and save themselves. Maud and those who followed him thus assumed that – with some crucial institutional support – all children and young people were capable of developing and expressing some personally distinguishing talents.

Demand-led or issue-based?

Over the service's 60-year history, the only substantial move away from the Maud formulation came in 1990 when the second of the ministerial conferences, again in a rare collective act, agreed a national statement of purpose. This did not in any way dilute the service's educational commitments: on the contrary, in crucial respects it reaffirmed them in very explicit terms. But, by adopting a social analysis which was much more critical than Maud's, it broadened and complicated these educational aspirations in ways which gave them a new relevance.

This major shift was not made overnight, nor did it come about by accident. It was the product of a struggle, itself at least a decade old, which in effect posited two ideal-type youth work approaches to young people. One emphasised that, to be motivating and to have an impact, youth work programmes must be demand-led to the extent that they arose directly out of and built onto the interests and concerns which young people brought to their youth service participation. The second model stressed that practice needed to give priority to addressing a range of issues of central importance to young people. These included, for example, health matters, particularly though not exclusively sexual health, and the environment. However, the ones which generated the greatest passion and energy for change were (with the notable exception of class) those which, stemming from the most abrasive social divisions within British society, were the source of young people's harshest experiences of discrimination and oppression.

On the ground, the two models were never as separate or as incompatible as the debate often implied. Demand-led policies and practice often sought deliberately to guide young people into considering, even confronting, the issues which had direct relevance to them, either as perpetrators or victims of oppression. For their part, if issue-based approaches were to get youth service users to 'own' the learning on offer, they too had to connect with where young people were starting, including wherever feasible their immediate interests and concerns, and then satisfy them that they had gained personally as well as politically.

Here as clearly as anywhere, the frequent introversion of the debate had its unintended negative consequences. The divisiveness which resulted, for example, encouraged impatient policy-makers, not always successfully, to press their own pragmatic solutions – a core curriculum for the service, managerial structures and procedures often only minimally adapted from the business world.

Nonetheless, during the 1980s and 1990s, the debate had a number of positive spin-offs. The defenders of demand-led approaches, for example, at least indirectly, provided a continuing defence of person-centred liberal educational values and principles at a time when school and further education curricula were being increasingly vocationalised. At the same time, those advocating issue-based work focused on young people's experience of discrimination helped the service survive political and media attacks on political correctness which often barely concealed an active collusion with individual prejudice and institutional oppression. Their effects particularly laid the ground for the 1990 statement of purpose which – notwithstanding severe ministerial chastisement – publicly committed the service to confronting just those attitudes and practices which produced such oppression.

Indeed, by the late 1990s the youth service had, in its own unobtrusive and still modest way, advanced on some fronts someway further than other state (or voluntary) services. In tackling racism, for example, it had apparently done better than the police service, certainly as revealed by the inquiry into the death of Stephen Lawrence. If comparative 1990s OFSTED evidence was any guide, it had also gone beyond the point reached by schools which were still disproportionately excluding Black (especially African-Caribbean) students and which in 1999 were told bluntly by one OFSTED report that they were institutionally racist. Indeed the forms and fierceness of the resistance to these findings by both these state institutions were in themselves evidence that, amidst its own internal anguishing, the youth service was perhaps doing better than it recognised.

Individual development plus collective identity

In the context of the education vs rescue debate the tension generated by the demand-led vs issue-based discourse had its most obvious, and positive, pay-off in the formulation of the second ministerial conference's statement of purpose. In asserting a need 'to redress all forms of inequality', this in effect questioned the long held and dominant assumption that British social policy had no need to address fundamental divisions within society. Indeed, by specifically inviting, even exhorting, youth workers to challenge oppressions such as racism and sexism, the statement drove home just how deep and conflict-laden some of these divisions were. In the process the statement also suggested that often highly formative personal experiences were not just individually constructed – the outcome of untrammelled choices freely made by one autonomous citizen after another. These choices were, at least by implication, seen as being shaped in crucial ways by the structures and institutions of the society in which the individual needed to 'make their way'.

The statement of purpose contained one other important premise: that for youth workers individual development, though important, was not sufficient. It talked, for example, of the need to celebrate the diversity and the strength which could arise out of precisely those divisions which attracted oppressive reactions – differences of culture, race, language, sexual identity, gender, disability, age, religion, class. The task being set the youth service seemed therefore to be not just to help young people realise their *own* potential. It was also to seek to liberate and actively nurture the potential within their *shared and collective* experiences and identities.

How politically wise or practically realisable such aspirations were is certainly open to question. Nonetheless, especially following the murder in the early 1990s of one child, Jamie Bulger, by two others, young people's more dangerous and least easily explicable actions again came increasingly to be explained as the result of intrinsic evil. The youth service statement of purpose at least offered some sort of counter to reviving analyses of young people's behaviour based on deficiency models of them and their personalities.

In a culturally diverse and more open society, the statement also carried some important positive messages. In particular it provided a long-overdue reworking of an educational mission whose given core values were uncompromisingly individualistic. By then these were seriously constraining the service's sensitivity, particularly to culturally distinct groups whose strong collective identities were often of great importance to them and which embodied considerable shared as well as personal untapped potential.

Educating an underclass?

Here as elsewhere, however, fundamental dilemmas remained, especially when the commitment to an educational purpose ran into the state's insistence on an increasingly refined targeting of society's losers. Indeed, by the late 1990s it was not immediately clear what might flow from the Labour Government's determination to further refine such selectivity.

Clearly much of this pressure still emanated from a concern, even a passion, to tackle social inequality and injustice. Nonetheless, the societal perspectives and analyses adopted had some serious, in-built limitations. New Labour's insistence

in particular on policies which emphasised rights less and responsibilities more all but eliminated any recognition of the possibility that a significant number of losers might be a meritocratic society's necessary price for guaranteeing that its winners really did succeed. With such structural explanations so severely downplayed – indeed at times all but rendered subversive – where else might state policy-makers then look for the targets of their best endeavours? To failing individuals and their perhaps inherently deficient personalities and upbringing?

For the youth service this route to targeting could have major implications. Albeit unintentionally, it could end up tipping its centre of gravity away from excitement at young people's possibilities to anxiety about their inadequacies, away from release of their untapped talent to their diversion from failure – that is, away from education and towards rescue. Moreover, the combination of the limited social analysis on which policies were being developed and the genuine urgency felt about getting the stragglers back into the race, could also put at risk the youth service's inherent commitment to young people's voluntary participation.

Professionalism vs volunteerism

The traditions of volunteering

Another of the youth service's long-standing dilemmas revolved around the question: how to integrate – even merely to achieve an acceptable reconciliation between – the volunteering tradition from which youth work had sprung and the ethos of professionalism which came as part of growing state sponsorship and the bureaucratic structures which accompanied this. Most obviously, volunteer and professional were separated by how much time each could give to the work and whether or not they were paid. However, over its 60 years the service was most tested by the deeper more ideological divergences which lay within the volunteer-professional dichotomy. This was further complicated by the institutionalised gulf which separated full and part-time paid staff for most of this period.

Volunteering became established within youth work as an integral element of the philanthropic impetus which produced the first charitable youth organisations. Underpinned by their sense of *noblesse oblige*, these original sponsors relied almost exclusively on men and women committed to 'mixing freely' with young people in order to pass on 'that subtle something which is called good form'. Quite explicitly, this 'gift' together with the opportunities to dispense it were conceived as essential qualities of 'the higher classes'.

The class basis of volunteering died hard, even though it was badly wounded by the depredations of the First World War. Not only did the conflict kill huge numbers of the men who were its life blood. Those who survived – including women – could no longer sustain at anything like its pre-war levels their investment of money and

time in activities like volunteer youth leadership.

Nonetheless, at least within the ideology and rhetoric inherited and sustained by the youth service, volunteering survived with many of its in-built (and in-bred) values and assumptions unchanged. At the very moment that the youth service was being launched in 1939, an influential report compiled for the King George Jubilee Trust dismissed as wholly unsuitable the 'less well educated leader' and the indigenous leadership emerging on the new housing estates. For the report's author, A. E. Morgan, the old response remained the best: encourage 'the younger members of the more privileged classes' – now pragmatically broadened out to include the professions, business and industry – 'in the spirit of service'.

During the 1950s, Peter Keunstler, one of youth work's most penetrating and systematic thinkers and analysts, offered a rare challenge to these class-based definitions of volunteering. His research report on voluntary youth leadership published in 1953 highlighted 'the magnificent "self-help" record of the trade unions and friendly societies'. From this insight he drew the conclusion – well evidenced but rarely enunciated – that 'the "lower orders" were indeed capable of high standards of social organisation and leadership'.

As in so many other areas of social policy and provision, during the 1960s and early 1970s class as a crucial variable in what the youth service was doing became increasingly masked within the 'neutral' pseudo-scientific language of welfarism and the welfare state. Nonetheless, through the 1970s and into the 1980s and 1990s (and notwithstanding the qualifications arising from concerns about abusers), volunteers and their contribution were repeatedly endorsed by state and other policy-makers.

Indeed, often for reasons of economy as much as principle, over these decades new sources of volunteering were identified – or rediscovered. These recognised and released that local 'indigenous' leadership (and even community activism) about which Morgan was so scornful. Working-class volunteers thus established themselves as highly competent practitioners, more and more in leadership positions. Moreover, they often got involved for reasons which contradicted the dominant volunteering ethic – for example, because their own children needed a club or youth group in the immediate area; or (dare it be admitted?) because they were looking for something personally satisfying and developmental beyond the stultifying experiences of industrial or domestic labour.

Among an unpaid workforce estimated by the Thompson Report in 1982 at around 525,000, less than a quarter were said to be working in the statutory sector. Most of the remainder – volunteer officers as well as workers – would have been located in one of the traditional voluntary organisations such as the Scouts and Guides, the Boys' or Girls' Brigades, the one night a week church club or in the independent voluntary sector. New volunteering opportunities also opened up for these 'ordinary' lay people (including young people), for example, as mentors and peer educators.

However, despite these shifts of practical expression, within the youth service the endorsed and dominant notion of volunteer retained many of its 19th century connotations. Though perhaps discussed in more careful and modest terms than in the past, volunteerism thus continued to be presented as an altruistic offering motivated by a sense of mission – what one youth service minister in 1986 called an 'unsung contribution'. The definitions offered particularly by state policy-makers and by those paid to manage and promote the major voluntary organisations thus still contained the message that the mere presence of volunteers somehow guaranteed a morally uplifting service for young people.

The day of the professional

As the state's engagement expanded, however, this traditional rhetoric became increasingly overlaid – indeed, many said sidelined. Most influential here were the attitudes and working practices of what, from Albemarle to Thompson, came to be called 'a professional cadre' of full-time paid workers. Though never totalling more than about 3,500 field practitioners and 1,500 officers, their influence on youth service thinking and priorities was soon far out of proportion to their numbers. By the 1970s, what the professionals were saying came increasingly to be read as what 'the youth service' was thinking, planning and doing.

Unfortunately, over time these pronounce-ments communicated sharply conflicting messages. Moreover, they did this in ways which were not always – some said were very rarely – clear or well argued. During the 1960s, the optimism (and the extra resources) generated by the Albemarle Report did for a time help to rally the new professionalism, particularly around the notion of social education as its distinctive practice. Once wider economic and social conditions deteriorated, however, this fragile coherence began to flake and even crack.

By the 1970s, the either-or debates on youth-versus-community and, in the 1980s, on demand-led-versus-issue-based exposed just how far this professionalism still was from clarifying and establishing a core and credible identity. What ultimately counted here was less that such debates actually occurred – they could be seen after all as evidence of a workforce intent on some vibrant and self-critical rethinking. It was much more that they were so often carried on in highly competitive ways which left those looking in – especially national and local politicians and policy-makers – far from convinced by the service's claims to be nurturing a new specialist profession.

Nor were such perceptions much altered by the quality of the arguments themselves. Still deeply infected by attitudes derived from its volunteering origins, even paid youth work continued to be seen and indeed often presented as an enterprise which thrived best on 'enthusiasm, spontaneity, intuition and good personal relationships'. Managers and policy-makers, no less than field workers, thus tended to be impatient with too much reflection, analysis

and evaluation – 'navel gazing' - and to reward doing rather than thinking.

Though the attempted professionalisation of the service did tip this balance some-what, it never shifted it fundamentally. Some embedded assumptions within the culture of the service worked against this. For one thing, sustained and systematic intellectual labour, including the research and reading which might stimulate and support it, was widely treated as for student days only – as something of a luxury to be indulged only until the real work began.

Secondly, despite notable individual exceptions, as a body even its professional educators – normally referred to anyway as trainers – failed over some 40 years to add substantially to the service's analysed collective wisdom. Even though their numbers grew with the expansion of qualifying routes, they gathered and published relatively little evidence-based theory and indulged in little philosophical dialogue intentionally constructed to prompt and sharpen practitioners' thinking and action. Indeed, some of the sectarianism which characterised the service's less tolerant debates could be traced back to hardline positions in which workers were confirmed, or into which they were inducted, by their training. Their over-concentration on critical appraisal of social policy – in itself an important skill for youth workers – sometimes also encouraged knee-jerk oppositional stances to new (especially state-sponsored) initiatives, resulting in the professional service being left behind by events.

Nor was the credibility of the trainers helped by what was widely judged to be the poor return on the service's training investment. Though sometimes based on substantive evidence, this conclusion was also drawn by those who – unrealistically and unreasonably – looked to professional training to overcome organisational limitations, management weaknesses and inadequate resources.

From professionalism to trade unionism

By the 1980s efforts to clarify and underpin the unifying elements of the service's claimed professional identity slackened still further as scepticism about the very concept spread on both the left and the right of the political spectrum. Far from resulting in a renewed convergence with volunteering, however, the increasingly attractive alternative among paid staff in the youth service – a heightened trade union consciousness – deepened the gulf still more.

In part this commitment to trade unionism was the outcome, post-Albemarle, of the recruitment of staff (particularly men) who had given up 'artisan' jobs in order to be able to work full-time at their (part-time paid or unpaid) preferred option – working with young people. Many thus came into the youth service with a sense of themselves primarily as workers in an (at best) uncongenial labour market. In some cases this was accompanied by a strong commitment to workplace organising which did not fall away just because they had become white collar and professional in a 'helping' service.

Most of these new recruits arrived sharing their professionalised colleagues' definition of youth leadership inherited from the volunteering tradition – for example, as a calling requiring great dedication. However, as the ideological shifts to market forces brought budget cuts, hardened managerial styles and real threats to jobs, these workers' definition of themselves changed. Reflecting the new realities of their status and material situation, they came more and more to see themselves as insecure and disempowered employees for whom trade union responses were both logical and necessary. With this view shared increasingly by their part-time paid colleagues, the tension between the traditions of the volunteer and the paid professional/worker, though in some important respects changing focus and shape, thus remained unresolved.

Voluntary vs state sponsorship

Voluntary organisation – official and hidden

Though (somewhat inconsistently) the charitable youth organisations which nurtured volunteerism had been courted before, they gained their most explicit state recognition in the 1939 Circular 1486, *The Service of Youth*. The roots of this voluntary sector lay in that 19th century period when, it was assumed, the educational and welfare needs of 'the lower orders' could and should be met only through philanthropic action by concerned individuals and groups. The mirror image of this position was a deep-seated suspicion of state intervention, particularly in areas of personal and family relationships. Even though the action being mounted was over-whelmingly sponsored by the privileged and the powerful, its insulation from state control allowed it to be defined, and to define itself, as an example of British democracy and freedom at work.

Other providers of youth work existed. However, to a greater or lesser degree they remained hidden from history, in part because it did not suit the more dominant interests within youth work (or more widely) to validate their 'alternative' values, aims and perspectives. Keunstler's research (quoted above) produced evidence on the labour movement acting as one such voluntary sponsor. His findings and interpretations also threw a passing light on the way that the very concept of youth work as handed down through the 20th century was socially constructed (and reconstructed). The resultant commonsense definition included and endorsed only some versions of such work with young people – and therefore firmly excluded others.

Nor were the versions highlighted by Keunstler the only alternative forms of organisational sponsorship for youth work to be marginalised or masked by official definitions. Often, too, the local self-help groups which surfaced during more radical periods of community activism fell into this category. By the late 20th century these had acquired sufficient profile and coherence to encourage a state paper like the 1991 Coopers Lybrand report on the

youth service to give them their own collective label: the independent voluntary sector. From the 1960s on, their role was significantly extended and strengthened by the emergence of Black and Asian youth groups for whom autonomy both from the long established national voluntary youth organisations and from the state was often a matter of principle and of pride.

The 'traditional' voluntary youth organisation

Nonetheless, the movement which, most publicly and largely unchallenged, carried the flag for youth work into local and national policy-making circles prior to 1939 was the 'traditional' voluntary youth sector as defined in Circular 1486. This had experienced some erosion of its dominance during and immediately after the First World War as governments sought to encourage the coordination and more systematic development of youth provision both centrally and through local authorities. However, the main organisations making up this voluntary sector continued to play the controlling roles within the juvenile organisation committees which resulted – and which on the whole anyway merely stumbled along when they did not actually fail.

It was thus not until the late 1930s, when the threat of a second world war again produced national agonising about the condition of youth, that the national voluntary youth organisations felt the need to react to the state's stirring interest in youth work. As an undisguised defensive measure, in 1936 they created their standing conference, SCNVYO. This reiterated their opposition to 'any element of compulsion' and restated as a central principle of youth work provision 'the value of variety and competition' as a safeguard against 'administrative convenience and simplicity'.

Throughout the history of the youth service, SCNVYO and its 1970s successor NCVYS, as well as national organisations individually, continued to mount a defence of traditional voluntaryism and against the creeping incursions of the state. As late as 1990, for example, they were able to exert sufficient backstairs pressure to prompt the junior minister with youth service responsibility into a damage-limitation exercise against the, for them, unappealing statement of purpose just agreed at a widely representative ministerial conference.

Realities of partnership

Nonetheless, throughout these 60 years the traditional voluntary sector had to accept the somewhat compromised position of partner to state agencies. Particularly following the Albemarle Report in 1960, this statutory sector took on the role of direct provider with increasing vigour and considerably more resources than the voluntary organisations could command. More and more over this period these organisations in effect became clients of the state as, locally and nationally, they came to rely on public funds to develop – even often just to maintain – their core facilities and activities.

As the impact of the Manpower Services Commission in the late 1970s and early 1980s illustrated particularly vividly, the sources of these public funds diversified well beyond the LEA and the Department for Education and Employment and all its earlier embodiments. Even after the MSC was abolished in the late 1980s, this trend continued – indeed probably accelerated. By the time the 1998 youth service audit was carried out, the service had become very heavily dependent on other state sources of funding – particularly Single Regeneration Budgets and Training and Enterprise Councils.

The extent to which this relationship to the state trimmed voluntary organisations' autonomy was perhaps most sharply exposed in the late 1980s by the Thatcher Government's insistence that they adjust their programmes to fit ministerial objectives. State policy-makers felt the need to do this even though, within the set parameters of its traditional values, the voluntary sector had over the previous half century reinvented itself many times – in some cases more effectively than its statutory partners. Indeed it was here often that the service most clearly demonstrated its capacity for devising imaginative prototypes for meeting young people's changing needs – and its lack of resources for putting many of these into production.

In fact, at national level, the state partner as embodied in the Ministry or Department of Education could never be relied upon to take a coherent or developmental approach to the service. Moreover, this remained true even after, from the mid-1980s, it was overseen by a specialist Youth Service Unit.

It was at local level, however, where partnership needed to deliver the most concrete results and so to be at its most authentic, that it was most unpredictable and questionable – and most consistently questioned. Reassuring rhetoric (on both sides) – labelled by one influential Director of Education during the 1960s as mere 'lip service' – often seemed to belie this. Voluntary organisation and local authority were, it was repeatedly said, working well (or at least better) together they were experiencing few, and then only superficial, difficulties.

In some areas this was true, and remained so for long periods. Beneath the cosmetics, however, disfiguring wrinkles were reflected back to the service at almost every stage of its development. As early as 1948 an independent think tank was reporting that 'LEAs have managed the service of youth with the minimum consultation with the voluntary bodies'. As a result, it seemed, 'the traditionalists of youth work, being stout champions of the voluntary principle … (were feeling) themselves moved by a certain claustrophobia'.

In 1965 SCNVYO's general secretary was able confidently to assert that partnership 'in almost every case … has been a successful enterprise' which had enabled the statutory and voluntary organisations 'to like and respect each other'. Yet only two years later the YSDC's investigation into the training of part-time workers bluntly reported 'certain attitudes in groups, and in individuals, which can militate against full partnership'. It pointed, too, to 'rivalries (real or imaginary), inadequacy of communication within and between voluntary organisations themselves, and between voluntary organisations and statutory bodies'.

Similar sentiments were being expressed by relatively objective commentators nearly a decade later: a 1975 review of the voluntary sector, for example, revealed 'a tendency to gloss over the disagreements, disparities and differences in approach and values'. The same concerns were still around in 1996 when a report on the youth service in London noted that 'the views emerging of these two sectors were in sharp contrast'. Whereas the local authorities saw their involvement with the voluntary sector as having 'greatly strengthened' over the previous five years, for their part the voluntary organisations were able to see 'very little' change in this relationship.

With partnership at the core of the very definition of the youth service, the tensions within it most obviously focused on practical, logistical and especially resource issues. This happened most uncomfortably when the partner agencies were required actually to do things together rather than just talk about doing them or develop good committee or working party rapport. Thus the 1967 criticisms quoted above came after three years of effort to establish joint training agencies for part-time workers – and then to base the planned courses on the 'common element' of youth work which was said to straddle both voluntary and statutory provision. In this period the two sectors had also had to work locally on

joint building programmes to be submitted to central government. In these
cases proximity did not apparently lead to
increased fondness.

Below these immediate and practical
pressures, however, deeper ideological
divisions seemed to lurk which were at
least in part rooted in the same kinds of
class differences which underpinned the
volunteer-professional tensions. In 1951, a
well-placed and sharp-eyed commentator
tactfully pointed these out to a national
audience celebrating the partnership's first
10 years. 'Local authorities,' he recalled,
'(had) belonged traditionally to the
servants' hall.' As a result, in the eyes of
those running the voluntary organisations
'their unsympathetic bureaucrats were the
last people to be trusted with so delicate
and esoteric a mystery as youth
leadership'. For their part, these same
officials 'were terrified (justifiably) lest
these strange voluntary members of youth
committees might prove to be that
dreadful thing, enthusiasts'.

The voluntary sector – even the traditional
voluntary sector – was of course never
monolithic. With their changing visions,
their search for new methods and
responses, their different patterns of
recruitment and training and much else
that divided rather than united them, the
national voluntary organisations' dealings
with state bodies over the next half
century were never uniform. Moreover,
given their long and conventional chains
of command, few of their (largely
volunteer) workers had significant contact
with or gave much thought to the state
and all it represented.

As power tilted decisively away from the
traditionalists and towards the bureaucrats,
it was often politic, too, for both groups to
allow differences in social background and
attitudes to go underground or at least to be
left unacknowledged. Nonetheless, value
differences between voluntary and state
conceptions of youth work persisted and
continued to feed, if not actually to cause,
both the overt conflicts and the quieter
evasions of cooperation which characterised
much of their 60-year partnership.

The other youth service partner

This, however, has not been the only
partnership which has, notionally,
underpinned the youth service since its
inception in 1939. Alongside national and
local government and the voluntary sector,
the Albemarle Report specifically called
young people 'the fourth partner' – a
notion which went back at least to a 1942
Youth Advisory Council report. It was
then reiterated in different forms by all the
subsequent major review documents
including Milson-Fairbairn, Thompson
and Coopers Lybrand (see Chapter 7) as
well as in most other mission statements.
Indeed, for the youth service it constitutes
a core commitment – not, as for most other
services, merely a useful and welcome by-
product of fulfilling other core tasks but an
integral element of its raison d'etre.

Ways of implementing such participation
have varied from period to period. They
have included proposals for a youth parliament and for involving young people in
local authority youth committees,
instituting local youth councils or forums,
giving users some responsibility for running

their clubs and centres through members' committees, encouraging self-programming groups and developing peer education projects. As the 1998 youth service audit showed, more recent efforts within local authorities have provided young people with local complaints procedures and have given them a place in the inspection of local facilities. Some national voluntary organisations, too, have persisted with local, regional and even national members' councils while since the mid 1960s BYC has consistently staked its claim to act as the national voice of youth. New Labour's concern to increase young people's social inclusion and to regenerate local communities in human as well as material ways again made participatory approaches flavour of the month.

Here too, however, considerable and persisting gaps between rhetoric and reality have persisted. Many of these, it would seem, have stemmed particularly from the tension of building empowerment for this age group into the structures, procedures and time-frames required by a youth service in which the state rapidly became the dominant power holder. The complex interaction within this process of democratic accountability, bureaucratic decision-making and professional practice has together produced an environment in which active and creative participation by a client group with often minimal interest in 'jam tomorrow' has been difficult to stimulate – and even harder to sustain.

Realities of state sponsorship

In 1966 – a mere generation from the time when the voluntary organisations had

simply assumed that youth work belonged to them – Andrew Fairbairn, Director of Education for Leicestershire and influential member of the Youth Service Development Council, put the changing balance in their relationship on the line. In the process he also made explicit the link between the growing dominance of the state and the professionalisation of the service's workforce. 'Voluntary bodies,' he pointed out, 'must realise that authorities are willy-nilly going to be the main pace-makers because of their increasing number of full-time professionals and the size of their financial outlay.'

Over the years commentators did occasionally – exceptionally – point to potential dangers in this situation: the Conservative Party's Bow Group in the 1960s, the former director of NYB John Ewen in the 1970s, David Marsland of the New Right in the 1980s. However, nothing happened in the following decades to prove Fairbairn wrong or to reverse the trend he identified. It was true that responsibility for running the service and actually carrying out its practice continued to be substantially devolved both to autonomous voluntary organisations and the full range of idiosyncratic local authorities whose plurality of priorities and structures went largely unchecked for much of its history. Nonetheless over six decades from 1939, and especially post-Albemarle, state leverage on policy and provision grew and grew.

The refusal of governments – both Conservatives and Labour – to strengthen the service's legislative basis only masked the less direct ways in which they exercised their control. Once Albemarle had given its authoritative stamp to the centrality of state leadership in developing youth work, a taken-for-granted consensus on this took firm root. Even the Thatcherite challenge to the whole post-1945 'welfare settlement' in the 1980s did little to substantially uproot it.

Indeed, despite their anti-statist rhetoric, Thatcher's governments showed great determination and imagination in strengthening the state's role in the social policy field, including even in a service as marginal as the youth service. Their complex financial mechanisms for containing local government spending not only reduced the money directly available to the youth service via LEAs. They also withdrew other resources from local authorities and then partially reallocated them via special programmes with sharply focused and monitored priorities determined by ministers. Even though only very modest amounts of these funds came to the youth service, the long-term effect was still to shape the service's programmes and forms of delivery with increasing specificity and on government terms.

From time to time, usually as a result of an outside stimulus, the central state would expend short spurts of proactive energy on the service – for example, immediately post-Albemarle and when (with strong encouragement from the NYA) in the late 1980s it suddenly discovered the service needed a core curriculum. For much of the service's 60-year development, however, national policy-makers preferred to play their

controlling and shaping roles in much more hands-off ways. This approach was usually defended on grounds of principle – that the voluntary sector was of course autonomous and that local authorities needed to determine policy locally. More often, however, their reticence could be traced to indifference to or lack of conviction about a service which, within a large central government department's overall educational responsibilities, was messy and hard to comprehend. The result was, for most of these years, if not an absence of mind, then certainly an absence of any central developmental vision.

At the end of the 1990s the arrival of a New Labour Government with a clear youth policy agenda and a determination if necessary to push this through from the top down, promised to sharpen and harden the debate about the state's role and power in the youth service. Decisive interventions were made quickly across all the main areas of youth provision – schooling, employment and employment training, the judicial system, social security, health. As they were said to be planned to produce 'joined-up-responses', they came close to constituting an overarching youth strategy.

Machinery which came to see youth as one of its greatest concerns – a Social Exclusion Unit – was put in place to stimulate, coordinate and monitor these policies. In due course the youth service and its promised development were made increasingly subject to the concerns of the Unit's planning, requiring it to commit itself to priorities which were compatible with the wider governmental youth strategy and to make specified contributions to achieving this. In a way which would certainly have surprised, perhaps even shocked, Andrew Fairbairn 30 years before, the central state, unambiguously and unashamedly, now seemed intent on setting – and in precise terms – not just pace but direction, too.

When examined in a historical perspective, particularly in relation to the voluntary dominance which 60 years before had been so entirely taken for granted, the sponsorship of youth work had indeed been turned on its head – much of it via an unremarked process of osmosis. Post-Albemarle few openly or from a coherently ideological or political position questioned what was happening. Most, even when as policy-makers they were regretfully imposing cuts, simply treated the growth of state influence, indeed control, as proper and inevitable. Suspicious anyway of charitable (or indeed corporate) funders liable to want some moral or even material return on their investment, most in effect concluded that, in sufficient quantity, the extra resources needed for the service to realise its potential could only come via the state.

By the 1970s therefore a broad if largely silent consensus existed on the need for and the appropriateness of state sponsor-ship for the youth service. If anything this was re-invigorated by the ideological and financial assaults of Thatcherism. Other powerful state education and welfare agencies might put themselves forward as potential safe havens for youth work –

indeed, as relatively generous funders. Nonetheless, as some guarantee that, in such bad times, youth work's distinctiveness could survive, the continuing existence of a specialised institution with an explicit state mandate for sponsoring and developing just this form of practice was still broadly treated as essential.

However, this balance of advantage was not set in stone. As historical conditions changed, it could turn from credit to debit. After all, as even many who were part of the consensus recognised, state support was coming with a series of price tags. Over and above even that of hardening state priorities and targets for the work, these included increased bureaucracy, tighter managerial controls and more rigid forms of profession-alisation. All of these to some degree impeded the delivery of promises to involve young people as 'the fourth partner' in the service's decision-making. More generally, they also reduced its and youth work's responsiveness to a clientele whose needs and demands rarely stayed still for long.

Moreover these doubts were if anything being fuelled by the initiatives of the central state led by a Labour Government confident that it knew what was needed to deal with the historic youth crisis. As the 20th century closed, therefore, the inheritance both of a distinctive form of practice known as youth work and of a youth service specifically mandated to guarantee this was looking more brittle than at almost any time in its 60-year history.

Key Youth Service Events 1979–99

Date	Youth service developments	The wider world
1979	Youth Service Forum abolished Skeet Youth and Community Service Bill Joint Council for Gay Teenagers set up	General election: Conservative Government
1980	Skeet Bill defeated Thompson Review Group set up Youth Service Partners' Group formed NAYC sets up Rural Youth Work Education Project London Union of Youth Clubs girls' work dispute	Community Relations Council publishes *Fire Next Time*
1981	Thompson Review Group interim report published Youth Call launched to lobby for young people's national community service Youth Choice launched to oppose compulsory service for young people NAYC start *Working with Girls* newsletter NAYC Report: *In the Service of Black Youth* published NYB: *Reader's Route Map* on work with girls published	Urban disturbances ('race riots') Scarman Report: *Brixton Disorders* published 'Sus' laws repealed British Council of Disabled People founded
1982	Thompson Report published	DES circular: *YTS – Implications*

1982	CETYCW established	*for the Education Service* published
1983	Commons Select Committee questions Secretary of State for Education Keith Joseph on youth service	General election: Conservative Government
	Wall private member's bill	YTS launched: 'military option' offered
	Cockerill review of NYB	HMI reports published
	DES: *Young People in the '80s* published	
	National Organisation for Work with Girls and Young Women (NOW) set up	
	CYSA becomes CYWU	
1984	DES response to Thompson Report	GLC and metropolitan counties abolished
	Bolger and Smith: *Starting from Strengths* published	Police and Criminal Evidence Act
	CETYCW (Kuper) report on future staffing	
1985	DES circular	International Youth Year
	National Advisory Council for the Youth Service (NACYS) established	Rate capping introduced
	Youth Exchange Centre set up	
	Willis: *Social Condition of Young People in Wolverhampton* published	
	London Gay Teenage Group report on young people and the youth service	
1986	LEATGS scheme for funding in-service training introduced	Disabled Persons Act
1987	NAYC closes down its Girls' Work Unit	General election: Conservative Government
	Certificate course for deaf youth workers starts	
1987	NAYC becomes Youth Clubs UK	
1988	National Advisory Council for	Education Reform Act: national

1988	the Youth Service abolished	schools curriculum; local management of schools; 'opting out' for schools
	CETYCW (Jardine) Report on future staffing	
		MSC abolished
	HMI Report: *Effective Youth Work* published	
		Section 28 of Local Government Act bans teaching of homosexuality
		Macdonald Report on murder of Asian pupil at Manchester Burnage High
1989	First Ministerial Conference on a core curriculum for the youth service	Berlin Wall down: end of Cold War, suggested 'peace dividend'
	DES reforms HQ grants system to voluntary organisations	Children Act
	GEST in-service training funding introduced	
	ESG apprenticeship schemes started	
	The Prince's Trust announces plans for Young Volunteers in the Community scheme	
	National Association of Lesbian and Gay Youth Workers formed	
1990	Second Ministerial Conference: statement of purpose for youth service agreed	ILEA abolished
	BYC, NCVYS and NAYPCAS become 'voluntary sector organisations'	
	National Black Workers' conference	
	Three-year Changing Attitudes Project on work with disabled young people started	
	National Youth and Community Work Alliance formed	
1991	Coopers and Lybrand Report: *Management of Youth Service in 1990s* published	Institute for Public Policy Research Report on young people's voluntary service
	Ministerial response to youth	Disabled people's Direct Action

	service Statement of Purpose published	Network formed
	NYB and CETYCW merge to form the NYA	
	1st Youth Information shop opened	
	41 youth volunteer schemes started	
1992	Third Ministerial Conference	General election: Conservative Government
	CYWU takes Warwickshire to High Court	DES becomes DfE
		Further and Higher Education Act
		OFSTED created
		Criminal Justice and Public Order Act
		Health of the Nation White Paper published
		Foyer Federation established
1993	DES review of NYA	
	Lloyd youth service bill	
	Lords debate on London Youth Service	
	DES three-year Youth Action schemes started	
	NYA promotes first Youth Work Week	
	NAYC Rural Links Project started	
	NABC adds 'Clubs for Young People' to title	
1994	Sufficiency Working Party Report published	Labour Party forms Youth Task Group
1994	OFSTED: *Inspecting Youth Work … A Framework* published	SRB 'round' prioritises young people
	National Organisation for Work with Girls and Young Women wound up	Henley Centre Report for CSV on young people's voluntary service

1994		Development Education Association set up
1995	Kilfoyle youth service bill	DfE becomes DfEE
	Standing Conference of Principal Youth and Community Officers formed	Disabled Discrimination Act
		White Paper *Rural England* published
	CYWU gets TUC membership	Health of the Young Nation campaign
		Cullen inquiry into Dunblane primary school murders
1996	UK Youth Work Alliance: *Agenda for a Generation* published	First National Lottery grants to youth work
	NYA reconstituted	Audit Commission: *Misspent Youth* published
	Part-time workers' JNC parity with full-timers	
1997	Global Youth Work Advisory Service started	General election: Labour Government
		White Paper: *Excellence in Schools* published
	National Forum for Development of Rural Youth Work formed	New Deal for young unemployed
1998	Youth service audit	Crime and Disorder Act
		Social Exclusion Unit established
		Green Paper on lifelong learning
		Young people's minimum wage set below adult level
		Drugs Tsar appointed
1999		Millennium Volunteers scheme launched

Main reference

Doug Nicholls, *CYWU: An Outline History
of Youth and Community Work in the
Union, 1834–1997*, Pepar Publications,
1997

Index

Hughes, Simon 157
Hunt Report 103
Hutton, Will 95

I

identity of the youth service
    9, 32, 36, 91, 166-7, 183-4,
    189
ideology 8, 11, 19, 36-7, 93-4,
    184
ILEA (Inner London
    Education Authority)
    abolition of 30-1
    expenditure on youth
    service 30
    multi-ethnic policy 104
income support 13, 83
independent sector 138-9,
    148, 182, 185
individual development 7,
    16-17, 38, 135, 136, 139,
    142, 177, 179-80
Industrial Society 32
information for young
    people 17, 76, 110, 117,
    119-20, 156
information/research into
    the youth service 7, 45,
    115, 124, 126, 127, 163,
    173
    NYB and 47-50, 128
inner cities 37, 46, 91, 119
in-service training 45, 64, 65,
    71-3, 116
    grants for 64-5, 72, 123-4
    validation of 63, 71
inspection (see also HMI;
    OFSTED) 45-7, 141-2
    of schools 77, 83, 85
INSTEP (In-Service Training
    and Education Panel)
    63, 71, 72
Institute for Public Policy
    Research 81
integration
    of Black and Asian
    young people 103, 104,
    107-8
    of disabled young people
    109, 111
INTEP (Initial Training and
    Education Panel) 62-3

Interaction 38
Interface 64
intermediate treatment see IT
international work 52, 120,
    133
issue-based provision 9, 42,
    60, 93-118, 178-9, 183
IT (intermediate treatment)
    13, 20, 32, 44, 86, 176

J

Jackson, Mark 130
James, Walter 43, 45
Jardine Report 60, 66
Jeffs, Tony and Smith, Mark
    97, 126
Jigsaw Youth Integration
    Project 111
JNC (Joint Negotiating
    Committee) 61, 62, 127
joint training agencies 68,
    188
Joseph, Keith 11, 19, 21, 56,
    65, 77, 175
    and ILEA 30-1
    and NACYS 42
    and Thompson Report
    22-3, 49
Joseph Rowntree Foundation
    79, 88, 123
juvenile delinquency (see also
    young offenders) 43, 55,
    76, 84, 86, 96, 117, 169,
    172, 174
    avoiding 50, 87, 88, 101
    Thompson Report and 15
juvenile organisation
    committees 185

K

Keele University conferences
    76
Kennedy, Allan 116
Kent, cuts in youth service
    28
Kent-Baguley, Peter 112-13
Keunstler, Peter 181, 185
Kilfoyle, Peter 155, 156, 157,
    161-2

King George Jubilee Trust
    147, 181
Kingston, youth service in
    31
Kirklees, youth service
    resources 28
Kuper Report 59-60

L

Labour Government (see also
    New Labour) 10, 128,
    129, 147, 157, 175
Labour Research 149
Lancashire, rural youth
    work 116
law, youth service and 84-8
Lawler, Geoff 22
LEAs 27, 69, 71-2, 138, 140,
    153
    Thompson Report on
    20, 22
    and training 68, 69
    variations in provision
    34, 164-5
    and voluntary sector see
    partnership
LEATGS (LEA Training
    Grants Scheme) 71-2
legislative/statutory basis
    20, 21, 22-3, 43-4, 51, 56,
    129, 150-7, 167-9, 172,
    175, 190
Leicestershire, youth
    services in 28
leisure activities, survey of
    16, 104
leisure/recreation, youth
    work defined as 31, 32,
    150, 177
Lesbian Caucus 113
Lewisham, youth service in
    31
Liberal Democratic Party 82,
    157
liberal education, youth
    work as 176-7, 178
lifelong learning 160, 168
Liverpool, support for
    voluntary sector 34
Lloyd, Tony 154, 155
Lloyd, Trefor, 96